Truth may seem, but cannot be:
Beauty brag, but 'tis not she;
Truth and beauty buried be.

To this urn let those repair
That are either true or fair;
For these dead birds sigh a prayer.

Bacon

English Men of Letters

EDITED BY JOHN MORLEY

THOMAS CARLYLE

Carlyle

by

JOHN NICHOL, LL.D.

AUTHOR OF

"AMERICAN LITERATURE"
" LORD BYRON"

English Men of Letters

EDITED BY

JOHN MORLEY

HARPER & BROTHERS PUBLISHERS
NEW YORK AND LONDON
1901

PREFATORY NOTE

THE following record of the leading events of Carlyle's life and attempt to estimate his genius rely on frequently renewed study of his work, on slight personal impressions—"vidi tantum"—and on information supplied by previous narrators. Of these the great author's chosen literary legatee is the most eminent and, in the main, the most reliable. Every critic of Carlyle must admit as constant obligations to Mr. Froude as every critic of Byron to Moore or of Scott to Lockhart. The works of these masters in biography remain the ample storehouses from which every student will continue to draw. Each has, in a sense, made his subject his own, and each has been similarly arraigned.

I must here be allowed to express a feeling akin to indignation at the persistent, often virulent attacks directed against a loyal friend, betrayed, it may be, by excess of faith and the defective reticence that often belongs to genius, to publish too much about his hero. But Mr. Froude's quotation, in defence, from the essay on *Sir Walter Scott* requires no supplement: it should be remembered that he acted with the most ample authority; that the restrictions under which he was at first entrusted with the MSS. of the *Reminiscences* and the *Letters and Memorials* (annotated by Carlyle himself, as if for publi-

cation) were withdrawn; and that the initial permission
to select finally approached a practical injunction to communicate the whole.   The worst that can be said is that,
in the last years of Carlyle's career, his own judgment as
to what should be made public of the details of his domestic life may have been somewhat obscured; but, if so,
it was a weakness easily hidden from a devotee.

My acknowledgments are due for several of the Press
comments which appeared shortly after Carlyle's death,
more especially that of the *St. James's Gazette,* giving
the most philosophical brief summary of his religious
views which I have seen; and for the kindness of Dr.
Eugene Oswald, President of the Carlyle Society, in re-
vising my proof-sheets, and supplying me with numerous
valuable hints, especially in matters relating to German
History and Literature.   I have also to thank the Editor
of the *Manchester Guardian* for permitting me to repro-
duce the substance of my article in its columns of February, 1881.   That article was largely based on a contribution on the same subject, in 1859, to Mackenzie's *Imperial
Dictionary of Biography.*

I may add that in the distribution of material over the
comparatively short space at my command, I have endeavoured to give prominence to facts less generally
known, and passed over slightly the details of events
previously enlarged on, as the terrible accident to Mrs.
Carlyle and the incidents of her death.   To her inner
history I have only referred in so far as it had a direct
bearing on her husband's life.   As regards the itinerary
of Carlyle's foreign journeys, it has seemed to me that it
might be of interest to those travelling in Germany to
have a short record of the places where the author sought
his " studies " for his greatest work.

CONTENTS.

THOMAS CARLYLE.

CHAPTER I.

INTRODUCTORY SUMMARY.

FOUR SCOTCHMEN, born within the limits of the same hundred years, all in the first rank of writers, if not of thinkers, represent much of the spirit of four successive generations. They are leading links in an intellectual chain.

DAVID HUME (1711 – 1776) remains the most salient type, in our island, of the scepticism, half conservative, half destructive, but never revolutionary, which marked the third quarter of the eighteenth century. He had some points of intellectual contact with Voltaire, though substituting a staid temper and passionless logic for the incisive brilliancy of a mocking Mercury; he had no relation, save an unhappy personal one, to Rousseau.

ROBERT BURNS (1759–1796), last of great lyrists inspired by a local genius, keenest of popular satirists, narrative poet of the people, spokesman of their higher as of their lower natures, stood on the verge between two eras. Half Jacobite, nursling of old minstrelsy, he was also half Jacobin, an early-born child of the upheaval that closed

1

the century; as essentially a foe of Calvinism as Hume himself. Master musician of his race, he was, as Thomas Campbell notes, severed, for good and ill, from his fellow Scots by an utter want of their protecting or paralysing caution.

WALTER SCOTT (1771–1832), broadest and most generous, if not loftiest of the group—" no sounder piece of British manhood," says Carlyle himself in his inadequate review, " was put together in that century "—the great revivalist of the mediæval past, lighting up its scenes with a magic glamour, the wizard of northern tradition, was also, like Burns, the humorist of contemporary life. Dealing with Feudal themes, but in the manner of the Romantic school, he was the heir of the Troubadours, the sympathetic peer of Byron, and in his translation of Goetz von Berlichingen he laid the first rafters of our bridge to Germany.

THOMAS CARLYLE (1795–1881) is on the whole the strongest, though far from the finest spirit of the age succeeding—an age of criticism threatening to crowd creation out, of jostling interests and of surging streams, some of which he has striven to direct, more to stem. Even now what Mill twenty-five years ago wrote of Coleridge is still true of Carlyle: "The reading public is apt to be divided between those to whom his views are everything and those to whom they are nothing." But it is possible to extricate from a mass of often turbid eloquence the strands of his thought and to measure his influence by indicating its range.

Travellers in the Hartz, ascending the Brocken, are in certain atmospheres startled by the apparition of a shadowy figure—a giant image of themselves, thrown on the horizon by the dawn. Similar is the relation of Carlyle to the

common types of his countrymen. Burns, despite his perfervid patriotism, was in many ways "a starry stranger."
Carlyle was Scotch to the core and to the close, in every
respect a macrocosm of the higher peasant class of the
Lowlanders. Saturated to the last with the spirit of a dismissed creed, he fretted in bonds from which he could
never get wholly free.   Intrepid, independent, steadfast,
frugal, prudent, dauntless, he trampled on the pride of
kings with the pride of Lucifer. He was clannish to excess, painfully jealous of proximate rivals, self-centred if
not self-seeking, fired by zeal and inflamed by almost mean
emulations, resenting benefits as debts, ungenerous—with
one exception, that of Goethe—to his intellectual creditors;
and, with reference to men and manners around him at
variance with himself, violently intolerant.   He bore a
strange relation to the great poet, in many ways his predecessor in influence, whom with persistent inconsistency
he alternately eulogised and disparaged, the half Scot
Lord Byron. One had by nature many affinities to the
Latin races, the other was purely Teutonic: but the power
of both was Titanic rather than Olympian; both were
forces of revolution; both protested, in widely different
fashion, against the tendency of the age to submerge Individualism; both were to a large extent egoists: the one
whining, the other roaring against the "Philistine" restraints of ordinary society.   Both had hot hearts, big
brains, and an exhaustless store of winged and fiery words;
both were wrapt in a measureless discontent, and made
constant appeal against what they deemed the shallows of
Optimism; Carlylism is the prose rather than "the male
of Byronism." The contrasts are, however, obvious; the
author of *Sartor Resartus*, however vaguely, defended the
System of the Universe; the author of *Cain*, with an

audacity that in its essence went beyond that of Shelley, arraigned it. In both we find vehemence and substantial honesty; but, in the one, there is a dominant faith, tempered by pride, in the "caste of Vere de Vere," in Freedom for itself—a faith marred by shifting purposes, the garrulous incontinence of vanity, and a broken life; in the other unwavering belief in Law. The record of their fame is diverse. Byron leapt into the citadel, awoke and found himself the greatest inheritor of an ancient name. Carlyle, a peasant's son, laid slow siege to his eminence, and, only after outliving twice the years of the other, attained it. His career was a struggle, sterner than that of either Johnson or Wordsworth, from obscurity, almost from contempt, to a rarely challenged renown. Fifty years ago few "so poor as do him reverence:" at his death, in a sunset storm of praise, the air was full of him, and deafening was the Babel of the reviews; for the progress of every original thinker is accompanied by a stream of commentary that swells as it runs till it ends in a dismal swamp of platitude. Carlyle's first recognition was from America, his last from his own countrymen. His teaching came home to their hearts "late in the gloamin'." In Scotland, where, for good or ill, passions are in extremes, he was long howled down, lampooned, preached at, prayed for: till, after his Edinburgh Inaugural Address, he of a sudden became the object of an equally blind devotion; and was, often by the very men who had tried and condemned him for blasphemy, as senselessly credited with essential orthodoxy. "The stone which the builders rejected became the headstone of the corner," the terror of the pulpit its text. Carlyle's decease was marked by a dirge of rhapsodists whose measureless acclamations stifled the voice of sober criticism. In the realm of contemporary English prose he has left no adequate successor;' the throne that does not pass by primogeniture is vacant, and the bleak northern skies seem colder and grayer since that venerable head was laid to rest in the village church, far from the smoke and din of the great city on whose streets his figure was long familiar and his name was at last so honored.

Carlyle first saw the world tempest-tossed by the events he celebrates in his earliest History. In its opening pages, we are made to listen to the feet and chariots of "Dubarrydom" hurrying from the "Armida Palace," where Louis XV. and the *ancien régime* lay dying; later to the ticking of the clocks in Launay's doomed Bastile; again to the tocsin of the steeples that roused the singers of the *Marseillaise* to march from "their bright Phocæan city" and grapple with the Swiss guard, last Bulwark of the Bourbons. "The Swiss would have won," the historian characteristically quotes from Napoleon, "if they had had a commander." Already, over little more than the space of the author's life—for he was a contemporary of Keats, born seven months before the death of Burns, Shelley's junior by three, Scott's by four, Byron's by seven years— in the year when Goethe went to feel the pulse of the "cannon-fever" at Argonne—already these sounds are like sounds across a sea. Two whole generations have passed with the memory of half their storms. "Another race has been, and other palms are won." Old policies, governments, councils, creeds, modes and hopes of life have been sifted in strange fires. Assaye, Trafalgar, Austerlitz, Jena, Leipzig, Inkermann, Sadowa, Waterloo when he was twenty and Sedan when he was seventy-five, have been

The nearest being the now foremost prose writers of our time, Mr. Ruskin and Mr. Froude.

fought and won. Born under the French Directory and
the Presidency of Washington, Carlyle survived two
French empires, two kingdoms, and two republics; elsewhere partitions, abolitions, revivals and deaths of States
innumerable. During his life our sway in the East
doubled its area, two peoples (the German with, the Italian without, his sympathy) were consolidated on the Continent, while another across the Atlantic developed to a
magnitude that amazes and sometimes alarms the rest.
Aggressions were made and repelled, patriots perorated
and fought, diplomatists finessed with a zeal worthy of
the world's most restless, if not its wisest, age. In the
internal affairs of the leading nations the transformation
scenes were often as rapid as those of a pantomime. The
Art and Literature of those eighty-six years—stirred to
new thought and form at their commencement by the so-
called Romantic movement, more recently influenced by
the Classic reaction, the Pre-Raphaelite protest, the Æs-
thetic *môde*—followed various even contradictory standards. But, in one line of progress, there was no shadow
of turning. Over the road which Bacon laid roughly
down and Newton made safe for transit, Physical Science,
during the whole period, advanced without let and beyond
the cavil of ignorance. If the dreams of the *New Atlantis* have not even in our days been wholly realised,
Science has been brought from heaven to earth, and the
elements made ministers of Prospero's wand. This apparent, and partially real, conquest of matter has doubtless done much to "relieve our estate," to make life in
some directions run more smoothly, and to multiply re-
sources to meet the demands of rapidly-increasing multitudes: but it is in danger of becoming a conquest of
matter over us; for the agencies we have called into ac

most fearful activity threaten, like Frankenstein's mis-created goblin, to beat us down to the same level. Sanguine spirits who

> "throw out acclamations of self-thanking, self-admiring,
> With, at every mile run faster, O the wondrous, wondrous age,"

are apt to forget that the electric light can do nothing to dispel the darkness of the mind; that there are strict limits to the power of prosperity to supply man's wants or satisfy his aspirations. This is a great part of Carlyle's teaching. It is impossible, were it desirable, accurately to define his religious, social, or political creed. He swallows formulæ with the voracity of Mirabeau, and like Proteus escapes analysis. No printed labels will stick to him: when we seek to corner him by argument he thunders and lightens. Emerson complains that he failed to extract from him a definite answer about Immortality. Neither by syllogism nor by crucible could Bacon himself have made the "Form" of Carlyle to confess itself. But call him what we will—essential Calvinist or recalcitrant Neologist, Mystic, Idealist, Deist or Pantheist, practical Absolutist, or "the strayed reveller" of Radicalism—he is consistent in his even bigoted antagonism to all Utilitarian solutions of the problems of the world. One of the foremost physicists of our time was among his truest and most loyal friends; they were bound together by the link of genius and kindred political views; and Carlyle was himself an expert in mathematics, the mental science that most obviously subserves physical research: but of Physics themselves (astronomy being scarcely a physical science) his ignorance was profound, and his abusive criticisms of such men as Darwin are infantile. This intellectual defect, or rather vacuum, left him free to denounce material views of life

with unconditioned vehemence. " Will the whole uphol-
sterers," he exclaims in his half comic, sometimes nonsensi-
cal, vein, " and confectioners of modern Europe undertake
to make one single shoeblack happy !" And more seriously
of the railways, without whose noisy aid he had never been
able to visit the battle-fields of Friedrich II.:

> Our stupendous railway miracles I have stopped short in admir-
> ing. . . . The distances of London to Aberdeen, to Ostend, to Vienna,
> are still infinitely inadequate to me. Will you teach me the winged
> flight through immensity, up to the throne dark with excess of
> bright? You unfortunate, you grin as an ape would at such a ques-
> tion: you do not know that unless you can reach thither in some
> effectual most veritable sense, you are lost, doomed to Hela's death-
> realm and the abyss where mere brutes are buried. I do not want
> cheaper cotton, swifter railways; I want what Novalis calls " God,
> Freedom, and Immortality." Will swift railways and sacrifices to
> Hudson help me towards that?

The ECONOMIC AND MECHANICAL SPIRIT of the age, faith
is mere steel or stone, was one of Carlyle's red rags. The
others were INSINCERITY in Politics and in Life, DEMOCRACY
without Reverence, and PHILANTHROPY without Sense. In
our time these two last powers have made such strides as
to threaten the Reign of Law. The Democrat without a
ruler, who protests that one man is by nature as good as
another, according to Carlyle is "shooting Niagara." In
deference to the mandate of the philanthropist the last
shred of brutality and much of decision has vanished from
our code. Sentiment is in office and Mercy not only
tempers, but threatens to gag Justice. When Sir Samuel
Romilly began his beneficent agitation, and Carlyle was
at school, talkers of treason were liable to be disembowelled
before execution; now the crime of treason is practically
erased, and the free use of dynamite brings so-called re-

forms "within the range of practical politics." Individualism was still a mark of the early years of the century. The spirit of "L'Etat c'est moi" survived in Mirabeau, "never name to me that *bête* of a word 'impossible;'" in the first Napoleon's threat to the Austrian ambassador, "I will break your empire like this vase;" in Nelson turning his blind eye to the signal of retreat at Copenhagen, and Wellington fencing Torres Vedras against the world: it lingered in Nicholas the Czar, and has found, perhaps, its latest political representative in Prince Bismarck.

This is the spirit to which Carlyle has always given his undivided sympathy. He has held out hands to Knox, Francia, Friedrich, to the men who have made manners, not to the manners which have made men, to the rulers of people, not to their representatives: and the not inconsiderable following he has obtained is the most conspicuous tribute to a power resolute to pull against the stream. How strong its currents may be illustrated by a few lines from our leading literary journal, the *Athenæum*, of the Saturday after his death:

"The future historian of the century will have to record the marvellous fact that while in the reign of Queen Victoria there was initiated, formulated, and methodised an entirely new cosmogony, its most powerful and highly-gifted man of letters was preaching a polity and a philosophy of history that would have better harmonised with the time of Queen Semiramis. . . . Long before he launched his sarcasms at human progress, there had been a conviction among thinkers that it was not the hero that developed the race, but a deep mysterious energy in the race that produced the hero; that the wave produced the bubble, and not the bubble the wave. But the moment a

theory of evolution saw the light it was a fact. The old
cosmogony, on which were built *Sartor Resartus* and the
Calvinism of Ecclefechan, was gone. Ecclefechan had declared that the earth did not move; but it moved nevertheless. The great stream of modern thought has advanced;
the theory of evolution has been universally accepted; nations, it is acknowledged, produce kings, and kings are
denied the faculty of producing nations."

Taliter, qualiter ; but one or two remarks on the incisive summary of this adroit and able theorist are obvious.
First, the implied assertion — " Ecclefechan had declared
that the earth did not move "—that Carlyle was in essential sympathy with the Inquisitors who confronted Galileo
with the rack, is perhaps the strangest piece of recent criticism extant: for what is his *French Revolution* but a can-
nonade in three volumes, reverberating, as no other book
has done, a hurricane of revolutionary thought and deed,
a final storming of old fortresses, an assertion of the necessity of movement, progress, and upheaval. Secondly,
every new discovery is apt to be discredited by new shib-
boleths, and one-sided exaggerations of its range. It were
platitude to say that Mr. Darwin was not only an almost
unrivalled student of nature, as careful and conscientious
in his methods, as fearless in stating his results, but—
pace Mr. Carlyle—a man of genius, who has thrown floods
of light on the inter-relations of the organic world. But
there are troops of serfs, "ullius addicti jurare in verba
magistri," who, accepting, without attempt or capacity to
verify the conclusions of the master mind, think to solve
all the mysteries of the universe by ejaculating the word
" Evolution." If I ask what was the secret of Dante's or
of Shakespeare's divining rod, and you answer " Evolution," 'tis as if, when sick in heart and sick in head, I were

referred, as medicine for "a mind diseased," to Grimm's Law or to the Magnetic Belt.

Let us grant that Cæsar was evolved from the currents in the air about the Roman Capitol, that Marcus Aurelius was a blend of Plato and Cleanthes, Charlemagne a graft of Frankish blood on Gallic soil, William I. a rill from Rollo filtered in Neustrian fields, Hildebrand a flame from the altar of the mediæval church, Barbarossa a plant grown to masterdom in German woods, or later — not to heap up figures whose memories still possess the world — that Columbus was a Genoan breeze, Bacon a *réchauffé* of Elizabethan thought, Orange the Silent a Dutch dyke, Chatham the frontispiece of eighteenth-century England, or Corsican Buonaparte the "armed soldier of Democracy." These men, at all events, were no bubbles on the froth of the waves which they defied and dominated.

This, and more, is to be said for Carlyle's insistance that great men are creators as well as creatures of their age. Doubtless, as we advance in history, direct personal influence, happily or unhappily, declines. In an era of over-wrought activity, of superficial, however free, education, when we run the risk of being associated into nothingness and criticised to death, it remains a question whether, in the interests of the highest civilisation (which means opportunity for every capable citizen to lead the highest life), the subordination of the one to the many ought to be accelerated or retarded. It is said that the triumph of Democracy is a mere "matter of time." But time is in this case of the essence of the matter, and the party of resistance will all the more earnestly maintain that the defenders should hold the forts till the invaders have become civilised. "The individual withers and the world is more and more," preludes, though over a long interval, the cynic comment of the second "Locksley Hall" on the "increasing purpose" of the age. At an earlier date "Luria" had protested against the arrogance of mere majorities.

> A people is but the attempt of many
> To rise to the completer life of one;
> And those who live as models to the mass
> Are singly of more value than they all.

Carlyle set these notes to Tennyson and to Browning in his *Hero Worship*—in reality, in thought, and more in action, older than Buddha or than Achilles, but which he first, as a dogma, sprang on our recent times, clenched with the asseveration that on two men, Mirabeau and Napoleon, mainly hung the fates of the most nominally levelling of Revolutions. The stamp his teaching made is still graven on the minds of the men of light who *lead*, and cannot be wholly effaced by the tongues of the men of words who *orate*. If he leans unduly to the exaltation of personal power, Carlyle is on the side of those whose defeat can be beneficent only if it be slow. Otherwise, to account for his attitude, we must refer to his life and to its surroundings, *i.e.* to the circumstances amid which he was "evolved."

CHAPTER II.

ECCLEFECHAN AND EDINBURGH.

[1795–1826.]

In the introduction to one of his essays, Carlyle has warned us against giving too much weight to genealogy : but all his biographies, from the sketch of the Riquetti kindred to his full length *Friedrich*, prefaced by two volumes of ancestry, recognise, if they do not overrate, inherited influences; and similarly his fragments of autobiography abound in suggestive reference. His family portraits are to be accepted with the deductions due to the family fever that was the earliest form of his hero-worship. Carlyle, says the *Athenæum* critic before quoted, divides contemporary mankind into the fools and the wise : the wise are the Carlyles, the Welshes, the Aitkens, and Edward Irving; the fools all the rest of unfortunate mortals: a Fuseli stroke of the critic[1] rivalling any of the author criticised ; yet the comment has a grain of truth.

The Carlyles are said to have come from the English town somewhat differently spelt, to Annandale, with David II., and, according to a legend, which the great author did not disdain to accept, among them was a certain Lord of Torthorwald, so created for defences of the Border. The churchyard of Ecclefechan is profusely strewn with the

---

[1] Even the most adverse critics of Carlyle are often his imitators, their hands taking a dye from what they work in.

graves of the family, all with coats of arms—two griffins
with adders' stings.   More definitely we find Thomas, the
author's grandfather, settled in that dullest of county villages as a carpenter.   In 1745 he saw the rebel Highlanders
on their southward march : he was notable for his study of
Anson's Voyages and of the *Arabian Nights:* "a fiery man,
his stroke as ready as his word; of the toughness and
springiness of steel; an honest but not an industrious
man;" subsequently tenant of a small farm, in which
capacity he does not seem to have managed his affairs
with much effect; the family were subjected to severe pri-
vations, the mother having, on occasion, to heat the meal
into cakes by straw taken from the sacks on which the
children slept.   In such an atmosphere there grew and
throve the five sons known as the five fighting masons—
"a curious sample of folks," said an old apprentice of one
of them, "pithy, bitter speaking bodies, and awfu' fighters."
The second of the group, James, born 1757, married—first,
a cousin, Janet Carlyle (the issue of which marriage, John
of Cockermouth, died before his grandfather) ; second,
Margaret Aitken, by whom he had four sons—THOMAS,
1795–1881 ; Alexander, 1797–1876 ; John (Dr. Carlyle,
translator of Dante), 1801–1879 ; and James, 1805–1890 ;
also five daughters, one of whom, Jane, became the wife of
her cousin James Aitken of Dumfries, and the mother of
Mary, the niece who tended her famous uncle so faithfully
during the last years of his life.   Nowhere is Carlyle's
loyalty to his race shown in a fairer light than in the first
of the papers published under the name of *Reminiscences.*
It differs from the others in being of an early date and
free from all offence.   From this pathetic sketch, written
when on a visit to London in 1832 he had sudden news
of his father's death, we may, even in our brief space,

extract a few passages which throw light on the characters, *i.e.* the points of contact and contrast of the writer and his theme :

In several respects I consider my father as one of the most inter- esting men I have known, . . . of perhaps the very largest natural endowment of any it has been my lot to converse with. None of you will ever forget that bold flowing style of his, flowing free from his untutored soul, full of metaphors (though he knew not what a meta- phor was), with all manner of potent words. . . . Nothing did I ever hear him undertake to render visible which did not become almost ocularly so. Emphatic I have heard him beyond all men. In anger he had no need of oaths : his words were like sharp arrows that smote into the very heart. The fault was that he exaggerated (which tendency I also inherit), yet in description, and for the sake chiefly of humorous effect. He was a man of rigid, even scrupulous veracity. . . . He was never visited with doubt. The old Theorem of the Universe was sufficient for him . . . he stood a true man, while his son stands here on the verge of the new. . . . A virtue he had which I should learn to imitate : he never spoke of what was dis- agreeable and past. His was a healthy mind. He had the most open contempt for all "clatter." . . . He was irascible, choleric, and we all dreaded his wrath, but passion never mastered him. . . . Man's face he did not fear : God he always feared. His reverence was, I think, considerably mixed with fear—rather awe, as of utter- able depths of silence through which flickered a trembling hope. . . . Let me learn of him. Let me write my books as he built his houses, and walk as blamelessly through this shadow world. . . . Though genuine and coherent, living and life-giving, he was nevertheless but half developed. We had all to complain that we durst not freely love him. His heart seemed as if walled in : he had not the free means to unbosom himself. . . . It seemed as if an atmosphere of fear repelled us from him. To me it was especially so. Till late years I was ever more or less awed and chilled by him.

James Carlyle has been compared to the father of Burns. The failings of both leant to virtue's side, in different ways. They were at one in their integrity, independence, fighting

force at stress, and their command of winged words; but
the elder had a softer heart, more love of letters, a broader
spirit; the younger more power to stem adverse tides, he
was a better man of business, made of tougher clay, and a
grimmer Calvinist. "Mr. Lawson," he writes in 1817, "is
doing very well, and has given us no more paraphrases."
He seems to have grown more rigid as he aged, under the
narrowing influences of the Covenanting land; but he remained stable and compact as the Auldgarth Bridge, built
with his own hands. James Carlyle hammered on at
Ecclefechan, making in his best year £100, till, after the
first decade of the century, the family migrated to Mainhill,
a bleak farm two miles from Lockerby, where he so throve
by work and thrift that he left, on his death in 1832, about
£1000. Strong, rough, and eminently *straight*, intolerant
of contradiction and ready with words like blows, his un-
sympathetic side recalls rather the father of the Brontës on
the wild Yorkshire moor than William Burness by the ingle
of Mount Oliphant. Margaret Carlyle was in theological
theory as strict as her husband, and for a time made more
moan over the aberrations of her favourite son. Like most
Scotch mothers of her rank, she had set her heart on seeing
him in a pulpit, from which any other eminence seemed a
fall; but she became, though comparatively illiterate, having
only late in life learnt to write a letter, a student of his
books. Over these they talked, smoking together, in old
country fashion, by the hearth; and she was to the last
proud of the genius which grew in large measure under
the unfailing sunshine of her anxious love.

Book II. of *Sartor* is an acknowledged fragment of
autobiography, mainly a record of the author's inner life,
but with numerous references to his environment. There
is not much to identify the foster parents of Teufelsdröckh,

and the dramatic drollery of the child's advent takes the place of ancestry: Entefuhl is obviously Ecclefechan, where the ducks are paddling in the ditch that has to pass muster for a stream, to-day as a century gone: the severe frugality which (as in the case of Wordsworth and Carlyle himself) survived the need for it is clearly recalled; also the discipline of the Roman-like domestic law, "In an orderly house, where the litter of children's sports is hateful, your training is rather to bear than to do. I was forbid much, wishes in any measure bold I had to renounce; everywhere a strait bond of obedience inflexibly held me down. It was not a joyful life, yet . . . a wholesome one." The following oft-quoted passage is characteristic of his early love of nature and the humorous touches by which he was wont to relieve his fits of sentiment:

On fine evenings I was wont to carry forth my supper (bread crumb boiled in milk) and eat it out of doors. On the coping of the wall, which I could reach by climbing, my porringer was placed: there many a sunset have I, looking at the distant mountains, consumed, not without relish, my evening meal. Those hues of gold and azure, that hush of worldly expectation as day died, were still a Hebrew speech for me: nevertheless I was looking at the fair illumined letters, and had an eye for the gilding.

In all that relates to the writer's own education, the Dichtung of *Sartor* and the Wahrheit of the *Reminiscences* are in accord. By Carlyle's own account, an "insignificant portion" of it "depended on schools." Like Burns, he was for some years trained in his own parish, where home influences counted for more than the teaching of not very competent masters. He soon read eagerly and variously. At the age of seven he was, by an Inspector of the old order, reported to be "complete in English."

In his tenth year (1805) he was sent to the Grammar
School of Annan, the "Hinterschlag Gymnasium," where
his "evil days began." Every oversensitive child finds
the life of a public school one long misery. Ordinary
boys — those of the Scotch borderland being of the most
savage type — are more brutal than ordinary men ; they
hate singularity as the world at first hates originality, and
have none of the restraints which the later semi-civilisa-
tion of life imposes. "They obey the impulse of rude
Nature which bids the deerherd fall upon any stricken
hart, the duck flock put to death any broken-winged
brother or sister, and on all hands the strong tyrannise
over the weak." Young Carlyle was mocked for his
moody ways, laughed at for his love of solitude, and
called "Tom the Tearful" because of his habit of crying.
To add much to his discomfort, he had made a rash promise to his pious mother, who seems, in contrast to her
husband's race, to have adopted non-resistance principles
— a promise to abstain from fighting, provocative of many
cuffs till it was well broken by a hinterschlag, applied to
some blustering bully. Nor had he refuge in the sympathy of his teacher's "bide-bound pedants, who knew
Syntax enough, and of the human soul thus much : that
it had a faculty called Memory, which could be acted on
through the muscular integument by appliance of birch
rods." At Annan, however, he acquired a fair knowledge
of Latin and French, the rudiments of algebra, the Greek
alphabet, began to study history, and had his first glimpse
of Edward Irving, the bright prize-taker from Edinburgh,
later his Mentor and then life-long friend. On Thomas's
return home it was decided to send him to the University,
despite the cynical warning of one of the village cronies,
"Educate a boy, and he grows up to despise his ignorant

parents." "Thou hast not done so," said old James in after years; "God be thanked for it," and the son plays due tribute to the tolerant patience and substantial generosity of the father: "With a noble faith he launched me forth into a world which he himself had never been permitted to visit." Carlyle walked through Moffat all the way to Edinburgh with a senior student, Tom Smail (who owes to this fact the preservation of his name), with eyes open to every shade on the moors, as is attested in two passages of the *Reminiscences.* The boys, as is the fashion still, clubbed together in cheap lodgings, and Carlyle attended the curriculum from 1809 to 1814. Comparatively little is known of his college life, which seems to have been for the majority of Scotch students much as it is now, a compulsorily frugal life, with too little variety, relaxation, or society outside Class Rooms, and within them a constant tug at Science, mental or physical, at the gateway to dissecting souls or bodies. We infer, from hints in later conversations and memorials, that Carlyle lived much with his own fancies, and owed little to any system. He is clearly thinking of his own youth in his account of Dr. Francia: "José must have been a loose-made tawny creature, much given to taciturn reflection, probably to crying humours, with fits of vehement ill nature—subject to the terriblest fits of hypochondria." His explosion in *Sartor,* "It is my painful duty to say that out of England and Spain, ours was the worst of all hitherto discovered Universities," is the first of a long series of libels on things and persons he did not like. The Scotch capital was still a literary centre of some original brilliancy, in the light of the circle of Scott, which followed that of Burns, in the early fame of Cockburn and Clark (Lord Eldin), of the *Quarterly* and *Edinburgh Reviews,* and of the elder Alison. The Chairs of the University were con-spicuously well filled by men of the sedate sort of ability required from Professors, some of them — conspicuously Brown, the more original if less "sound" successor of Dugald Stewart, Playfair, and Leslie—rising to a higher rank. But great Educational institutions must adapt themselves to the training of average minds by require-ments and retractions against which genius always rebels. Biography more than History repeats itself, and the mur-murs of Carlyle are, like those of Milton, Gibbon, Locke, and Wordsworth, the protests or growls of irrepressible individuality kicking against the pricks. He was never in any sense a classic; read Greek with difficulty—Æschylus and Sophocles mainly in translations—and while appre-ciating Tacitus disparaged Horace. For Scotch Meta-physics, or any logical system, he never cared, and in his days there was written over the Academic entrances " No Mysticism." He distinguished himself in Mathematics, and soon found, by his own vaunt,[1] the *Principia* of Newton prostrate at his feet: he was a favourite pupil of Leslie, who escaped the frequent penalty of befriending him, but he took no prizes: the noise in the class room hindered his answers, and he said later to Mr. Froude that thoughts only came to him properly when alone. The social leader of a select set of young men in his own rank, by choice and necessity *integer vitæ* he divided his time be-tween the seclusion of study and writing letters, in which kind of literature he was perhaps the most prolific writer of his time. In 1814 Carlyle completed his course with-out taking a degree, did some tutorial work, and, in the

[1] He went so far as to say in 1847 that "the man who had mastered the first forty-seven propositions of Euclid stood nearer to God than he had done before."

same year, accepted the post of Mathematical Usher at
Annan as successor to Irving, who had been translated to
Haddington.   Still in formal pursuit of the ministry,
though beginning to fight shy of its fences, he went up
twice a year to deliver addresses at the Divinity Hall, one
of which, "on the uses of affliction," was afterwards by
himself condemned as flowery; another was a Latin thesis
on the theme, "num detur religio naturalis." The posthumous publication of some of his writings, *e.g.* of the
fragment of the novel *Wotton Reinfred*, reconciles us to
the loss of those which have not been recovered.

In the vacations, spent at Mainhill, he began to study
German, and corresponded with his College friends. Many
of Carlyle's early letters, reproduced in the volumes edited
by Mr. Charles E. Norton, are written in what Sydney
Smith asserts to be the only unpermissible style, "the
tiresome;" and the thought, far from being precocious, is
distinctly commonplace, *e.g.* the letter to Robert Mitchell
on the fall of Napoleon; or the following to his parents:
"There are few things in this world more valuable than
knowledge, and youth is the season for acquiring it;" or
to James Johnstone the trite quotation, "Truly pale death
overturns with impartial foot the hut of the poor man and
the palace of the king." Several are marred by the egotism which in most Scotch peasants of aspiring talent
takes the form of perpetual comparison of themselves with
others; refrains of the ambition against which the writer
elsewhere inveighs as the "kettle tied to the dog's tail."
In a note to Thomas Murray he writes:

Ever since I have been able to form a wish, the wish of being
known has been the foremost.   O Fortune! bestow coronets and
crowns and principalities and purses and pudding and power, upon
the great and noble and fat ones of the earth.   Grant me that, with

a heart unyielding to thy favours and unbending to thy frowns, I may attain to literary fame.

That his critical and literary instincts were yet undeveloped there is ample proof. Take his comment, at the age of nineteen, on the verses of Leyden:

> Shout, Britons, for the battle of Assaye,
> For that was a day
> When we stood in our array
> Like the lions might at bay.

"Can anything be grander?" To Johnstone (who with Mitchell consumes a whole volume) he writes: "Read Shakespeare. If you have not, then I desire you read it (*sic*) and tell me what you think of *him*," etc. Elsewhere the dogmatic summary of Hume's "Essays" illustrates the lingering eighteenth-century Latinism that had been previously travestied in the more stilted passages of the letters of Burns. "Many of his opinions are not to be adopted. How odd does it look to refer all the modifications of national character to the influence of moral causes. Might it not be asserted with some plausibility that even those which he denominates moral causes originate from physical circumstances." The whole first volume of this somewhat over-expanded collection overflows with ebullitions of bile, in comparison with which the misanthropy of Byron's early romances seems philanthropy, *e.g.* :

How weary, flat, stale, and unprofitable seems to me all the uses of this world. For what are its inhabitants? Its great men and its little, its fat ones and its lean . . . pitiful automatons, despicable Yahoos, yea, they are altogether an insufferable thing. "O! for a lodge in some vast wilderness, some boundless continuity of shade, where the scowl of the purse-proud nabob, the sneer and strut of the coxcomb, the bray of the ninny and the clodpole might never reach me more."

On the other hand, there are frequent evidences of the imperial intrepidity, the matchless industry, and the splendid independence of the writer.   In his twenty-first year Carlyle again succeeded his Annan predecessor (who seems to have given dissatisfaction by some vagaries of severity) as mathematical teacher in the main school of Kirkcaldy. The *Reminiscences* of Irving's generous reception of his protégé present one of the pleasantest pictures in the records of their friendship.   The same chapter is illustrated by a series of sketches of the scenery of the east coast rarely rivalled in descriptive literature.   It is elsewhere enlivened, if also defaced, by the earliest examples of the cynical criticisms of character that make most readers rejoice in having escaped the author's observation.

During the two years of his residence in Fifeshire, Carlyle encountered his first romance, in making acquaintance with a well-born young lady, "by far the brightest and cleverest" of Irving's pupils—Margaret Gordon—"an acquaintance which might easily have been more" had not relatives and circumstances intervened.   Doubtless Mr. Froude is right in asserting this lady to have been the original of *Sartor's* "Blumine," and in leaving him to marry "Herr Towgood," ultimately Governor of Nova Scotia, she bequeathed, though in formal antitheses, advice that reflects well on her discrimination of character. "Cultivate the milder dispositions of the heart, subdue the mere extravagant visions of the brain.   Genius will render you great.   May virtue render you beloved.   Remove the awful distance between you and other men by kind and gentle manners.   Deal gently with their inferiority, and be convinced that they will respect you as much and like you more."   To this advice, which he never even tried to take, she adds, happily perhaps for herself, "I give you not my address, because I dare not promise to see you." In 1818 Carlyle, always intolerant of work imposed, came to the conclusion that "it were better to perish than to continue schoolmastering," and left Kirkcaldy, with £90 saved, for Edinburgh, where he lived over three years, taking private pupils, and trying to enter on his real mission through the gates of literature — gates constantly barred, for even in those older days of laxer competition, obstinacy, and outré-ness, unredeemed by any social advantages, were guarantees of frequent failure. Men with the literary form of genius highly developed have rarely much endurance of defeat. Carlyle, even in his best moods, resented real or fancied injuries, and at this stage of his career complained that he got nothing but vinegar from his fellows, comparing himself to a worm that, trodden on, would turn into a torpedo. He had begun to be tormented by the dyspepsia, which "gnawed like a rat" at its life-long tenement, his stomach, and by sleeplessness, due in part to internal causes, but also to the "Bedlam" noises of men, machines, and animals, which pestered him in town and country from first to last. He kept hesitating about his career, tried law, mathematical teaching, contributions to magazines and dictionaries, everything but journalism, to which he had a rooted repugnance, and the Church, which he had definitely abandoned. How far the change in his views may have been due to his reading of Gibbon,[1] Rousseau, Voltaire, etc., how far to self-reflection is uncertain, but he already found himself unable, in a plain sense, to subscribe to the Westminster Confession or any so-called orthodox

[1] He refers to Gibbon's *Decline and Fall* as "of all books the most impressive on me in my then stage of investigation and state of mind. His winged sarcasms, so quiet and yet so conclusively transpiercing, were often admirably potent and illustrative to me."

articles, and equally unable by any philosophical reconciliation of contraries to write black with white on a ground
of neutral gray.   Mentally and physically adrift he was
midway in the valley of the shadow, which he represents
as "The Everlasting No," and beset by "temptations in
the wilderness."   At this crisis he writes, "the biographies
of men of letters are the wretchedest chapters in our history, except perhaps the Newgate Calendar," a remark that
recalls the similar cry of Burns, "There are not among the
martyrologies so rueful a narrative as the lives of the
poets."   Carlyle, reverting to this crisis, refers with constant bitterness to the absence of a popularity which he
yet professes to scorn.

I was entirely unknown in Edinburgh circles; solitary eating my
own heart, misgivings as to whether there shall be presently anything else to eat, fast losing health, a prey to numerous struggles
and miseries . . . three weeks without any kind of sleep, from im-
possibility to be free of noise, . . . wanderings through mazes of
doubt, perpetual questions unanswered, etc.

What is this but Byron's cry, "I am not happy?" which
his afterwards stern critic compares to the screaming of a
meat-jack.

Carlyle carried with him from town to country the same
dismal mood.   "Mainhill," says his biographer, "was never
a less happy home to him than it was this summer (1819).
He could not conceal the condition of his mind; and to
his family, to whom the truth of their creed was no more
a matter of doubt than the presence of the sun in the sky,
he must have seemed as if possessed."

Returning to Edinburgh in the early winter, he for a
time wrote hopefully about his studies.   "The law I find
to be a most complicated subject, yet I like it pretty well.

Its great charm in my eyes is that no mean compliances are requisite for prospering in it." But this strain soon gave way to a fresh fit of perversity, and we have a record of his throwing up the cards in one of his most ill-natured notes.

I did read some law books, attend Hume's lectures on Scotch law, and converse with and question various dull people of the practical sort. But it and they and the admired lecturing Hume himself appeared to me mere denizens of the kingdom of dulness, pointing towards nothing but money as wages for all that bogpost of disgust.

The same year (that of Peterloo) was that of the Radical rising in Glasgow against the poverty which was the natural aftermath of the great war, oppressions, half real, half imaginary, of the military force, and the yeomaury in particular. Carlyle's contribution to the reminiscences of the time is doubly interesting because written (in the article on Irving, 1836) from memory, when he had long ceased to be a Radical. A few sentences suffice to illustrate this phase or stage of his political progress:

A time of great rages and absurd terrors and expectations, a very fierce Radical and anti-Radical time. Edinburgh, endlessly agitated by it all around me . . . gentry people full of zeal and foolish terror and fury, and looking *disgustingly busy and important*. . . . One bleared Sunday morning I had gone out for my walk. At the riding house in Nicholson Street was a kind of straggly group, with red-coats interspersed. They took their way, not very dangerous-looking men of war ; but there rose from the little crowd the strangest shout I have heard human throats utter, not very loud, but it said as plain as words, and with infinitely more emphasis of sincerity, "May the devil go with you, ye peculiarly contemptible, and dead to the distresses of your fellow-creatures." Another morning . . . I met an advocate slightly of my acquaintance hurrying along, musket in hand, towards the Links, there to be drilled as item of the "gentlemen" volunteers now a-foot. " You should have the like of this," said he, cheerily patting his musket.   " Hm, yes ; but I haven't yet quite settled on which side "—which probably he hoped was quiz, though it really expressed my feeling . . . mutiny and revolt being a light matter to the young.

This period is illustrated by numerous letters from Irving, who had migrated to Glasgow as an assistant to Dr. Chalmers, abounding in sound counsels to persevere in some profession and make the best of practical opportunities.   None of Carlyle's answers have been preserved, but the sole trace of his having been influenced by his friend's advice is his contribution (1820–1823) of sixteen[1]

[1] The subjects of these were—Lady Mary Wortley Montagu, Montaigne, Montesquieu, Montfaucon, Dr. Moore, Sir John Moore, Necker, Nelson, Netherlands, Newfoundland, Norfolk, Northamptonshire, Northumberland, Mungo Park, Lord Chatham, William Pitt.   These articles, on the whole, judiciously omitted from the author's collected works, are characterised by marks of great industry, commonplace and general fairness, with a style singularly formal, like that of the less impressive pages of Johnson.   The following, among numerous passages, are curious as illustrating the comparative orthodoxy of the writer's early judgments : " The brilliant hints which ' Montesquieu' scatters round him with a liberal hand have excited or assisted the speculations of others in almost every department of political economy, and he is deservedly mentioned as a principal founder of that important service."   " Mirabeau confronted him (' Necker ') like his evil genius ; and being totally without scruple in the employment of any expedient, was but too successful in overthrowing all reasonable proposals, and conducting the people to that state of anarchy out of which his own ambition was to be rewarded," etc. Similarly the verdicts on Pitt, Chatham, Nelson, Park, Lady Montagu, etc., are those of an ordinary intelligent Englishman of conscientious research, fed on the " Lives of the Poets " and Trafalgar memories.   The morality, as in the Essay on Montaigne, is unexceptionable ; the following would commend itself to any boarding-

articles to the *Edinburgh Encyclopædia* under the editorship of Sir David Brewster. The scant remuneration obtained from these .was well timed, but they contain no
original matter, and did nothing for his fame. Meanwhile
it appears from one of Irving's letters that Carlyle's
thoughts had been, as later in his early London life, turning towards emigration. " He says," writes his friend, " I
have the ends of my thoughts to bring together . . . my
views of life to reform, my health to recover, and then
once more I shall venture my bark on the waters of this
wide realm, and if she cannot weather it I shall steer west
and try the waters of another world."

The resolves, sometimes the efforts of celebrated Englishmen, " nos manet oceanus," as Cromwell, Burns, Coleridge, and Southey (allured, some critic suggests, by the
poetical sound of Susquehanna), Arthur Clough, Richard
Hengist Horne, and Browning's " Waring,"[1] to elude " the
fever and the fret " of an old civilisation, and take refuge
in the fancied freedom of wild lands, when more than
dreams have been failures. Puritan patriots, it is true,
made New England and the scions of the Cavaliers Vir-
ginia; but no poet or imaginative writer has ever been
successfully transplanted, with the dubious exception of
Heinrich Heine. It is certain that, despite his first warm
recognition coming from across the Atlantic, the author of
the *Latter-Day Pamphlets* would have found the " States "

school: " Melancholy experience has never ceased to show that great
warlike talents, like great talents of any kind, may be united with a
coarse and ignoble heart."

[1] Cf. the American Bryant himself, in his longing to leave his
New York Press and " plant him where the red deer feed, in the
green forest," to lead the life of Robin Hood and Shakespeare's
banished Duke.

more fruitful in food for cursing than either Edinburgh or London.

The spring of 1820 was marked by a memorable visit to Irving, on Carlyle's way to spend, as was his wont, the summer months at home. His few days in Glasgow are recorded in a graphic sketch of the bald-headed merchants at the Tontine, and an account of his introduction to Dr. Chalmers, to whom he refers always with admiration and a respect but slightly modified. The critic's praise of British contemporaries, other than relatives, is so rare that the following sentences are worth transcribing :

He (Chalmers) was a man of much natural dignity, ingenuity, honesty, and kind affection, as well as sound intellect and imagination. . . . He had a burst of genuine fun too. . . . His laugh was ever a hearty, low guffaw, and his tones in preaching would reach to the piercingly pathetic. No preacher ever went so into one's heart. He was a man essentially of little culture, of narrow sphere all his life. Such an intellect, professing to be educated, and yet . . . ignorant in all that lies beyond the horizon in place or time I have almost nowhere met with—a man capable of so much soaking indolence, lazy brooding . . . as a first stage of his life well indicated, . . . yet capable of impetuous activity and braying audacity, as his later years showed. I suppose there will never again be such a preacher in any Christian church. "The truth of Christianity," he said, "was all written in us already in sympathetic ink. Bible awakens it and you can read."

A sympathetic image but of no great weight as an argument addressed to doubting Thomas. Chalmers, whose originality lay rather in his quick insight and fire than in his, mainly commonplace, thought, had the credit of recognising the religious side of his (Carlyle's) genius, when to the mass of his countrymen he was a rock of offence. One of the great preacher's criticisms of the great writer is notably just: "He is a lover of earnestness more than a lover of truth."

There follows in some of the first pages of the *Reminiscences* an account of a long walk with Irving, who had arranged to accompany Carlyle for the first stage, *i.e.* fifteen miles of the road of his, for the most part, pedestrian march from Glasgow to Ecclefechan, a record among many of similar excursions over dales and hills, and "by the beached margent," revived for us in sun and shade by a pen almost as magical as Turner's brush. We must refer to the pages of Mr. Froude for the picture of Drumclog moss—"a good place for Cameronian preaching, and dangerously difficult for Claverse (*sic*) and horse soldiery if the suffering remnant had a few old muskets among them"—for the graphic glimpse of Ailsa Craig, and the talk by the dry stone fence, in the twilight. "It was just here, as the sun was sinking, Irving drew from me by degrees, in the softest manner, that I did not think as he of the Christian religion, and that it was vain for me to expect I ever could or should. This, if this was so, he had pre-engaged to take well of me, like an elder brother, if I would be frank with him. And right loyally he did so." They parted here: Carlyle trudged on to the then "utterly quiet little inn" at Muirkirk, left next morning at 4 A.M., and reached Dumfries, a distance of fifty-four miles, at 8 P.M., "the longest walk I ever made." He spent the summer at Mainhill, studying modern languages, "living riotously with Schiller and Goethe," at work on the *Encyclopædia* articles, and visiting his friend at Annan, when there came an offer of the charge of a son of a Yorkshire farmer, which Irving urged him to accept, advancing the old plea, "You live too much in an ideal world," and wisely adding, "try your hand with the respectable illit-

erate men of middle life. You may be taught to forget
. . . the splendours and envies . . . of men of literature."

This exhortation led to a result recorded with much
humour, egotism, and arrogance in a letter to his intimate
friend Dr. John Fergusson, of Kelso Grammar School,
which, despite the mark "private and confidential," was
yet published, several years after the death of the recipi-
ent and shortly after that of the writer, in a gossiping
memoir. We are, therefore, at liberty to select from the
letter the following paragraphs:

I delayed sending an answer till I might have it in my power to
communicate what seemed then likely to produce a considerable
change in my stile (*sic*) of life, a proposal to become a "travelling
tutor," as they call it, to a young person in the North Riding, for
whom that exercise was recommended on account of bodily and
mental weakness. They offered me £150 per annum, and withal invited me to come and examine things on the spot before engaging.
I went accordingly, and happy was it I went; from description I
was ready to accept the place; from inspection all Earndale would
not have hired me to accept it. This boy was a dotard, a semi-vege-
table, the elder brother, head of the family, a two-legged animal
without feathers, intellect, or virtue, and all the connections seemed
to have the power of eating pudding but no higher power. So I left
the barbarous people. . . . York is but a heap of bricks. Jonathan
Dryasdust (see *Ivanhoe*) is justly named. York is the Bœotia of
Britain. . . . Upon the whole, however, I derived great amusement
from my journey, . . . I conversed with all kinds of men, from
graziers up to knights of the shire, argued with them all, and broke
specimens from their souls (if any,) which I retain within the museum of my cranium. I have no prospects that are worth the name.
I am like a being thrown from another planet on this dark terres-
trial ball, an alien, a pilgrim . . . and life is to me like a pathless, a
waste, and a howling wilderness. Do not leave your situation if you
can possibly avoid it. Experience shows it to be a fearful thing to
be swept in by the roaring surge of life, and then to float alone un-
directed on its restless, monstrous bosom. Keep ashore while yet

you may, or if you must to sea, sail under convoy; trust not the waves without a guide. You and I are but pinnaces or cork boats, yet hold fast by the Manilla ship, *and do not let go the painter.*

Towards the close of this year Irving, alarmed by his friend's despondency, sent him a most generous and delicately-worded invitation to spend some months under his roof; but Carlyle declined, and in a letter of March, 1821, he writes to his brother John : "Edinburgh, with all its drawbacks, is the only scene for me," on which follows one of his finest descriptions, that of the view from Arthur's Seat.

According to the most probable chronology, for many of Carlyle's dates are hard to fix, the next important event of his life, his being introduced, on occasion of a visit to Haddington, to Miss Jane Welsh by her old tutor, Edward Irving—an event which marks the beginning of a new era in his career—took place towards the close of May or in the first week of June. To June is assigned the incident, described in *Sartor* as the transition from the Everlasting No to the Everlasting Yea, a sort of revelation that came upon him as he was in Leith Walk—Rue St. Thomas de l'Enfer in the Romance—on the way to cool his distempers by a plunge in the sea. The passage proclaiming this has been everywhere quoted; and it is only essential to note that it resembled the "illuminations" of St. Paul and of Constantine merely by its being a sudden spiritual impulse. It was in no sense a conversion to any belief in person or creed, it was but the assertion of a strong manhood against an almost suicidal mood of despair; a condition set forth with a superabundant paraphernalia of eloquence easily condensed. Doubt in the mind of Teufelsdröckh had darkened into disbelief in divine or human justice, freedom, or himself. If there be a God, He sits

on the hills "since the first Sabbath," careless of mankind.
Duty seems to be but a "phantasm made up of desire and
fear;" virtue "some bubble of the blood," absence of vitality perhaps.

What in these days are terrors of conscience to diseases of the
liver? Not on morality but on cookery let us build our stronghold.
... Thus has the bewildered wanderer to stand, shouting question
after question into the Sibyl cave, and receiving for answer an echo.

From this scepticism, deeper than that of *Queen Mab*,
fiercer than that of *Candide*, Carlyle was dramatically rescued by the sense that he was a servant of God, even when
doubting His existence.

After all the nameless woe that inquiry had wrought me, I nevertheless still loved truth, and would bait no jot of my allegiance. ...
Truth I cried, though the heavens crush me for following her; no
falsehood! though a whole celestial lubberland were the price of
apostacy.

With a grasp on this rock, Carlyle springs from the slough
of despond and asserts himself:

> Ich bin ein Mensch geboren
> Und das muss ein Kämpfer seyn.

He finds in persistent action, energy, and courage a present
strength, and a lamp of at least such partial victory as he
lived to achieve.

> He would not make his judgment blind;
> He faced the spectres of the mind—

but he never "laid them," or came near the serenity of his
master, Goethe; and his teaching, public and private, remained half a wail. The Leith Walk revolt was rather
the attitude of a man turning at bay than of one making
a leap.

2*

Death?   Well, Death . . . let it come then, and I will meet it and defy it.   And as so I thought there rushed a stream of fire over my soul, and I shook base fear away.   Ever from that time the temper of my misery was changed; not . . . whining sorrow . . . but grim defiance.

Yet the misery remained, for two years later we find him writing :

I could read the curse of Ernulphus, or something twenty times as fierce, upon myself and all things earthly. . . . The year is closing. This time eight and twenty years I was a child of three weeks ago. . . .

> Oh! little did my mother think,
>   That day she cradled me,
> The lands that I should travel in,
>   The death I was to dee.

My curse seems deeper and blacker than that of any man: to be immured in a rotten carcase, every avenue of which is changed into an inlet of pain.   How have I deserved this? . . . I know not.   Then why don't you kill yourself, sir?   Is there not arsenic, is there not ratsbane of various kinds, and hemp, and steel?   Most true, Satha-nas . . . but it will be time enough to use them when I have *lost* the game I am but *losing*, . . . and while my friends, my mother, father, brothers, sisters live, the duty of not breaking their hearts would still remain. . . . I want health, health, health!   On this subject I am becoming quite furious: my torments are greater than I am able to bear.

Nowhere in Carlyle's writing, save on the surface, is there any excess of Optimism; but after the Leith Walk inspiration he had resolved on "no surrender;" and that, henceforth, he had better heart in his work we have proof in its more regular, if not more rapid, progress.   His last hack service was the series of articles for Brewster, unless we add a translation, under the same auspices, of Legendre's Geometry, begun, according to some reports, in the Kirkcaldy period, finished in 1822, and published in 1824. For this task, prefixed by an original *Essay on Proportion*, much commended by De Morgan, he obtained the respectable sum of £50. Two subsequent candidatures for Chairs of Astronomy showed that Carlyle had not lost his taste for Mathematics; but this work was his practical farewell to that science. His first sustained efforts as an author were those of an interpreter. His complete mastery of German has been said to have endowed him with "his sword of sharpness and shoes of swiftness;" it may be added, in some instances also, with the "fog-cap." But in his earliest substantial volume, the *Life of Schiller*, there is nothing either obscure in style or mystic in thought. This work began to appear in the *London Magazine* in 1823, was finished in 1824, and in 1825 published in a separate form. Approved during its progress by an encouraging article in the *Times*, it was, in 1830, translated into German on the instigation of Goethe, who introduced the work by an important commendatory preface, and so first brought the author's name conspicuously before a continental public. Carlyle himself, partly, perhaps, from the spirit of contradiction, was inclined to speak slightingly of this high-toned and sympathetic biography: "It is," said he, "in the wrong vein, laborious, partly affected, meagre, bombastic." But these are sentences of a morbid time, when, for want of other victims, he turned and rent himself. *Pari passu*, he was toiling at his translation of *Wilhelm Meister's Apprenticeship*. This was published in Edinburgh in 1824. Heartily commended in *Blackwood*, it was generally recognised as one of the best English renderings of any foreign author; and Jeffrey, in his absurd review of Goethe's great prose drama, speaks in high terms of the skill displayed by the translator. The virulent at-

tack of De Quincey—a writer as unreliable as brilliant—in
the *London Magazine* does not seem to have carried much
weight even then, and has none now. The *Wanderjahre*,
constituting the third volume of the English edition, first
appeared as the last of four on German Romance—a series
of admirably selected and executed translations from Mu-
sæus, Fouqué, Tieck, Hoffmann, Richter, and Goethe, prefaced by short biographical and critical notices of each—
published in Edinburgh in 1827. This date is also that
of the first of the more elaborate and extensive criticisms
which, appearing in the Edinburgh and Foreign reviews,
established Carlyle as the English pioneer of German literature. The result of these works would have been enough
to drive the wolf from the door and to render their author
independent of the oatmeal from home; but another
source of revenue enabled him not only to keep himself,
but to settle his brother Alick in a farm, and to support
John through his University course as a medical student.
This and similar services to the family circle were rendered
with gracious disclaimers of obligation. "What any
brethren of our father's house possess, I look on as a common stock from which all are entitled to draw."

For this good fortune he was again indebted to his
friend of friends. Irving had begun to feel his position
at Glasgow unsatisfactory, and at the close of 1821 he was
induced to accept an appointment to the Caledonian Chap-
el at Hatton Garden. On migrating to London, to make
a greater, if not a safer, name in the central city, and finally, be lost in its vortex, he had invited Carlyle to follow
him, saying, "Scotland breeds men, but England rears
them." Shortly after, introduced by Mrs. Strachey, one
of his worshipping audience, to her sister, Mrs. Buller, he
found the latter in trouble about the education of her sons.

Charles, the elder, was a youth of bright but restive intelligence, and it was desired to find some transitional training for him on his way from Harrow to Cambridge. Irving urged his being placed, in the interim, under Carlyle's charge. The proposal, with an offer of £200 a year, was accepted, and the brothers were soon duly installed in George Square, while their tutor remained in Moray Place, Edinburgh. The early stages of this relationship were eminently satisfactory; Carlyle wrote that the teaching of the Bullers was a pleasure rather than a task; they seemed to him " quite another set of boys than I have been used to, and treat me in another sort of manner than tutors are used. The eldest is one of the cleverest boys I have ever seen." There was never any jar between the teacher and the taught. Carlyle speaks with unfailing regard of the favourite pupil, whose brilliant University and Parliamentary career bore testimony to the good practical guidance he had received. His premature death at the entrance on a sphere[1] of wider influence made a serious blank in his old master's life.

But as regards the relation of the employer and employed, we are wearied by the constantly recurring record of kindness lavishly bestowed, ungraciously received, and soon ungratefully forgotten. The elder Bullers — the mother a former beauty and woman of some brilliancy, the father a solid and courteous gentleman retired from the Anglo-Indian service—came to Edinburgh in the spring of the tutorship, and recognising Carlyle's abilities, welcomed him to the family circle, and treated him, by his own confession, with a " degree of respect " he " did not de-

---

[1] Charles Buller became Carlyle's pupil at the age of fifteen. He died as Commissioner of the Poor in 1848 (*æt.* forty-two).

serve ;" adapting their arrangements, as far as possible, to his hours and habits; consulting his convenience and humouring his whims. Early in 1823 they went to live together at Kinnaird House, near Dunkeld, when he continued to write letters to his kin still praising his patrons; but the first note of discord is soon struck in satirical references to their aristocratic friends and querulous complaints of the servants. During the winter, for greater quiet, a room was assigned to him in another house near Kinnaird; a consideration which met with the award: "My bower is the most polite of bowers, refusing admittance to no wind that blows." And about this same time he wrote, growling at his fare: "It is clear to me that I shall never recover my health under the economy of Mrs. Buller."

In 1824 the family returned to London, and Carlyle followed in June by a sailing yacht from Leith. On arrival he sent to Miss Welsh a letter, sneering at his fellow passengers, but ending with a striking picture of his first impressions of the capital:

We were winding slowly through the forests of masts in the Thames up to our station at Tower Wharf. The giant bustle, the coal heavers, the bargemen, the black buildings, the ten thousand times ten thousand sounds and movements of that monstrous harbour formed the grandest object I had ever witnessed. One man seems a drop in the ocean; you feel annihilated in the immensity of that heart of all the world.

On reaching London he first stayed for two or three weeks under Irving's roof and was introduced to his friends. Of Mrs. Strachey and her young cousin Kitty, who seems to have run the risk of admiring him to excess, he always spoke well: but the Basil Montagues, to whose hospitality and friendship he was made welcome, he has maligned in such a manner as to justify the retaliatory

pamphlet of the sharp-tongued eldest daughter of the
house, then about to become Mrs. Anne Procter.   By letter and "reminiscence" he is equally reckless in invective
against almost all the eminent men of letters with whom
he then came in contact, and also, in most cases, in ridicule
of their wives.   His accounts of Hazlitt, Campbell, and
Coleridge have just enough truth to exasperate the libels,
in some cases perhaps whetted by the consciousness of their
being addressed to a sympathetic listener: but it is his
frequent travesty of well-wishers and creditors for kindness that has left the deepest stain on his memory.   Settled with his pupil Charles in Kew Green lodgings he
writes: "The Bullers are essentially a cold race of people.
They live in the midst of fashion and external show.   They
love no living creature."   And a fortnight later, from Irving's house at Pentonville, he sends to his mother an account of his self-dismissal.   Mrs. Buller had offered him
two alternatives—to go with the family to France or to remain in the country preparing the eldest boy for Cambridge.   He declined both, and they parted, shaking hands
with dry eyes.   "I feel glad," he adds in a sentence that
recalls the worst egotism of Coleridge,[1] "that I have done
with them. . . . I was selling the very quintessence of my
spirit for £200 a year."

There followed eight weeks of residence in or about
Birmingham, with a friend called Badams, who undertook
to cure dyspepsia by a new method and failed without being reviled.   Together, and in company with others, as
the astronomer Airy, they saw the black country and the
toiling squads, in whom Carlyle, through all his shifts from
radical democracy to Platonic autocracy, continued to take

---

[1] *Vide* Carlyle's *Life of Sterling*, chap. viii., p. 79.

a deep interest; on other days they had pleasant excursions to the green fields and old towers of Warwickshire. On occasion of this visit he came in contact with De Quincey's review of *Meister*, and in recounting the event credits himself with the philosophic thought, "This man is perhaps right on some points; if so let him be admonitory." But the description that follows of "the child that has been in hell," however just, is less magnanimous. Then came a trip, in company with Mr. Strachey and Kitty and maid, by Dover and Calais along Sterne's route to Paris, "The Vanity Fair of the Universe," where Louis XVIII. was then lying dead in state. Carlyle's comments are mainly acid remarks on the Palais Royal, with the refrain, "God bless the narrow seas." But he saw Legendre and Laplace, heard Cuvier lecture and Talma act, and what was of more moment, had his first sight of the Continent and the city of one phase of whose history he was to be the most brilliant recorder. Back in London for the winter, where his time was divided between Irving's house and his own neighbouring room in Southampton Street; he was cheered by Goethe's own acknowledgment of the translation of *Meister*, and wrote more epistolary satires, welcome at Haddington.

In March, 1825, Carlyle again set his face northward, and travelling by coach through Birmingham, Manchester, Bolton, and Carlisle, established himself, in May, at Hoddam Hill; a farm near the Solway, three miles from Mainhill, which his father had leased for him. His brother Alexander farmed, while Thomas toiled on at German translations and rode about on horseback. For a space, one of the few contented periods of his life, there is a truce to complaining. Here, free from the noises, which are the pests of literary life, he was building up his character and

forming the opinions which, with few material changes, he
long continued to hold.   Thus he writes from over a distance of forty years:

With all its manifold petty troubles, this year at Hoddam Hill
has a rustic beauty and dignity to me, and lies now like a not ignoble
russet-coated idyll in my memory; one of the quietest on the whole,
and perhaps the most triumphantly important of my life. . . . I found
that I had conquered all my scepticisms, agonising doubtings, fearful wrestlings with the foul and vile and soul-murdering mud-gods of
my epoch, and was emerging free in spirit into the eternal blue of
ether.   I had in effect gained an immense victory. . . . Once more,
thank Heaven for its highest gift, I then felt and still feel endlessly indebted to Goethe in the business.   He, in his fashion, I perceived, had travelled the steep road before me, the first of the moderns.   Bodily health itself seemed improving. . . . Nowhere can I
recollect of myself such pious musings, communings silent and
spontaneous with Fact and Nature as in these poor Annandale localities.   The sound of the Kirk bell once or twice on Sunday morn-
ings from Hoddam Kirk, about a mile off on the plain below me,
was strangely touching, like the departing voice of eighteen hundred years.

Elsewhere, during one of the rare gleams of sunshine in
a life of lurid storms, we have the expression of his passionate independence, his tyrannous love of liberty:

It is inexpressible what an increase of happiness and of consciousness—of inward dignity—I have gained since I came within
the walls of this poor cottage—my own four walls.   They simply
admit that I am *Herr im Hause*, and act on this conviction.   There
is no grumbling about my habitudes and whims.   If I choose to dine
on fire and brimstone, they will cook it for me to their best skill,
thinking only that I am an unintelligible mortal, *fâcheux* to deal
with, but not to be dealt with in any other way.   My own four walls.

The last words form the refrain of a set of verses, the
most characteristic, as Mr. Froude justly observes, of the
D

writer, the actual composition of which seems, however, to
belong to the next chapter of his career, beginning:

> The storm and night is on the waste,
>   Wild through the wind the huntsman calls,
> As fast on willing nag I haste
>   Home to my own four walls.

The feeling that inspires them is clenched in the defiance:

> King George has palaces of pride,
>   And armed grooms must ward those halls;
> With one stout bolt I safe abide
>   Within my own four walls.

> Not all his men may sever this;
>   It yields to friends', not monarchs' calls;
> My whinstone house my castle is—
>   I have my own four walls.

> When fools or knaves do make a rout,
>   With jigmen, dinners, balls, cabals,
> I turn my back and shut them out:
>   These are my own four walls.

CHAPTER III.

CRAIGENPUTTOCK.

[1826–1834.]

"Ah, when she was young, she was a fleein', dancin', light-heartit thing, Jeannie Welsh, that naething would hae dauntit. But she grew grave a' at ance. There was Maister Irving, ye ken, that had been her teachor; and he cam' aboot her. Then there was Maister ——. Then there was Maister Carlyle himsel', and *he* cam' to finish her off like."—HADDINGTON NURSE.

"My broom, as I sweep up the withered leaves, might be heard at a furlong's distance."—T. CARLYLE, from Craigenputtock, Oct., 1830.

DURING the last days at Hoddam Hill, Carlyle was on the verge of a crisis of his career, *i.e.* his making a marriage, for the chequered fortune of which he was greatly himself to blame.

No biography can ignore the strange conditions of a domestic life, already made familiar in so many records that they are past evasion. Various opinions have been held regarding the lady whom he selected to share his lot. Any adequate estimate of this remarkable woman belongs to an account of her own career, such as that given by Mrs. Ireland in her judicious and interesting abridgment of the material amply supplied. Jane Baillie Welsh (*b.* 1801, *d.* 1866)—descended on the paternal side from Elizabeth, the youngest daughter of John Knox; on the maternal owning to an inheritance of gipsy blood—belonged to a family long esteemed in the borders. Her father, a distinguished Edinburgh student, and afterwards eminent surgeon at Haddington, noted alike for his humanity and skill, made a small fortune, and purchased in advance from his father his inheritance of Craigenputtock, a remnant of the once larger family estate. He died in 1819, when his daughter was in her eighteenth year. To her he left the now world-famous farm and the bulk of his property. Jane, of precocious talents, seems to have been, almost from infancy, the tyrant of the house at Haddington, where her people took a place of precedence in the small county town. Her grandfathers, John of Penfillan and Walter of Templand, also a Welsh, though of another the gipsy stock, vied for her baby favours, while her mother's quick and shifty tempers seem at that date to have combined in the process of "spoiling" her. The records of the schooldays of the juvenile Jane all point to a somewhat masculine strength of character. Through life, it must be acknowledged, this brilliant creature was essentially "a mocking-bird," and made game of every one till she met her mate. The little lady was learned, reading Virgil at nine, ambitious enough to venture a tragedy at fourteen, and cynical ; writing to her life-long friend, Miss Eliza Stodart, of Haddington as a "bottomless pit of dulness," where "all my little world lay glittering in tinsel at my feet." She was ruthless to the suitors—as numerous, says Mr. Froude, "as those of Penelope"—who flocked about the young beauty, wit, and heiress. Of the discarded rivals there was only one of note—George Rennie, long afterwards referred to by Carlyle as a "clever, decisive, very ambitious, but quite unmelodious young fellow whom we knew here (in Chelsea) as sculptor and M.P." She dismissed him in 1821 for some cause of displeasure, "due to pride, reserve, and his soured temper about the world;" but when he came to take leave, she confesses, "I scarcely heard a word he said, my own heart beat so loud." Years after, in London, she went by request of his wife to Rennie's death-bed.

Meanwhile she had fallen under the spell of her tutor, Edward Irving, and, as she, after much *finesse* and evasion admitted, came to love him in earnest. Irving saw her weak points, saying she was apt to turn her powers to "arts of cruelty which satire and scorn are," and "to contemplate the inferiority of others rather from the point of view of ridicule and contempt than of commiseration and relief." Later she retaliated, "There would have been no 'tongues' had Irving married me." But he was fettered by a previous engagement, to which, after some struggle for release, he held, leaving in charge of his ward, as guide, philosopher, and friend, his old ally and successor, Thomas Carlyle. Between this exceptional pair there begun in 1821 a relationship of constant growth in intimacy, marked by frequent visits, conversations, confidences, and a correspondence, long, full, and varied, starting with interchange of literary sympathies, and sliding by degrees into the dangerous friendship called Platonical. At the outset it was plain that Carlyle was not the St. Preux or Wolmar whose ideas of elegance Jane Welsh—a hasty student of Rousseau — had set in unhappy contrast to the honest young swains of Haddington. Uncouth, ungainly in manner and attire, he first excited her ridicule even more than he attracted her esteem, and her written descriptions of him recall that of Johnson by Lord Chesterfield. "He scrapes the fender, . . . only his tongue should be left at liberty, his other members are most fantastically awkward;" but the poor mocking-bird had met her fate.

The correspondence falls under two sections, the critical and the personal. The critical consists of remarks, good, bad, and indifferent, on books and their writers. Carlyle began his siege by talking German to her, now extolling Schiller and Goethe to the skies, now, with a rare stretch of deference, half conniving at her sneers. Much also passed between them about English authors, among them comments on Byron, notably inconsistent. Of him Carlyle writes (April 15th, 1824) as "a pampered lord," who would care nothing for the £500 a year that would make an honest man happy; but later, on hearing of the death at Mesolonghi, more in the vein of his master Goethe, he exclaims:

Alas, poor Byron! the news of his death came upon me like a mass of lead; and yet the thought of it sends a painful twinge through all my being, as if I had lost a brother. O God! that so many souls of mud and clay should fill up their base existence to the utmost bound; and this, the noblest spirit in Europe, should sink before half his course was run. . . . Late so full of fire and generous passion and proud purposes, and now for ever dumb and cold. . . . Had he been spared to the age of three-score and ten what might he not have been! what might he not have been! . . . I dreamed of seeing him and knowing him; but . . . we shall go to him, he shall not return to us.

This in answer to her account of the same intelligence: " I was told it all alone in a room full of people. If they had said the sun or the moon was gone out of the heavens, it could not have struck me with the idea of a more awful and dreary blank in the creation than the words 'Byron is dead.' " Other letters of the same period, from London, are studded or disfigured by the incisive ill-natured sarcasms above referred to, or they relate to the work and prospects of the writer. Those that bear on the progress of his suit mark it as the strangest and, when we look before and after, one of the saddest courtships in literary history. As early as 1822 Carlyle entertained the idea of making Jane Welsh his wife; she had begun to yield to the fascinations of his speech—a fascination akin to that of Burns—when she wrote, " I will be happier contemplating my beau-ideal than a real, substantial, eating, drinking, sleeping, honest husband." In 1823 they were half-declared lovers, but there were recalcitrant fits on both sides. On occasion of a meeting at Edinburgh there was a quarrel, followed by a note of repentance, in which she confessed, " Nothing short of a devil could have tempted me to torment you and myself as I did on that unblessed day." Somewhat earlier she had written in answer to his first distinct avowal, " My friend, I love you. But were you my brother I should love you the same. No. Your friend I will be . . . while I breathe the breath of life; but your wife never, though you were as rich as Crœsus, as honoured and renowned as you yet shall be." To which Carlyle answered with characteristic pride, " I have no idea of dying in the Arcadian shepherd's style for the disappointment of hopes which I never seriously entertained, and had no right to entertain seriously." There was indeed nothing of Corydon and Phillis in this struggle of two strong wills, the weaker giving way to the stronger, the gradual but inexorable closing of an iron ring. Backed by h e natural repugnance of her mother to the match, Miss Welsh still rebelled, bracing herself with the reflection, " Men and women may be very charming without having any genius;" and to his renewed appeal (1825), " It lies with you whether I shall be a right man or only a hard and bitter Stoic," retorting, " I am not in love with you . . . my affections are in a state of perfect tranquillity."

But she admitted he was her "only fellowship and support," and confiding at length the truth about Irving, surrendered in the words, "Decide, and woe to me if your
reason be your judge and not your love." In this duel of
Puck and Theseus, the latter felt he had won and pressed
his advantage, offering to let her free and adding warnings
to the blind, "Without great sacrifices on both sides, the
possibility of our union is an empty dream." At the
eleventh hour, when, in her own words, she was "married
past redemption," he wrote, "If you judge fit, I will take
you to my heart this very week. If you judge fit, I will
this very week forswear you for ever;" and replied to her
request that her widowed mother might live under their
wedded roof in terms that might have become Petruchio:
"It may be stated in a word. The man should bear rule
in the house, not the woman. This is an eternal axiom,
the law of nature which no mortal departs from unpun-
ished. . . . Will your mother consent to make me her
guardian and director, and be a second wife to her daughter's husband?"

> Was ever woman in this humour woo'd,
> Was ever woman in this humour won?

Miss Welsh at length reluctantly agreed to come to start
life at Scotsbrig, where his family had migrated; but
Carlyle pushed another counter: "Your mother must not
visit mine: the mere idea of such a visit argued too plainly
that you *knew nothing* of the family circle in which for
my sake you were willing to take a place." It being agreed
that Mrs. Welsh was to leave Haddington, where the alliance
was palpably unpopular, Carlyle proposed to begin married
life in his step-mother's vacant house, saying in effect to
his bride-elect that as for intrusive visitors he had "nerve

enough" to kick her old friends out of doors. The line of
complaisance being drawn here, the bridegroom-elect had
to soothe his sense of even this slight submission by a
scolding letter; while in answer to the question of finance
he pointed out that he had £200 to start with, and that a
labourer and his wife had been known to live on £14 a
year.

On the edge of the great change in her life, Jane Welsh
writes, "I am resolved in spirit, in the face of every horrible fate," and says she has decided to put off mourning for
her father, having found a second father. Carlyle proposed
that after the "dreaded ceremony" he and his bride and
his brother John should travel together by the stage-coach
from Dumfries to Edinburgh. In "the last dying speech
and marrying words" she objects to this arrangement, and
after the event (October 17th, 1826) they drove in a post-
chaise to 21 Comely Bank, where Mrs. Welsh, now herself
settled at Templand, had furnished a house for them.
Meanwhile the Carlyle family migrated to Scotsbrig. There
followed eighteen comparatively tranquil months, an oasis
in the wilderness, where the anomalous pair lived in some
respects like other people. They had seats in church, and
social gatherings—Wednesday "At Homes," to which the
celebrity of their brilliant conversational powers attracted
the brightest spirits of the northern capital, among them
Sir William Hamilton, Sir David Brewster, John Wilson,
De Quincey, forgiven for his review, and above all Jeffrey,
a friend, though of opposite character, nearly as true as
Irving himself. Procter had introduced Carlyle to the
famous editor, who, as a Scotch cousin of the Welshes, took
from the first a keen interest in the still struggling author,
and opened to him the door of the *Edinburgh Review.*
The appearance of the article on *Richter,* 1827, and that,

in the course of the same year, on *The State of German Literature*, marks the beginning of a long series of splendid historical and critical essays—closing in 1855 with the *Prinzenraub*—which set Carlyle in the front of the reviewers of the century. The success in the *Edinburgh* was an "open sesame;" and the conductors of the *Foreign* and *Foreign Quarterly* Reviews, later, those of *Frazer* and the *Westminster*, were ready to receive whatever the new writer might choose to send.

To the *Foreign Review* he contributed from Comely Bank the *Life and Writings of Werner*, a paper on *Helena*, the leading episode of the second part of "Faust," and the first of the two great Essays on *Goethe*, which fixed his place as the interpreter of Germany to England. In midsummer, 1827, Carlyle received a letter from Goethe cordially acknowledging the *Life of Schiller*, and enclosing presents of books for himself and his wife. This, followed by a later inquiry as to the author of the article on *German Literature*, was the opening of a correspondence of sage advice on the one side and of lively gratitude on the other, that lasted till the death of the veteran in 1832. Goethe assisted, or tried to assist, his admirer by giving him a testimonial in a candidature for the Chair (vacant by the promotion of Dr. Chalmers) of Moral Philosophy at St. Andrews. Jeffrey, a frequent visitor and host of the Carlyles, still regarded as "a jewel of advocates . . . the most lovable of little men," urged and aided the canvass, but in vain. The testimonials were too strong to be judicious, and "it was enough that" the candidate "was described as a man of original and extraordinary gifts to make college patrons shrink from contact with him." Another failure, about the same date and with the same backing, was an application for a Professorship in London Uni-

versity, practically under the patronage of Brougham; yet
another, of a different kind, was Carlyle's attempt to write
a novel, which having been found — better before than
after publication—to be a failure, was for the most part
burnt. "He could not," says Froude, " write a novel any
more than he could write poetry. He had no *invention*.[1]
His genius was for fact; to lay hold on truth, with all his
intellect and all his imagination. He could no more in-
vent than he could lie."

The remaining incidents of Carlyle's Edinburgh life are
few: a visit from his mother; a message from Goethe
transmitting a medal for Sir Walter Scott; sums generously sent for his brother John's medical education in Germany; loans to Alexander, and a frustrate scheme for starting a new Annual Register, designed to be a literary *résumé*
of the year, make up the record. The "rift in the lute,"
Carlyle's incapacity for domestic life, was already showing
itself. Within the course of an orthodox honeymoon he
had begun to shut himself up in interior solitude, seldom
saw his wife from breakfast till 4 P.M., when they dined
together and read *Don Quixote* in Spanish. The husband
was half forgotten in the author beginning to prophesy:
he wrote alone, walked alone, thought alone, and for the
most part talked alone, *i.e.* in monologue that did not wait
or care for answer. There was respect, there was affection,

---

[1] Carlyle's verses also demonstrate that he had no metrical ear.
The only really good lines he ever wrote, save in translations where
the rhythm was set to him, are those constantly quoted about the
dawn of "another blue day." Those sent to his mother on "Proud
Hapsburg," and to Jane Welsh before marriage are unworthy of
Macaulay's school-boy, "Non di non homines," but it took much
hammering to persuade Carlyle of the fact, and when persuaded he
concluded that verse-writing was a mere tinkling of cymbals!

but there was little companionship. Meanwhile, despite the *Review* articles, Carlyle's other works, especially the volumes on German romance, were not succeeding, and the mill had to grind without grist. It seemed doubtful if he could longer afford to live in Edinburgh; he craved after greater quiet, and when the farm, which was the main Welsh inheritance, fell vacant, resolved on migrating thither. His wife yielding, though with a natural repugnance to the extreme seclusion in store for her, and the Jeffreys kindly assisting, they went together in May, 1828, to the Hill of the Hawks.

Craigenputtock is by no means "the dreariest spot in all the British dominions." On a sunny day it is an inland home, with wide billowy straths of grass around, inestimable silence broke only by the placid bleating of sheep, and the long rolling ridges of the Solway hills in front. But in the "winter wind," girt by drifts of snow, no post or apothecary within fifteen miles, it may be dreary enough. Here Carlyle allowed his wife to serve him through six years of household drudgery; an offence for which he was never quite forgiven, and to estimate its magnitude here seems the proper place. He was a model son and brother, and his conjugal fidelity has been much appraised, but he was as unfit, and for some of the same reasons, to make "a happy fireside clime" as was Jonathan Swift; and less even than Byron had he a share of the mutual forbearance which is essential to the closest of all relations.

"Napoleon," says Emerson, "to achieve his ends risked everything and spared nothing, neither ammunition, nor money, nor troops, nor generals, nor himself." With a slight change of phrase the same may be said of Carlyle's devotion to his work. There is no more prevailing refrain in his writing, public and private, than his denunciation of

literature as a profession, nor any wiser words than those
in which the veteran warns the young men, whose questions
he answers with touching solicitude, against its adoption.
"It should be," he declares, "the wine not the food of life,
the ardent spirits of thought and fancy without the bread
of action parches up nature and makes strong souls like
Byron dangerous, the weak despicable." But it was nevertheless the profession of his deliberate choice, and he soon
found himself bound to it as Ixion to his wheel. The most
thorough worker on record, he found nothing easy that
was great, and he would do nothing little. In his determination to pluck out the heart of the mystery, be it of
himself, as in *Sartor ;* of Germany, as in his Goethes and
Richters ; the state of England, as in *Chartism* and *Past
and Present ;* of *Cromwell* or of *Friedrich*, he faced all
obstacles and overthrew them. Dauntless and ruthless, he
allowed nothing to divert or to mar his designs, least of all
domestic cares or even duties. "Selfish he was"—I again
quote from his biographer—"if it be selfish to be ready
to sacrifice every person dependent on him as completely
as he sacrificed himself." What such a man wanted was a
house-keeper and a nurse, not a wife, and when we consider that he had chosen for the latter companionship a
woman almost as ambitious as himself, whose conversation
was only less brilliant than his own, of delicate health and
dainty ways, loyal to death, but, according to Mr. Froude,
in some respects "as hard as flint," with "dangerous sparks
of fire," whose quick temper found vent in sarcasms that
blistered and words like swords, who could declare during
the time of the engagement, to which in spite of warnings
manifold she clung, "I will not marry to live on less than
my natural and artificial wants ;" who, ridiculing his accent
to his face and before his friends, could write, "apply your

31

talents to gild over the inequality of our births;" and who found herself obliged to live sixteen miles from the nearest neighbour, to milk a cow, scour floors and mend shoes— when we consider all this we are constrained to admit that the 17th October, 1826, was a *dies nefastus*, nor wonder that thirty years later Mrs. Carlyle wrote, "I married for ambition, Carlyle has exceeded all that my wildest hopes ever imagined of him, and I am miserable"—and to a young friend, "My dear, whatever you do, never marry a man of genius."

Carlyle's own references to the life at Craigenputtock are marked by all his aggravating inconsistency. "How happy we shall be in this Craig o' Putta," he writes to his wife from Scotsbrig, April 17th, 1827; and later to Goethe:

Here Rousseau would have been as happy as on his island of Saint Pierre. My town friends indeed ascribe my sojourn here to a similar disposition, and forbode me no good results. But I came here solely with the design to simplify my way of life, and to secure the independence through which I could be enabled to be true to myself. This bit of earth is our own; here we can live, write, and think as best pleases ourselves, even though Zoilus himself were to be crowned the monarch of literature. From some of our heights I can descry, about a day's journey to the west, the hill where Agricola and the Romans left a camp behind them. At the foot of it I was born, and there both father and mother still live to love me. . . . The only piece of any importance that I have written since I came here is an Essay on Burns.

This Essay, modified at first then let alone by Jeffrey, appeared in the *Edinburgh* in the autumn of 1828. We turn to Carlyle's journal and find the entry, "Finished a paper on Burns at this Devil's Den," elsewhere referred to as a "gaunt and hungry Siberia." Later still he confesses, when preparing for his final move south, "Of solitude I have really had enough."

Romæ Tibur amem ventosus, Tibure Romam.

Carlyle in the moor was always sighing for the town, and in the town for the moor.   During the first twenty years of his London life, in what he called "the Devil's oven," he is constantly clamouring to return to the den.   His wife, more and more forlorn though ever loyal, consistently disliked it; little wonder, between sluttish maid-servants, and owl-like solitude : and she expressed her dislike in the pathetic verses, "To a Swallow Building under our Eaves," sent to Jeffrey in 1832, and ending :

> God speed thee, pretty bird; may thy small nest
>   With little ones all in good time be blest;
>   I love thee much,
> For well thou managest that life of thine,
> While I! Oh, ask not what I do with mine,
>   Would I were such!   *The Desert.*

The monotony of the moorland life was relieved by visits of relations and others made and repaid, an excursion to Edinburgh, a residence in London, and the production of work, the best of which has a chance of living with the language.   One of the most interesting of the correspondences of this period is a series of letters, addressed to an anonymous Edinburgh friend who seems to have had some idea of abandoning his profession of the Law for Literature, a course against which Carlyle strenuously protests. From these letters, which have only appeared in the columns of the *Glasgow Herald,* we may extract a few sentences :

Don't disparage the work that gains your bread.   What is all work but a drudgery ? no labour for the present joyous, but grievous.   A

man who has nothing to admire except himself is in the minimum
state.   The question is, Does a man really love Truth, or only the
market price of it?   Even literary men should have something else
to do.   Kames was a lawyer, Roscoe a merchant, Hans Sachs a cob-
bler, Burns a gauger, etc.

The following singular passage, the style of which suggests an imitation of Sterne, is the acme of unconscious
self-satire: .

You are infinitely unjust to Blockheads, as they are called.   Ask
yourself seriously within your own heart—what right have you to
live wisely in God's world, and they not to live a little wisely?   Is
there a man more to be condoled with, nay, I will say to be cherished
and tenderly treated, than a man that has no brain.   My Purse is
empty, it can be filled again; the Jew Rothschild could fill it; or I
can even live with it very far from full.   But, gracious heavens!
what is to be done with my *empty Head?*

Three of the visits of this period are memorable.   Two
from the Jeffreys (in 1828 and 1830) leave us with the
same uncomfortable impression of kindness ungrudgingly
bestowed and grudgingly received.   Jeffrey had a double
interest in the household at Craigenputtock—an almost
brotherly regard for the wife, and a belief, restrained by
the range of a keen though limited appreciation, in the
powers of the husband, to whom he wrote: "Take care
of the fair creature who has entrusted herself so entirely
to you," and with a half truth, "You have no mission
upon earth, whatever you may fancy, half so important as
to be innocently happy."   And again: "Bring your
blooming Eve out of your blasted Paradise, and seek
shelter in the lower world."   But Carlyle held to the
"banner with a strange device," and was either deaf or indignant.   The visits passed, with satirical references from

both the host and hostess; for Mrs. Carlyle, who could herself abundantly scoff and scold, would allow the liberty to no one else. Jeffrey meanwhile was never weary of well-doing. Previous to his promotion as Lord Advocate and consequent transference to London, he tried to negotiate for Carlyle's appointment as his successor in the editorship of the *Review*, but failed to make him accept the necessary conditions. The paper entitled *Signs of the Times* was the last production that he had to revise for his eccentric friend. Those following on Taylor's *German Literature* and the *Characteristics* were brought out in 1831 under the auspices of Macvey Napier. The other visit was from the most illustrious of Carlyle's English-speaking friends, in many respects a fellow-worker, yet "a spirit of another sort," and destined, though a transcendental mystic, to be the most practical of his benefactors. Twenty-four hours of Ralph Waldo Emerson (often referred to in the course of a long and intimate correspondence) are spoken of by Mrs. Carlyle as a visit from the clouds, brightening the prevailing gray. He came to the remote inland home with "the pure intellectual gleam" of which Hawthorne speaks, and "the quiet night of clear fine talk" remained one of the memories which led Carlyle afterwards to say, "Perhaps our happiest days were spent at the Craig." Goethe's letters, especially that in which he acknowledges a lock of Mrs. Carlyle's hair, "eine unvergleichliche schwarze Haar locke," were also among the gleams of 1829. The great German died three years later, after receiving the birthday tribute in his 82d year from English friends; and it is pleasant to remember that in this instance the disciple was to the end loyal to his master. To this period belong many other correspondences. "I am scribble scribbling," he says in a

3*   E

letter of 1832, and mere scribbling may fill many pages
with few headaches; but Carlyle wrestled as he wrote, and
not a page of those marvellous *Miscellanies* but is red with
his life's blood.   Under all his reviewing, he was set on a
work whose fortunes were to be the strangest, whose result
was, in some respects, the widest of his efforts.   The plan
of *Sartor Resartus* is far from original.   Swift's *Tale of
a Tub* distinctly anticipated the Clothes Philosophy; there
are besides manifest obligations to Reinecke Fuchs, Jean
Paul Richter, and other German authors: but in our days
originality is only possible in the handling; Carlyle has
made an imaginary German professor the mere mouth-
piece of his own and the higher aspiration of the Scotland
of his day, and it remains the most popular as surely as
his *Friedrich* is the greatest of his works.   The author
was abundantly conscious of the value of the book, and
superabundantly angry at the unconsciousness of the literary patrons of the time.   In 1821 he resolved if possible to go up to London to push the prospects of this
first-born male child.   The *res angusta* stood in the way.
Jeffrey, after asking his friend "what situation he could
get him that he would detest the least," pressed on him
"in the coolest, lightest manner the use of his purse."
This Carlyle, to the extent of £50 as a loan (carefully returned), was induced ultimately to accept.   It has been
said that "proud men never wholly forgive those to whom
they feel themselves obliged," but their resenting of benefits is the worst feature of their pride.   Carlyle made his
second visit to London to seek types for *Sartor*, in vain.
Always preaching reticence with the sound of artillery,
he vents in many pages the rage of his chagrin at the
"Arimaspian" publishers, who would not print his book,
and the public which, "dosed with froth," would not buy

it. The following is little softened by the chiaroscuro of five and thirty years:

Done, I think, at Craigenputtock between January and August, 1830, *Teufelsdröckh* was ready, and I decided to make for London; night before going, how I remember it! . . . The beggarly history of poor *Sartor* among the blockheadisms is not worth recording or remembering, least of all here! In short, finding that I had got £100 (if memory serve) for *Schiller* six or seven years before, and for *Sartor*, at least twice as good, I could not only not get £200, but even get no Murray or the like to publish it on half profits. Murray, a most stupendous object to me, tumbling about eyeless, with the evidently strong wish to say "Yes" and "No"—my first signal experience of that sad human predicament. I said, We will make it "No," then; wrap up our MS., and carry it about for some two years from one terrified owl to another; published at last experimentally in *Fraser*, and even then mostly laughed at, nothing coming of the volume except what was sent by Emerson from America.

This summary is unfair to Murray, who was inclined, on Jeffrey's recommendation, to accept the book; but on finding that Carlyle had carried the MS. to Longmans and another publisher, in hopes of a better bargain, and that it had been refused, naturally wished to refer the matter to his "reader," and the negotiation closed. *Sartor* struggled into half life in parts of the magazine to which the writer had already contributed several of his German essays, and it was even then published with reluctance, and on half pay. The reception of this work, a nondescript, yet among the finest prose poems in our language, seemed to justify bookseller, editor, and readers alike, for the British public in general were of their worst opinion. "It is a heap of clotted nonsense," pronounced the *Sun*. "Stop that stuff or stop my paper," wrote one of *Fraser's* constituents. "When is that stupid series of articles by the crazy tailor going to end?" cried another. At this time

Carlyle used to say there were only two people who found anything in his book worth reading—Emerson and a priest in Cork, who said to the editor that he would take the magazine when anything in it appeared by the author of *Sartor*. The volume was only published in 1838, by Saunders and Otley, after the *French Revolution* had further raised the writer's name, and then on a guarantee from friends willing to take the risk of loss. It does not appear whether Carlyle refers to this edition or to some slighter reissue of the magazine articles when he writes in the *Reminiscences:* "I sent off six copies to six Edinburgh literary friends, from not one of whom did I get the smallest whisper even of receipt—a thing disappointing more or less to human nature, and which has silently and insensibly led me never since to send any copy of a book to Edinburgh. . . . The plebs of literature might be divided in their verdicts about me; though by count of heads I always suspect the guilty clear had it; but the conscript fathers declined to vote at all."[1] In America *Sartor* was pieced together from *Fraser*, published in a volume introduced by Alexander Everett, extolled by Emerson as "A criticism of the spirit of the age in which we live; exhibiting in the most just and novel light the present aspect of religion, politics, literature, and social life." The editors add: "We believe no book has been published for many years . . . which discovers an equal mastery over all the riches of the language. The author makes ample amends for the occasional eccentricity of his genius not only by frequent bursts of pure splendour, but by the wit and sense which never fail him."

[1] *Tempora mutantur.* A few months before Carlyle's death a cheap edition of *Sartor* was issued, and 30,000 copies were sold within a few weeks.

Americans are intolerant of honest criticism on themselves, but they are, more than any other nation, open to appreciate vigorous expressions of original views of life and ethics—all that we understand by philosophy—and equally so to new forms of art. The leading critics of the New England have often been the first and best testers of the fresh products of the Old. A land of experiment in all directions, ranging from Mount Lebanon to Oneida Creek, has been ready to welcome the suggestions, physical or metaphysical, of startling enterprise. Ideas which filter slowly through English soil and abide for generations, flash over the electric atmosphere of the West. Hence Coleridge, Carlyle, and Browning were already accepted as prophets in Boston while their own countrymen were still examining their credentials. To this readiness, as of a photographic plate, to receive, must be added the fact that the message of *Sartor* crossed the Atlantic when the hour to receive it had struck. To its publication has been attributed the origin of a movement that was almost simultaneously inaugurated by Emerson's *Harvard Discourse*. It was a revolt against the reign of Commerce in practice, Calvinism in theory, and precedent in Art that gave birth to the Transcendentalism of *The Dial*—a Pantheon in which Carlyle had at once assigned to him a place. He meanwhile was busy in London making friends by his conspicuous, almost obtrusive, genius, and sowing the seeds of discord by his equally obtrusive spleen. To his visit of 1831–1832 belongs one of the worst of the elaborate invectives against Lamb which have recoiled on the memory of his critic—to the credit of English sympathies with the most lovable of slightly erring men— with more than the force of a boomerang. A sheaf of sharp sayings of the same date owe their sting to their half truth, *e.g.* to a man who excused himself for profligate journalism on the old plea, " I must live, sir." " No, sir, you need not live, if your body cannot be kept together without selling your soul." Similarly he was abusing the periodicals — " mud," " sand," and " dust magazines "—to which he had contributed, *inter alia*, the great Essay on *Voltaire* and the consummate sketch of *Novalis ;* with the second paper on *Richter* to the *Foreign Review*, the reviews of *History* and of *Schiller* to *Fraser*, and that on *Goethe's Works* to the *Foreign Quarterly*. During this period he was introduced to Molesworth, Austin, and J. S. Mill. On his summons, October 1st, 1832, Mrs. Carlyle came up to Ampton Street, where he then resided, to see him safe through the rest of his London time. They lamented over the lapse of Irving, now lost in the delirium of tongues, and made a league of friendship with Mill, whom he describes as " a partial disciple of mine," a friendship that stood a hard test, but was broken when the author of *Liberty* naturally found it impossible to remain a disciple of the writer of *Latter-Day Pamphlets*. Mill, like Napier, was at first staggered by the *Characteristics*, though he afterwards said it was one of Carlyle's greatest works, and was enthusiastic over the review of Boswell's *Johnson*, published in *Fraser* in the course of this year. Meanwhile Margaret, Carlyle's favourite sister, had died, and his brightest, Jean, "the Craw," had married her cousin, James Aitken. In memory of the former he wrote as a master of threnody: to the bridegroom of the latter he addressed a letter reminding him of the duties of a husband, "to do as he would be done by to his wife !" In 1832 John, again by Jeffrey's aid, obtained a situation at £300 a year as travelling physician to Lady Clare, and was enabled, as he promptly did, to pay back his debts. Alexander seems to have been still struggling with an imperfectly successful farm. In the same year, when Carlyle was in London, his father died at Scotsbrig, after a residence there of six years. His son saw him last in August, 1831, when, referring to his Craigenputtock solitude, he said: "Man, it's surely a pity that thou shouldst sit yonder with nothing but the eye of Omniscience to see thee, and thou with such a gift to speak."

The Carlyles returned in March, she to her domestic services, baking bread, preserving eggs, and brightening grates till her eyes grew dim; he to work at his *Diderot*, doing justice to a character more alien to his own than even Voltaire's, reading twenty-five volumes, one per day, to complete the essay; then at *Count Cagliostro*, also for *Fraser*, a link between his last Craigenputtock and his first London toils. The period is marked by shoals of letters, a last present from Weimar, a visit to Edinburgh, and a candidature for a University Chair,[1] which Carlyle thought Jeffrey could have got for him; but the advocate did not, probably could not, in this case satisfy his client. In excusing himself he ventured to lecture the applicant on what he imagined to be the impracticable temper and perverse eccentricity which had retarded and might continue to retard his advancement. Carlyle, never tolerant of rebuke however just, was indignant, and though an open quarrel was avoided by letters on both sides of courteous compromise, the breach was in reality never healed, and Jeffrey has a niche in the *Reminiscences* as a "little man who meant well, but did not see far or know much." Carlyle went on, however, like Thor, at the *Diamond Neck-*

---

[1] The last was in 1836, for the Chair of Astronomy in Glasgow.

lace, which is a proem to the *French Revolution*, but inly growling, " My own private impression is that I shall never get any promotion in this world." " A prophet is not readily acknowledged in his own country ;" "Mein Leben gebt sehr übel: all dim, misty, squally, disheartening at times, almost heart-breaking." This is the prose rather than the male of Byron. Of all men Carlyle could least reck his own rede. He never even tried to consume his own smoke. His *Sartor* is indeed more contained, and takes at its summit a higher flight than Rousseau's *Confessions*, or the *Sorrows of Werther*, or the first two cantos of *Childe Harold:* but reading Byron's letters is mingling with a world gay and grave ; reading Goethe's walking in the Parthenon, though the Graces in the niches are sometimes unclad ; reading Carlyle's is travelling through glimpses of sunny fields and then plunging into coal-black tunnels. At last he decided, " Puttock is no longer good for *me*," and his brave wife approving, and even inciting, he resolved to burn his ships and seek his fortune—sink or swim—in the metropolis. Carlyle, for once taking the initiative of practical trouble, went in advance on a house-hunt to London, and by advice of Leigh Hunt fixed on the now famous house in Chelsea, near the Thames.

CHAPTER IV.

CHEYNE ROW.

[1834–1842.]

THE curtain falls on Craigenputtock, the bleak farm by the bleak hills, and rises on Cheyne Row, a side street off the river Thames, winding as slowly by the reaches of Barnes and Battersea as Cowper's Ouse, dotted with brown-sailed ships and holiday boats in place of the excursion steamers that now stop at Carlyle Pier; hard by the Carlyle Statue on the new (1874) Embankment, in front the "Carlyle mansions," a stone's-throw from "Carlyle Square." Turning up the row, we find over No. 24, formerly No. 5, the Carlyle medallion in marble, marking the house where the Chelsea prophet, rejected, recognised, and adulated of men, lived over a stretch of forty-seven years. Here were his headquarters, but he was a frequent wanderer. About half the time was occupied in trips almost yearly to Scotland, one to Ireland, one to Belgium, one to France, and two to Germany; besides, in the later days, constant visits to admiring friends, more and more drawn from the higher ranks in English society, the members of which learnt to appreciate his genius before he found a hearing among the mass of the people.

The whole period falls readily under four sections marking as many phases of the author's outer and inner life, while the same character is preserved throughout:

I. 1834–1842—When the death of Mrs. Welsh and the late success of Carlyle's work relieved him from a long, sometimes severe struggle with narrow means. It is the period of the *French Revolution*, *The Lectures*, and *Hero-Worship*, and of *Chartism*, the last work with a vestige of adherence to the Radical creed.

II. 1842–1853—When the death of his mother loosened his ties to the North. This decade of his literary career is mainly signalised by the writing and publication of the *Life and Letters of Cromwell*, of Carlyle's political works, *Past and Present* and the *Latter-Day Pamphlets*, and of the *Life of Sterling*, works which mark his now consummated disbelief in democracy, and his distinct abjuration of adherence, in any ordinary sense, to the "Creed of Christendom."

III. 1853–1866—When the laurels of his triumphant speech as Lord Rector at Edinburgh were suddenly withered by the death of his wife. This period is filled with the *History of Fredrich II.*, and marked by a yet more decidedly accentuated trust in autocracy.

IV. 1866–1881—Fifteen years of the setting of the sun.

The Carlyles, coming to the metropolis in a spirit of rarely realised audacity on a reserve fund of from £200 to £300 at most, could not propose to establish themselves in any centre of fashion. In their circumstances their choice of abode was on the whole a fortunate one. Chelsea,

Not wholly in the busy world, nor quite
Beyond it,

was, even in those days of less constant communication, within measurable distance of the centres of London life: it had then and still preserves a host of interesting historic and literary traditions. Among the men who in old times lived or met together in that outlying region of London, we have memories of Sir Thomas More and of Erasmus, of the Essayists Addison and Steele, and of Swift. Hard by is the tomb of Bolingbroke and the square of Sir Hans Sloane; Smollett lived for a time in Laurence Street; nearer our own day, Turner resided in Cheyne Walk, later George Eliot, W. B. Scott, Dante Rossetti, Swinburne for a season, and George Meredith. When Carlyle came to settle there, Leigh Hunt[1] in Upper Cheyne Row, an almost next-door neighbour, was among the first of a series of visitors; always welcome, despite his "hugger-mugger" household and his borrowing tendencies, his "unpractical messages" and "rose-coloured reform processes," as a bright "singing bird, musical in flowing talk," abounding in often subtle criticisms and constant good-humour. To the Chelsea home, since the Mecca of many pilgrims, there also flocked other old Ampton Street friends, drawn thither by genuine regard. Mrs. Carlyle, by the testimony of Miss Cushman and all competent judges, was a "*raconteur* unparalleled." To quote the same authority, "that wonderful woman, able to live in the full light of Carlyle's genius without being overwhelmed by it," had a peculiar skill in drawing out the most brilliant conversationalist of the age.

[1] Cf. Byron's account of the same household at Pisa. Carlyle deals very leniently with the malignant volume on Byron which amply justified the epigram of Moore. But he afterwards spoke more slightly of his little satellite, attributing the faint praise, in the *Examiner*, of the second course of lectures to Hunt's jealousy of a friend now " beginning to be somebody."

Burns and Wilson were his Scotch predecessors in an art of
which the close of our century—when every fresh thought
is treasured to be printed and paid for—knows little but
the shadow. Of Carlyle, as of Johnson, it might have been
said, "There is no use arguing with him, for if his pistol
misses fire he knocks you down with the butt;" both men
would have benefited by revolt from their dictation, but
the power to contradict either was overborne by a superior
power to assert. Swift's occasional insolence, in like manner, prevailed by reason of the colossal strength that made
him a Gulliver in Lilliput. Carlyle in earlier, as in later
times, would have been the better of meeting his mate, or
of being overmatched ; but there was no Wellington found
for this "grand Napoleon of the realms" of prose. His
reverence for men, if not for things, grew weaker with the
strengthening of his sway, a sway due to the fact that men
of extensive learning are rarely men of incisive force, and
Carlyle—in this respect more akin to Johnson than to
Swift—had the acquired material to serve as fuel for the
inborn fire. Hence the least satisfactory of his criticisms
are those passed on his peers. Injustices of conversation
should be pardoned to an impulsive nature, even those of
correspondence in the case of a man who had a mania for
pouring out his moods to all and sundry ; but where Carlyle has carefully recarved false estimates in cameo, his
memory must abide the consequence. Quite late in life,
referring to the Chelsea days, he says, "The best of those
who then flocked about as was Leigh Hunt," who never
seriously said him nay ; "and the worst Lamb," who was
not among the worshippers. No one now doubts that
Carlyle's best adviser and most candid critic might have
been John Stuart Mill, for whom he long felt as much regard as it was possible for him to entertain towards a

proximate equal. The following is characteristic: "He
had taken a great attachment to me (which lasted about
ten years and then suddenly ended, I never knew how), an
altogether clear, logical, honest, amicable, affectionate young
man, and respected as such here, though sometimes felt to
be rather colourless, even aqueous, no religion in any form
traceable in him." And similarly of his friend, Mrs. Taylor, "She was a will-o'-the-wispish iridescence of a creature;
meaning nothing bad either;" and again of Mill himself,
"His talk is sawdustish, like ale when there is no wine to
be had." Such criticisms, some ungrateful, others unjust,
may be relieved by reference to the close of two friendships to which (though even these were clouded by a touch
of personal jealousy) he was faithful in the main; for the
references of both husband and wife to Irving's "delira-
tious" are the tears due to the sufferings of errant minds.
Their last glimpse of this best friend of earlier days was
in October, 1834, when he came on horseback to the door
of their new home, and left with the benediction to his
lost Jane, "You have made a little Paradise around you."
He died in Glasgow in the December of the same year,
and his memory is pathetically embalmed in Carlyle's
threnody. The final phases of another old relationship
were in some degree similar. During the first years of
their settlement, Lord Jeffrey frequently called at Cheyne
Row, and sent kind letters to his cousin, received by her
husband with the growl, "I am at work stern and grim,
not to be interrupted by Jeffrey's theoretic flourish of epistolary trumpeting." Carlyle, however, paid more than one
visit to Craigcrook, seeing his host for the last time in the
autumn of 1849, "worn in body and thin in mind," "grown
lunar now and not solar any more." Three months later
he heard of the death of this benefactor of his youth, and

32

wrote the memorial which finds its place in the second volume of the *Reminiscences.*

The work " stern and grim " was the *French Revolution,* the production of which is the dominant theme of the first chapter of Carlyle's London life.   Mr. Froude, in the course of an estimate of this work which leaves little room for other criticism, dwells on the fact that it was written for a purpose, *i.e.* to show that rulers, like those of the French in the eighteenth century, who are solely bent on the pleasures and oblivious of the duties of life, must end by being " burnt up."   This, doubtless, is one of the morals of the *French Revolution*—the other being that anarchy ends in despotism—and unquestionably a writer who never ceased to be a preacher must have had it in his mind.   But Carlyle's peculiarity is that he combined the functions of a prophet and of an artist, and that while now the one, now the other, was foremost, he never wholly forgot the one in the other.   In this instance he found a theme well fit for both, and threw his heart into it, though under much discouragement.   Despite the Essays, into each of which he had put work enough for a volume, the Reviews were shy of him ; while his *Sartor* had, on this side of the Atlantic, been received mainly with jeers.   Carlyle, never unconscious of his prerogative and apostolic primogeniture, felt like a knight who had performed his vigils, and finding himself still ignored, became a knight of the rueful countenance.   Thoroughly equipped, adept enough in ancient tongues to appreciate Homer, a master of German and a fluent reader of French, a critic whose range stretched from Diderot to John Knox, he regarded his treatment as "tragically hard," exclaiming, " I could learn to do all things I have seen done, and am forbidden to try any of them." The efforts to keep the wolf from his own doors were harder

than any but a few were till lately aware of. Landed in
London with his £200 reserve, he could easily have made
way in the usual ruts; but he would have none of them,
and refused to accept the employment which is the most
open, as it is the most lucrative, to literary aspirants. To
nine out of ten the "profession of literature" means Journalism; while Journalism often means dishonesty, always
conformity. Carlyle was, in a sense deeper than that of
the sects, essentially a nonconformist; he not only disdained to write a word he did not believe, he would not
suppress a word he did believe—a rule of action fatal to
swift success. During these years there began an acquaintance, soon ripening into intimacy, the memories of which
are enshrined in one of the most beautiful of biographies.
Carlyle's relation to John Sterling drew out the sort of affection which best suited him—the love of a master for a
pupil, of superior for inferior, of the benefactor for the
benefited; and consequently there is no line in the record
of it that jars. Sterling once tried to benefit his friend,
and perhaps fortunately failed. He introduced Carlyle to
his father, then the editor of the *Times*, and the latter
promptly invited the struggling author to contribute to its
columns, but, according to Mr. Froude, "on the implied
conditions . . . when a man enlists in the army, his soul as
well as his body belong to his commanding officer." Carlyle talked, all his life, about what his greatest disciple
calls "The Lamp of Obedience;" but he himself would
obey no one, and found it hard to be civil to those who
did not see with his eyes. He rejected—we trust in polite
terms—the offer of "the Thunderer." "In other respects
also," says our main authority, "he was impracticable, un-
malleable, and as independent and wilful as if he were the
heir to a peerage. He had created no 'public' of his

own; the public which existed could not understand his
writings and would not buy them; and thus it was that in
Cheyne Row he was more neglected than he had been in
Scotland." Welcome to a limited range of literary society, he astonished and amused by his vehement eloquence,
but when crossed he was not only "sarcastic" but rude,
and speaking of people, as he wrote of them, with various
shades of contempt, naturally gave frequent offence. Those
whose toes are trodden on, not by accident, justifiably re-
taliate. "Are you looking for your t-t-turban?" Charles
Lamb is reported to have said in some entertainer's lobby
after listening for an evening to his invectives, and the
phrase may have rankled in Carlyle's mind. Living in a
glass case, while throwing stones about, supersensitive to
criticism though professing to despise critics, he made at
least as many enemies as friends, and by his own confession became an Ishmaelite. In view of the reception of
Sartor, we do not wonder to find him writing in 1833:

It is twenty-three months since I earned a penny by the craft of
literature, and yet I know no fault I have committed. . . . I am tempted to go to America. . . . I shall quit literature, it does not invite me.
Providence warns me to have done with it. I have failed in the Divine Infernal Universe.

Or meditating, when at the lowest ebb, to go wandering
about the world like Teufelsdröckh, looking for a rest for
the sole of his foot. And yet all the time, with incompa-
rable naïveté, he was asserting:

The longer I live among this people the deeper grows my feeling
of natural superiority to them. . . . The literary world here is a thing
which I have no other course left me but to defy. . . . I can reverence
no existing man. With health and peace for one year, I could write
a better book than there has been in this country for generations.

All through his journal and his correspondence there is a perpetual alternation of despair and confidence, always closing with the refrain, " Working, trying is the only remover of doubt," and wise counsels often echoed from Goethe, "Accomplish as well as you can the task on hand, and the next step will become clear ;" on the other hand—

A man must not only be able to work but to give over working. ... If a man wait till he has entirely brushed off his imperfections, he will spin for ever on his axis, advancing no whither. ... The *French Revolution* stands pretty fair in my head, nor do I mean to investigate much more about it, but to splash down what I know in large masses of colours, that it may look like a smoke and flame conflagration in the distance.

The progress of this work was retarded by the calamity familiar to every reader, but it must be referred to as throwing one of the finest lights on his character. Carlyle's closest intellectual link with J. S. Mill was their common interest in French politics and literature ; the latter, himself meditating a history of the Revolution, not only surrendered in favour of the man whose superior pictorial genius he recognised, but supplied him freely with the books he had accumulated for the enterprise. His interest in the work was unfortunately so great as to induce him to borrow the MS. of the first volume, completed in the early spring of 1835, and his business habits so defective as to permit him to leave it lying about when read, so that, as appears from the received accounts, it was mistaken by the servant for waste paper ; certainly it was destroyed ; and Mill came to Cheyne Row to announce the fact in such a desperate state of mind that Carlyle's first anxiety seems to have been to console his friend. According to Mrs. Carlyle, as reported by Froude, "the first words her hus-

4　　　　　　　　　F

band uttered as the door closed were, 'Well, Mill, poor fellow, is terribly cut up; we must endeavour to hide from him how very serious this business is to us.'" This trait of magnanimity under the first blow of a disaster which seemed to cancel the work of years[1] should be set against his nearly contemporaneous criticisms of Coleridge, Lamb, Wordsworth, Sydney Smith, Macaulay, etc.

Mill sent a cheque of £200 as "the slightest external compensation" for the loss, and only, by urgent entreaty, procured the acceptance of half the sum. Carlyle here, as in every real emergency, bracing his resolve by courageous words, as "never tine heart or get provoked heart," set himself to re-write the volume with an energy that recalls that of Scott rebuilding his ruined estate; but the work was at first so "wretched" that it had to be laid aside for a season, during which the author wisely took a restorative bath of comparatively commonplace novels. The re-writing of the first volume was completed in September, 1835; the whole book in January, 1837. The mood in which it was written throws a light on the excellences as on the defects of the history. The *Reminiscences* again record the gloom and defiance of "Thomas the Doubter" walking through the London streets "with a feeling similar to Satan's stepping the burning marl," and scowling at the equipages about Hyde Park corner, sternly thinking, "Yes, and perhaps none of you could do what I am at. I shall finish this book, throw it at your feet, buy a rifle and spade, and withdraw to the Transatlantic wilderness." In an adjacent page he reports himself as having said to his wife:

---

[1] Carlyle had only been writing the volume for five months; but he was preparing for it during much of his life at Craigenputtock.

What they will do with this book none knows, my lass; but they have not had for two hundred years any book that came more truly from a man's very heart, and so let them trample it under foot and hoof as they see best. . . . "They cannot trample that," she would cheerily answer.

This passage points at once to the secret of the writer's spell and the limits of his lasting power. His works were written seldom with perfect fairness, never with the dry light required for a clear presentation of the truth; they have all "an infusion from the will and the affections;" but they were all written with a whole sincerity and utter fervour; they rose from his hot heart, and rushed through the air "like rockets druv' by their own burning." Consequently his readers confess that he has never forgot the Horatian maxim

> Si vis me flere dolendum est,
> Primum ipsi tibi.

About this time Carlyle writes, "My friends think I have found the art of living upon nothing," and there must, despite of Mill's contribution, have been "bitter thrift" in Cheyne Row during the years 1835–1837. He struggled through the unremunerative interval of waiting for the sale of a great work by help of fees derived from his essays on the *Diamond Necklace* (which, after being refused by the *Foreign Quarterly*, appeared in *Fraser*, 1837), that on *Mirabeau* in the *Westminster*, and in the following year, for the same periodical, the article on *Sir Walter Scott*. To the last work, undertaken against the grain, he refers in one of the renewed wails of the year: "O that literature had never been devised. I am scourged back to it by the whip of necessity." The circumstance may account for some of the manifest defects of one of the least satisfactory of Carlyle's longer reviews. Frequent

references in previous letters show that he never appreciated Scott, to whom he refers as a mere Restaurateur.

Meanwhile the appearance of the *French Revolution* had
brought the name of its author, then in his forty-third
year, for the first time prominently before the public.   It
attracted the attention of Thackeray, who wrote a generous review in the *Times*, of Southey, Jeffrey, Macaulay,
Hallam, and Brougham, who recognised the advent of an
equal, if sometimes an adverse power in the world of letters.   But, though the book established his reputation, the
sale was slow, and for some years the only substantial profits,
amounting to about £400, came from America, through
the indefatigable activity and good management of Emerson.   It is pleasant to note a passage in the interesting
volumes of their *Correspondence* which shows that in this
instance the benefited understood his financial relation to
the benefactor: "A reflection I cannot but make is that,
at bottom, this money was all yours; not a penny of it belonged to me by any law except that of helpful friendship.
I feel as if I could not examine it without a kind of crime."
Others who, at this period, made efforts to assist "the
polar Bear" were less fortunate.   In several instances good
intentions paved the palace of Momus, and in one led a
well-meaning man into a notoriously false position.   Mr.
Basil Montagu being in want of a private secretary offered
the post to his former guest, as a temporary makeshift, at
a salary of £200, and so brought upon his memory a tor-
rent of contempt.   Undeterred by this and similar warnings, the indefatigable philanthropist, Miss Harriet Martineau, who at first conciliated the Carlyles by her affection
for "this side of the street," and was afterwards an object
of their joint ridicule, conceived the idea of organising a
course of lectures to an audience collected by canvass to

hear the strange being from the moors talk for an hour on end about literature, morals, and history. He was then an object of curiosity to those who knew anything about him at all, and lecturing was at that time a lucrative and an honourable employment. The "good Harriet," so called by Cheyne Row in its condescending mood, aided by other kind friends of the Sterling and Mill circles—the former including Frederick Denison Maurice—made so great a success of the enterprise that it was thrice repeated. The *first* course of six lectures on "German Literature," May, 1857, delivered in Wills's Rooms, realised £135; the *second* of twelve, on the "History of European Literature," at 17 Edward Street, Portman Square, had a net result of £300; the *third*, in the same rooms, on "Revolutions," brought £200; the *fourth*, on "Heroes," the same. In closing this course Carlyle appeared for the last time on a public platform until 1866, when he delivered his Inaugural Address as Lord Rector to the students of Edinburgh.

The impression he produced on his unusually select audiences was that of a man of genius, but roughly clad. The more superficial auditors had a new sensation, those who came to stare remained to wonder; the more reflective felt that they had learnt something of value. Carlyle had no inconsiderable share of the oratorical power which he latterly so derided; he was able to speak from a few notes; but there were comments more or less severe on his manner and style. J. Grant, in his *Portraits of Public Characters*, says: "At times he distorts his features as if suddenly seized by some paroxysm of pain . . . he makes mouths; he has a harsh accent and graceless gesticulation." Leigh Hunt, in the *Examiner*, remarks on the lecturer's power of extemporising; but adds that he often touches only the mountain-tops of the subject, and that the impres-

sion left was as if some Puritan had come to life again,
liberalised by German philosophy. Bunsen, present at one
of the lectures, speaks of the striking and rugged thoughts
thrown at people's heads; and Margaret Fuller, afterwards
Countess D'Ossoli, referred to his arrogance redeemed by
" the grandeur of a Siegfried melting down masses of iron
into sunset red." Carlyle's own comments are for the
most part slighting. He refers to his lectures as a mixture
of prophecy and play-acting, and says that when about to
open his course on "Heroes" he felt like a man going to
be hanged. To Emerson, April 17th, 1839, he writes:

My lectures come on this day two weeks. O heaven! I cannot
"speak;" I can only gasp and writhe and stutter, a spectacle to
gods and fashionables—being forced to it by want of money. In
five weeks I shall be free, and then—! Shall it be Switzerland?
shall it be Scotland? nay, shall it be America and Concord?

Emerson had written about a Boston publication of the
Miscellanies (first there collected), and was continually
urging his friend to emigrate and speak to more appre-
ciative audiences in the States; but the London lectures,
which had, with the remittances from over sea, practically
saved Carlyle from ruin or from exile, had made him decide "to turn his back to the treacherous Syren"—the
temptation to sink into oratory. Mr. Froude's explanation
and defence of this decision may be clenched by a reference to the warning his master had received. He had announced himself as a preacher and a prophet, and been
taken at his word; but similarly had Edward Irving, who
for a season of sun or glamour gathered around him the
same crowd and glitter: the end came; twilight and clouds
of night. Fashion had flocked to the sermons of the elder
Annandale youth—as to the recitatives of the younger—

to see a wild man of the woods and hear him sing; but the novelty gone, they passed on "to Egyptian crocodiles, Iroquois hunters," and left him stranded with "unquiet fire" and "flaccid face." "O foulest Circæan draft," exclaimed his old admirer in his fine dirge, "thou poison of popular applause, madness is in thee and death, thy end is Bedlam and the grave," and with the fixed resolve, "De me fabula non narrabitur," he shut the book on this phase of his life.

The lectures on "Hero-Worship" (a phrase taken from Hume) were published in 1841, and met with considerable success, the name of the writer having then begun to run "like wildfire through London." At the close of the previous year he had published his long pamphlet on *Chartism*, it having proved unsuitable for its original destination as an article in the *Quarterly*. Here first he clearly enunciates, "Might is right"—one of the few strings on which, with all the variations of a political Paganini, he played through life. This tract is on the border line between the old modified Radicalism of *Sartor* and the less modified Conservatism of his later years. In 1840 Carlyle still speaks of himself as a man foiled; but at the close of that year all fear of penury was over, and in the following he was able to refuse a Chair of History at Edinburgh, as later another at St. Andrews. Meanwhile his practical power and genuine zeal for the diffusion of knowledge appeared in his foundation of the London Library, which brought him into more or less close contact with Tennyson, Milman, Forster, Helps, Spedding, Gladstone, and other leaders of the thought and action of the time. There is little in Carlyle's life at any time that can be called eventful. From first to last it was that of a retired

scholar, a thinker demanding sympathy while craving after
solitude, and the frequent inconsistency of the two require-
ments was the source of much of his unhappiness. Our
authorities, for all that we do not see in his published
works, are found in his voluminous correspondence, copious autobiographical jottings, and the three volumes of
his wife's letters and journal dating from the commencement of the struggle for recognition in London, and ex-
tending to the year of her death. Criticism of these remarkable documents, the theme of so much controversy,
belongs rather to a life of Mrs. Carlyle; but a few salient
facts may here be noted. It appears on the surface that
husband and wife had in common several marked peculiarities; on the intellectual side they had not only an extraordinary amount, but the same kind of ability, superhumanly
keen insight, and wonderful power of expression, both with
tongue and pen; the same intensity of feeling, thoroughness, and courage to look the ugliest truths full in the face;
in both, these high qualities were marred by a tendency to
attribute the worst motives to almost every one. Their
joint contempt for all whom they called "fools," i.e. the
immense majority of mankind, was a serious drawback to
the pleasure of their company. It is indeed obvious that,
whether or not it be correct to say that "his nature was
the soft one, hers the hard," Mrs. Carlyle was the severer
cynic of the two. Much of her writing confirms the impression of those who have heard her talk that no one, not
even her husband, was safe from the shafts of her ridicule.
Her pride in his genius knew no bounds, and it is improb-
able that she would have tolerated from any outsider a
breath of adverse criticism; but she herself claimed many
liberties she would not grant. Clannish almost as Carlyle
himself, even her relations are occasionally made to appear

ridiculous. There was nothing in her affections, save her
memory of her own father, corresponding to his devotion
to his whole family. With equal penetration and greater
scorn, she had no share of his underlying reverence. Such
limited union as was granted to her married life had only
soured the mocking-bird spirit of the child that derided
her grandfather's accent on occasion of his bringing her
back from a drive by another route to " varry the shane."
Carlyle's constant wailings take from him any claim to
such powers of endurance as might justify his later attacks
on Byron.

But neither had his wife any real reticence. Whenever
there were domestic troubles—flitting, repairing, building,
etc., on every occasion of clamour or worry, he, with scarce
pardonable oblivion of physical delicacy greater than his
own, went off, generally to visit distinguished friends, and
left behind him the burden and the heat of the day. She
performed her unpleasant work and all associated duties
with a practical genius that he complimented as "triumphant." She performed them, ungrudgingly perhaps, but
never without complaint; her invariable practice was to
endure and tell. " Quelle vie," she writes in 1837 to John
Sterling, whom she seems to have really liked, "let no
woman who values peace of soul ever marry an author;"
and again to the same in 1839, "Carlyle had to sit on a
jury two days, to the ruin of his whole being, physical,
moral, and intellectual," but " one gets to feel a sort of indifference to his growling." Conspicuous exceptions, as in
the case of the Shelleys, the Dobells, and the Brownings,
have been seen, within or almost within our memories, but
as a rule it is a risk for two supersensitive and nervous
people to live together; when they are sensitive in opposite ways the alliance is fatal; fortunately the Carlyles
  4*

were, in this respect, in the main sympathetic. With most
of the household troubles which occupy so exaggerated a
space in the letters and journals of both—papering, plas-
tering, painting, deceitful or disorderly domestics—general
readers have so little concern that they have reason to re-
sent the number of pages wasted in printing them; but
there was one common grievance of wider interest, to
which we have before and must here again finally refer,
premising that it affected not one period but the whole of
their lives, *i.e.* their constant, only half effectual struggle
with the modern Hydra-headed monster, the reckless and
needless Noises produced or permitted, sometimes increased
rather than suppressed by modern civilization. Mrs. Carlyle suffered almost as much as her husband from these
murderers of sleep and assassins of repose; on her mainly
fell the task of contending with the Cochin-chinas, whose
senseless shrieks went "through her like a sword," of
abating a " Der Freischütz of cats," or a pandemonium of
barrel-organs, of suppressing macaws for which Carlyle
" could neither think nor live;" now mitigating the scales
on a piano, now conjuring away, by threat or bribe, from
their neighbours a shoal of "demon fowls;" lastly, of super-
intending the troops of bricklayers, joiners, iron-hammerers
employed, with partial success, to convert the top story of
5 Cheyne Row into a sound-proof room. Her hard-won
victories in this field must have agreeably added to the
sense of personality to which she resolutely clung. Her
assertion, " Instead of boiling up individuals into the species, I would draw a chalk circle round every individuality,"
is the essence of much of her mate's philosophy; but, in
the following to Sterling, she somewhat bitterly protests
against her own absorption : "In spite of the honestest
efforts to annihilate my I—ity or merge it in what the

world doubtless considers my better half, I still find myself a self-subsisting, and, alas, self-seeking me." The ever
restive consciousness of being submerged is one of the
dominant notes of her journal, the other is the sense of
being even within the circle unrecognized. "C. is a domestic wandering Jew. . . . When he is at work I hardly
ever see his face from breakfast to dinner." . . . "Poor
little wretch that I am, . . . I feel as if I were already half-
buried . . . in some intermediate state between the living
and the dead. . . . Oh, so lonely!" These are among the
suspiria de profundis of a life which her husband compared
to "a great joyless stoicism," writing to the brother, whom
he had proposed as a third on their first home-coming.
"Solitude, indeed, is sad as Golgotha, but it is not mad
like Bedlam; absence of delirium is possible only for me
in solitude;" a sentiment almost literally acted on. In his
offering of penitential cypress, referring to his wife's de-
light in the ultimate success of his work, he says, "She
flickered round me like a perpetual radiance." But during
their joint lives their numerous visits and journeys were
made at separate times or apart. They crossed continually on the roads up and down, but when absent wrote to
one another often the most affectionate letters. Their at-
traction increased, contrary to Kepler's law, in the *direct*
ratio of the square of the distance, and when it was
stretched beyond the stars the long latent love of the sur-
vivor became a worship.

Carlyle's devotion to his own kin, blood of his blood
and bone of his bone, did not wait for any death to make
itself declared. His veneration for his mother was recip-
rocated by a confidence and pride in him unruffled from
cradle to grave, despite their widening theoretic differences, for with less distinct acknowledgment she seems to

have practically shared his belief, "it matters little what a man holds in comparison with how he holds it." But on his wife's side the family bond was less absolute, and the fact adds a tragic interest to her first great bereavement after the settlement in London. There were many callers—increasing in number and eminence as time went on—at Cheyne Row, but naturally few guests. Among these, Mrs. Carlyle's mother paid, in 1838, her first and last visit, unhappily attended by some unpleasant friction. Grace Welsh (through whom her daughter derived the gipsy vein) had been in early years a beauty and a woman of fashion, endowed with so much natural ability that Carlyle, not altogether predisposed in her favour, confessed she had just missed being a genius; but she was accustomed to have her way, and old Walter of Penfillan confessed to having seen her in fifteen different humours in one evening. Welcomed on her arrival, misunderstandings soon arose. Carlyle himself had to interpose with conciliatory advice to his wife to bear with her mother's humours. One household incident, though often quoted, is too characteristic to be omitted. On occasion of an evening party, Mrs. Welsh, whose ideas of hospitality, if not display, were perhaps larger than those suited for her still struggling hosts, had lighted a show of candles for the entertainment, whereupon the mistress of the house, with an air of authority, carried away two of them, an act which her mother resented with tears. The penitent daughter, in a mood like that which prompted Johnson to stand in the Uttoxeter market-place, left in her will that the candles were to be preserved and lit about her coffin, round which, nearly thirty years later, they were found burning. Carlyle has recorded their last sight of his mother-in-law in a few of his many graphic touches. It was at Dumfries, in 1841, where she had brought Jane down from Templand to meet and accompany him back to the south. They parted at the door of the little inn, with deep, suppressed emotion, perhaps overcharged by some presentiment, Mrs. Welsh looking sad but bright, and their last glimpse of her was the feather in her bonnet waving down the way to Lochmaben gate. Towards the close of February, 1842, news came that she had had an apoplectic stroke, and Mrs. Carlyle hurried north, stopping to break the journey at her uncle's house in Liverpool; when there she was so prostrated by the sudden announcement of her mother's death that she was prohibited from going further, and Carlyle came down from London in her stead. On reaching Templand he found that the funeral had already taken place. He remained six weeks, acting as executor in winding up the estate, which now, by the previous will, devolved on his wife. To her during the interval he wrote a series of pathetic letters. Reading these—which, with others from Haddington in the following years, make an anthology of tenderness and truth, reading them alongside of his angry invectives, with his wife's own accounts of the bilious earthquakes and peevish angers over petty cares; or worse, his ebullitions of jealousy assuming the masque of contempt, we again revert to the biographer who has said almost all that ought to be said of Carlyle, and more: "It seemed as if his soul was divided, like the Dioscuri, as if one part of it was in heaven, and the other in the place opposite heaven. But the misery had its origin in the same sensitiveness of nature which was so tremulously alive to soft and delicate emotion. Men of genius . . . are like the wind-harp which answers to the breath that touches it, now low and sweet, now rising into wild swell or angry scream, as the strings

33

are swept by some passing gush." This applies completely to men like Burns, Byron, Heine, and Carlyle, less to
the Miltons, Shakespeares, and Goethes of the world.

The crisis of bereavement, which promised to bind the
husband and wife more closely together, brought to an
end a dispute in which for once Mrs. Carlyle had her way.
During the eight years over which we have been glancing,
Carlyle had been perpetually grumbling at his Chelsea
life : the restless spirit, which never found peace on this
side of the grave, was constantly goading him with an impulse of flight and change, from land to sea, from shore to
hills; anywhere or everywhere, at the time, seemed better
than where he was. America and the Teufelsdröckh wanderings abandoned, he reverted to the idea of returning to
his own haunts. A letter to Emerson in 1839 best ex-
presses his prevalent feeling :

This foggy Babylon tumbles along as it was wont: and as for my
particular case uses me not worse but better than of old. Nay, there
are many in it that have a real friendliness for me. . . . The worst is
the sore tear and wear of this huge roaring Niagara of things on
such a poor, excitable set of nerves as mine. The velocity of all
things, of the very word you hear on the streets, is at railway rate;
joy itself is unenjoyable, to be avoided like pain; there is no wish
one has so pressingly as for quiet. Ah me! I often swear I will be
buried at least in free, breezy Scotland, out of this insane hubbub
. . . if ever the smallest competence of worldly means be mine, I will
fly this whirlpool as I would the Lake of Malebolge.

The competence had come, the death of Mrs. Welsh
leaving to his wife and himself practically from £200 to
£300 a year; why not finally return to the home of their
early married life, " in reductâ valle caniculæ," with no
noise around it but the trickle of rills and the nibbling of
sheep? Craigenputtock was now their own, and within its

"four walls" they would begin a calmer life. Fortunately, Mrs. Carlyle, whose shrewd practical instinct was never
at fault, saw through the fallacy, and set herself resolutely
against the scheme. Scotland had lost much of its charm
for her—a year later she refused an invitation from Mrs.
Aitken, saying, "I could do nothing at Scotsbrig or Dumfries but cry from morning to night." She herself had
enough of the Hill of the Hawks, and she knew that within a year Carlyle would again be calling it the Devil's Den
and lamenting Cheyne Row. He gave way with the protest, "I cannot deliberately mean anything that is harmful
to you," and certainly it was well for him.

There is no record of an original writer or artist coming
from the north of our island to make his mark in the
south, succeeding, and then retracing his steps. Had Carlyle done so, he would probably have passed from the
growing recognition of a society he was beginning to find
on the whole congenial, to the solitude of intellectual os-
tracism. Scotland may be breezy, but it is not conspicuously free. Erratic opinions, when duly veiled, are generally allowed; but this concession is of little worth. On
the tolerance of those who have no strong belief in anything, Carlyle, thinking possibly of rose-water Hunt and
the litterateurs of his tribe, expressed himself with incisive
and memorable truth: "It is but doubt and indifference.
*Touch the thing they do believe and value, their own self-
conceit: they are rattlesnakes then.*"[1] Tolerance for the
frank expression of views which clash with the sincere or
professed faith of the majority is rare everywhere; in
Scotland rarest. Episcopalians, high and broad, were content to condone the grim Calvinism that still infiltrated

---

[1] The italics are Mr. Froude's.

Carlyle's thoughts, and to smile, at worst, at his idolatry
of the iconoclast who said, "the idolater shall die the
death." But the reproach of "Pantheism" was for long
fatal to his reception across the Tweed.

Towards the close of this period he acknowledged that
London was "among improper places" the best for "writing books, after all the one use of living" for him ; its inhabitants "greatly the best" he "had ever walked with,"
and its aristocracy—the Marshalls, Stanleys, Hollands, Rus-
sells, Ashburtons, Lansdownes, who held by him through
life—its "choicest specimens." Other friendships equally
valued he made among the leading authors of the age.
Tennyson sought his company, and Connop Thirlwall.
Arnold of Rugby wrote in commendation of the *French
Revolution* and of *Chartism.* Thackeray admired and reviewed him well. Even in Macaulay, condemned to limbo
under the suspicion of having reviewed him ill, he found,
when the suspicion was proved unjust, a promise of better
things. As early as 1839 Sterling had written an article
in the *Westminster*, which gave him intense pleasure ; for
while contemning it in almost the same words as Byron did,
he loved praise equally well. In 1840 he had crossed the
Rubicon that lies between aspiration and attainment. The
populace might be blind or dumb, the "rattlesnakes"—the
"irresponsible indolent reviewers," who, from behind a
hedge pelt every wrestler till they found societies for the
victor — might still obscurely hiss; but Carlyle was at
length safe by the verdict of the "Conscript Fathers."

CHAPTER V.

THE bold venture of coming to London with a lean purse, few friends, and little fame had succeeded : but it had been a terrible risk, and the struggle had left scars behind it. To this period of his life we may apply Carlyle's words— made use of by himself at a later date—"The battle was over and we were sore wounded." It is as a maimed knight of modern chivalry, who sounded the *reveille* for an onslaught on the citadels of sham, rather than as a prophet of the future that his name is likely to endure in the history of English thought. He has also a place with Scott amongst the recreators of bygone ages, but he regarded their annals less as pictures than as lesson-books. His aim was that expressed by Tennyson to " steal fire from fountains of the past," but his design was to admonish rather than " to glorify the present." This is the avowed object of the second of his distinctly political works, which, following on the track of the first, *Chartism*, and written in a similar spirit, takes higher artistic rank. *Past and Present*, suggested by a visit to the almshouse of St. Ives and reading the chronicle of *Jocelin de Brakelond*, was undertaken as a duty, while he was mainly engaged on a greater work, the duty he felt laid upon him to say something that should bear directly on the welfare of the peo-

G

ple, especially of the poor around him. It was an impulse
similar to that which inspired *Oliver Twist*, but Carlyle's
remedies were widely different from those of Dickens.
Not merely more kindness and sympathy but paternal
government, supplying work to the idle inmates of the
workhouse, and insisting by force if need be on it being
done, was his panacea. It had been Abbot Samson's way
in his strong government of the Monastery of St. Ed-
munds, and he resolved, half in parable, half in plain sermon, to recommend it to the Ministers Peel and Russell.

In this mood the book was written off in the first seven
weeks of 1843, a *tour de force* comparable to Johnson's
writing of *Rasselas*, and published in April. It at once
made a mark by the opposition as well as by the approval
it excited. Criticism of the work—of its excellences, which
are acknowledged, and its defects as manifold—belongs to
a review of the author's political philosophy: it is enough
here to note that it was remarkable in three ways. *First*,
the object of its main attack, *laissez faire*, being a definite
one, it was capable of having and had some practical effect. Mr. Froude exaggerates when he says that Carlyle
killed the pseudo-science of orthodox political economy;
for the fundamental truths in the works of Turgot, Smith,
Ricardo, and Mill cannot be killed: but he pointed out
that, like Aristotle's leaden rule, the laws of supply and
demand must be made to bend; as Mathematics made
mechanical must allow for friction, so must Economics
leave us a little room for charity. There is ground to believe that the famous Factory Acts owed some of their
suggestions to *Past and Present*. Carlyle always speaks
respectfully of the future Lord Shaftesbury. "I heard
Milnes saying," notes the Lady Sneerwell of real life, " at
the Shuttleworths that Lord Ashley was the greatest man

alive: he was the only man that Carlyle praised in his
book. I dare say he knew I was overhearing him." But,
while supplying arguments and a stimulus to philanthropists, his protests against philanthropy as an adequate solution of the problem of human misery became more pronounced. About the date of the conception of this book
we find in the Journal:

Again and again of late I ask myself in whispers, is it the duty
of a citizen to paint mere heroisms. . . . Live to make others happy!
Yes, surely, at all times, so far as you can. But at bottom that is
not the aim of my life. . . . it is mere hypocrisy to call it such, as is
continually done nowadays. . . . Avoid cant. Do not think that
your life means a mere searching in gutters for fallen figures to wipe
and set up.

Past and Present, in the *second* place, is notable as the
only considerable consecutive book—unless we also except
the *Life of Sterling*—which the author wrote without
the accompaniment of wrestlings, agonies, and disgusts.
Thirdly, though marking a stage in his mental progress,
the fusion of the refrains of *Chartism* and *Hero-Worship*,
and his first clear breach with Mazzini and with Mill, the
book was written as an interlude, when he was in severe
travail with his greatest contribution to English history.
The last rebuff which Carlyle encountered came, by curious
accident, from the *Westminster*, to which Mill had engaged him to contribute an article on "Oliver Cromwell."
While this was in preparation, Mill had to leave the
country on account of his health, and gave the review in
charge of an Aberdonian called Robertson, who wrote to
stop the progress of the essay with the message that *he*
had decided to undertake the subject himself. Carlyle
was angry; but, instead of sullenly throwing the MS.

aside, he set about constructing on its basis a History of the Civil War.

Numerous visits and tours during the following three years, though bringing him into contact with new and interesting personalities, were mainly determined by the resolve to make himself acquainted with the localities of the war; and his knowledge of them has contributed to give colour and reality to the finest battle-pieces in modern English prose. In 1842 with Dr. Arnold he drove from Rugby fifteen miles to Naseby, and the same year, after a brief yachting trip to Belgium—in the notes on which the old Flemish towns stand out as clearly as in Longfellow's verse—he made his pilgrimage to St. Ives and Ely Cathedral, where Oliver two centuries before had called out to the recalcitrant Anglican in the pulpit, "Cease your fooling and come down." In July, 1843, Carlyle made a trip to South Wales; first to visit a worthy devotee called Redmond, and then to Bishop Thirlwall near Carmarthen. " A right solid, simple-hearted, robust man, very strangely swathed," is the visitor's meagre estimate of one of our most classic historians.

On his way back he carefully reconnoitred the field of Worcester. Passing his wife at Liverpool, where she was a guest of her uncle, and leaving her to return to London and brush up Cheyne Row, he walked over Snowdon from Llanberis to Beddgelert, with his brother John. He next proceeded to Scotsbrig, then north to Edinburgh, and then to Dunbar, which he contrived to visit on the 3d of September, an anniversary revived in his pictured page with a glow and force to match which we have to revert to Bacon's account of the sea-fight of the *Revenge*. From Dunbar he returned to Edinburgh, spent some time with his always admired and admiring friend Erskine, of Linlathen, a Scotch broad churchman of the type of F. D. Maurice and Macleod Campbell, and then went home to set in earnest to the actual writing of his work. He had decided to abandon the design of a History, and to make his book a Biography of Cromwell, interlacing with it the main features and events of the Commonwealth. The difficulties even of this reduced plan were still immense, and his groans at every stage in its progress were "louder and more loud," e.g., " My progress in *Cromwell* is frightful." " A thousand times I regretted that this task was ever taken up." " The most impossible book of all I ever before tried," and at the close, " *Cromwell* I must have written in 1844, but for four years previous it had been a continual toil and misery to me; four years of abstruse toil, obscure speculation, futile wrestling, and misery I used to count it had cost me." The book, issued in 1845, soon went through three editions, and brought the author to the front as the most original historian of his time. Macaulay was his rival, but in different paths of the same field. About this time Mr. Froude became his pupil, and has left an interesting account (iii. 290-300) of his master's influence over the Oxford of those days which would be only spoilt by selections. Oxford, like Athens, ever longing after something new, patronised the Chelsea prophet, and then calmed down to her wonted cynicism. But Froude and Ruskin were, as far as compatible with the strong personality of each, always loyal; and the capacity inborn in both, the power to breathe life into dry records and dead stones had at least an added impulse from their master.

The year 1844 is marked by the publication in the *Foreign Quarterly* of the essay on *Dr. Francia*, and by the death of John Sterling—loved with the love of David for

Jonathan — outside his own family losses, the greatest
wrench in Carlyle's life.   Sterling's published writings are
as inadequate to his reputation as the fragmentary remains
of Arthur Hallam ; but in friendships, especially unequal
friendships, personal fascination counts for more than half,
and all are agreed as to the charm in both instances of the
inspiring companionships.   Archdeacon Hare having given
a somewhat coldly correct account of Sterling as a clergy-
man, Carlyle three years later, in 1851, published his own
impressions of his friend as a thinker, sane philanthropist,
and devotee of truth, in a work that, written in a three
months' fervour, has some claim to rank, though faltering,
as prose after verse, with *Adonais, In Memoriam,* and Matthew Arnold's *Thyrsis.*

These years are marked by a series of acts of unobtru-
sive benevolence, the memory of which has been in some
cases accidentally rescued from the oblivion to which the
benefactor was willing to have them consigned.   Carlyle
never boasted of doing a kindness.   He was, like Wordsworth, frugal at home beyond necessity, but often as generous in giving as he was ungenerous in judging.   His
assistance to Thomas Cooper, author of the *Purgatory of
Suicides,* his time spent in answering letters of "anxious
enquirers"—letters that nine out of ten busy men would
have flung into the waste-paper basket—his interest in such
works as Samuel Bamford's *Life of a Radical,* and admirable advice to the writer;[1] his instructions to a young

[1] These letters to Bamford, showing a keen interest in the working-
men of whom his correspondent had written, point to the ideal of a
sort of Tory Democracy. Carlyle writes : " We want more knowledge
about the Lancashire operatives ; their miseries and gains, virtues
and vices.   Winnow what you have to say, and give us wheat free
from chaff.   Then the rich captains of workers will be willing to

student on the choice of books, and well-timed warning to another against the profession of literature, are sun-rifts in the storm, that show "a heart within blood-tinctured, of a veined humanity." The same epoch, however—that of the start of the great writer's almost uninterrupted triumph—brings us in face of an episode singularly delicate and difficult to deal with, but impossible to evade.

Carlyle, now generally recognised in London as having one of the most powerful intellects, and by far the greatest command of language among his contemporaries, was beginning to suffer some of the penalties of renown in being beset by bores and travestied by imitators; but he was also enjoying its rewards. Eminent men of all shades of opinion made his acquaintance; he was a frequent guest of the genial Mæcenas, an admirer of genius though no mere worshipper of success, R. Monckton Milnes; meeting Hallam, Bunsen, Pusey, etc., at his house in London, and afterwards visiting him at Fryston Hall in Yorkshire. The future Lord Houghton was, among distinguished men of letters and society, the one of whom he spoke with the most unvarying regard. Carlyle corresponded with Peel, whom he set almost on a par with Wellington as worthy of perfect trust, and talked familiarly with Bishop Wilberforce, whom he miraculously credits with holding at heart views much like his own. At a somewhat later date, in the circle of his friends, bound to him by various degrees of intimacy, History was represented by Thirlwall, Grote, and Froude;

listen to you. Brevity and sincerity will succeed. Be brief and select, omit much, give each subject its proper proportionate space ; and be exact without caring to round off the edges of what you have to say." Later, he declines Bamford's offer of verses, saying " verse is a bugbear to booksellers at present. These are prosaic, earnest, practical, not singing times."

Poetry by Browning, Henry Taylor, Tennyson, and Clough; Social romance by Kingsley ; Biography by James Spedding and John Forster; and Criticism by John Ruskin. His link to the last named was, however, their common distrust of political economy, as shown in *Unto This Last*, rather than any deep artistic sympathy. In Macaulay, a conversationalist more rapid than himself, Carlyle found a rival rather than a companion ; but his prejudiced view of physical science was forgotten in his personal affection for Tyndall and in their congenial politics. His society was from the publication of *Cromwell* till near his death increasingly sought after by the aristocracy, several members of which invited him to their country-seats, and bestowed on him all acceptable favours. In this class he came to find other qualities than those referred to in the *Sartor* inscription, and other aims than that of " preserving their game," the ambition to hold the helm of the State in stormy weather, and to play their part among the "captains of industry." In the *Reminiscences* the aristocracy are deliberately voted to be " for continual grace of bearing and of acting, steadfast honour, light address, and cheery stoicism, actually yet the best of English classes." There can be no doubt that his intercourse with this class, as with men of affairs and letters, some of whom were his proximate equals, was a fortunate sequel to the duck-pond of Ecclefechan and the lonely rambles on the Border moors.

> Es bildet ein Talent sich in der Stille,
> Sich ein Character in dem Strom der Welt.

The life of a great capital may be the crown of education, but there is a danger in homage that comes late and then without reserve. Give me neither poverty nor riches,

applies to praise as well as to wealth; and the sudden transition from comparative neglect to

honour, love, obedience, troops of friends,

is a moral trial passing the strength of all but a few of
the "irritable race" of writers. The deference paid to
Carlyle made him yet more intolerant of contradiction, and
fostered his selfishness, in one instance with the disastrous
result of clouding a whole decade of his domestic life.
In February, 1839, he speaks of dining—"an eight-o'clock
dinner which ruined me for a week"—with "a certain
Baring," at whose table in Bath House he again met Bunsen, and was introduced to Lord Mahon. This was the
beginning of what, after the death of Sterling, grew into
the most intimate friendship of his life. Baring, son of
Lord Ashburton of the American treaty so named, and
successor to the title on his father's death in 1848, was a
man of sterling worth and sound sense, who entered into
many of the views of his guest. His wife was by general
consent the most brilliant woman of rank in London, whose
grace, wit, refinement, and decision of character had made
her the acknowledged leader of society. Lady Harriet, by
the exercise of some overpowering though purely intellectual spell, made the proudest of men, the modern Diogenes,
our later Swift, so much her slave that for twelve years,
whenever he could steal a day from his work, he ran at her
beck from town to country, from castle to cot; from Addiscombe, her husband's villa in Surrey, to the Grange, her
father-in-law's seat in Hampshire; from Loch Luichart and
Glen Finnan, where they had Highland shootings, to the
Palais Royal. Mr. Froude's comment in his introduction
to the Journal is substantially as follows: Lady Harriet
Baring or Ashburton was the centre of a planetary system

5

in which every distinguished public man of genuine worth
then revolved.   Carlyle was naturally the chief among
them, and he was perhaps at one time ambitious of himself
taking some part in public affairs, and saw the advantage of
this stepping-stone to enable him to do something more for
the world, as Byron said, than write books for it.   But the
idea of entering Parliament, which seems to have once
suggested itself to him in 1849, was too vague and transient
to have ever influenced his conduct.   It is more correct to
say that he was flattered by a sympathy not too thorough
to be tame, pleased by adulation never gross, charmed by
the same graces that charmed the rest, and finally fascinated
by a sort of hypnotism.   The irritation which this strange
alliance produced in the mind of the mistress of Cheyne
Row is no matter of surprise.   Pride and affection together
had made her bear with all her husband's humours, and
share with him all the toils of the struggle from obscurity.
He had emerged, and she was still half content to be systematically set aside for his books, the inanimate rivals on
which he was building a fame she had some claim to share.
But her fiery spirit was not yet tamed into submitting to
be sacrificed to an animate rival, or passively permitting
the usurpation of companionship grudged to herself by
another woman, whom she could not enjoy the luxury of
despising.   Lady Harriet's superiority in *finesse* and geni-
ality, as well as advantages of station, were aggravations of
the injury, and this with a singular want of tact Carlyle
further aggravated when he insisted on his wife accepting
the invitations of his hostess.   These visits, always against
the grain, were rendered more irritating from a half conscious antagonism between the chief female actors in the
tragi-comedy ; the one sometimes innocently unobservant
of the wants of her guest, the other turning every acciden-

tal neglect into a slight, and receiving every jest as an
affront. Carlyle's "Gloriana" was to the mind of his wife
a "heathen goddess," while Mrs. Carlyle, with reference to
her favourite dog "Nero," was in her turn nicknamed
Agrippina.

In midsummer of 1846, after an enforced sojourn at
Addiscombe in worse than her usual health, she returned
to Chelsea with "her mind all churned to froth," opened it
to her husband with such plainness that "there was a violent scene;" she left the house in a mood like that of the
first Mrs. Milton, and took refuge with her friends the
Paulets at Seaforth, near Liverpool, uncertain whether or
not she would return. There were only two persons from
whom it would seem natural for her at such a crisis to ask
advice; one was Geraldine Jewsbury, a young Manchester
lady, authoress of a well-known novel, *The Half-Sisters*,
from the beginning of their acquaintance in 1841 till the
close in 1866 her most intimate associate and chosen con-
fidant, who, we are told, "knew all" her secrets;[1] the
other was the inspired Italian, pure patriot and Stoic moralist, Joseph Mazzini. To him she wrote twice—once apparently before leaving London, and again from Seaforth.
His letters in reply, tenderly sympathetic and yet rigidly
insistent on the duty of forbearance and endurance, availed
to avert the threatened catastrophe; but there are sentences
which show how bitter the complaints must have been.

It is only you who can teach yourself that, whatever the *present*
may be, you must front it with dignity. . . . I could only point out
to you the fulfilment of duties which can make life—not happy—

---

[1] Carlyle often speaks, sometimes slightingly, of Miss Jewsbury,
as a sensational novelist and admirer of George Sand, but he appreciated her genuine worth.

what can? but earnest, sacred, and resigned. . . . I am carrying a
burden even heavier than you, and have undergone even bitterer de-
ceptions. Your life proves an empty thing, you say. Empty! Do
not blaspheme. Have you never done good? Have you never
loved? . . . Pain and joy, deception and fulfilled hopes are just the
rain and the sunshine that must meet the traveller on his way.
Bless the Almighty if He has thought proper to send the latter to
you. . . . Wrap your cloak round you against the first, but do not
think a single moment that the one or the other have anything to do
with the *end* of the journey.

Carlyle's first letter after the rupture is a mixture of
reproach and affection. "We never parted before in such
a manner; and all for literally nothing. . . . Adieu,
dearest, for that is, and, if madness prevail not, may forever be, your authentic title;" and another, enclosing the
birthday present which he had never omitted since her
mother's death, softened his wife's resentment, and the
storm blew over for a time. But while the cause remained there was in the house at best a surface tranquillity, at worst an undertone of misery which finds voice
in Mrs. Carlyle's diary from October, 1855, to May, 1856,
not merely covered with "black spider webs," but steeped
in gall, the publication of which has made so much debate. It is like a page from *Othello* reversed. A few
sentences condense the refrain of the lament. "Charles
Buller said of the Duchess de Praslin, 'What could a poor
fellow do with a wife that kept a journal but murder
her?'" "That eternal Bath House! I wonder how many
thousand miles Mr. C. has walked between here and
there?" "Being an only child, I never wished to sew
men's trousers—no, never!

"I gin to think I've sold myself
For very little cas."

"To-day I called on my lady : she was perfectly civil, for a wonder." "Edward Irving ! The past is past and gone is gone—

> "O waly, waly, love is bonnie,
> A little while when it is new."

Quotations which, laid alongside the records of the writer's visit to the people at Haddington, "who seem all to grow so good and kind as they grow old," and to the graves in the church-yard there, are infinitely pathetic. The letters which follow are in the same strain, *e.g.* to Carlyle when visiting his sister at the Gill, "I never forget kindness, nor, alas, unkindness either :" to Luichart, "I don't believe thee, wishing yourself at home. . . . You don't, as weakly amiable people do, sacrifice yourself for the pleasure of others ;" to Mrs. Russell at Thornhill, "My London doctor's prescription is that I should be kept always happy and tranquil (! ! !)"

In the summer of 1856 Lady Ashburton gave a real ground for offence in allowing both the Carlyles, on their way north with her, to take a seat in an ordinary railway carriage, beside her maid, while she herself travelled in a special saloon. Partly, perhaps in consequence, Mrs. Carlyle soon went to visit her cousins in Fifeshire, and afterwards refused to accompany her ladyship on the way back. This resulted in another quarrel with her husband, who had issued the command from Luichart—but it was their last on the subject, for Gloriana died on the 4th of the following May, 1857, at Paris : "The most queen-like woman I had ever known or seen, by nature and by culture *facile princeps* she, I think, of all great ladies I have ever seen." This brought to a close an episode in which there were faults on both sides, gravely punished : the in

34

cidents of its course and the manner in which they were
received show, among other things, that railing at the
name of "Happiness" does little or nothing to reconcile
people to the want of the reality.   In 1858 Lord Ashburton married again—a Miss Stuart Mackenzie, who became the attached friends of the Carlyles, and remained on
terms of unruffled intimacy with both till the end: she
survived her husband, who died in 1864, leaving a legacy
of £2000 to the household at Cheyne Row.   *Sic transit.*

From this date we must turn back over nearly twenty
years to retrace the main steps of the great author's
career.   Much of the interval was devoted to innumerable
visits, in acceptance of endless hospitalities, or in pay-
ing his annual devotions to Annandale—calls on his time
which kept him rushing from place to place like a comet.
Two facts are notable about those expeditions: they rarely
seemed to give him much pleasure, even at Scotsbrig he
complained of sleepless nights and farm noises; and he
was hardly ever accompanied by his wife.   She, too, was
constantly running north to her own kindred in Liverpool
or Scotland, but their paths did not run parallel, they almost always insected, so that when the one was on the
way north the other was homeward bound, to look out
alone on "a horizon of zero."   Only a few of these visits
are worth recording as of general interest.   Most of them
were paid, a few received.   In the autumn of 1846, Margaret Fuller, sent from Emerson, called at Cheyne Row,
and recorded her impression of the master as "in a very
sweet humour, full of wit and pathos, without being over-
bearing," adding that she was "carried away by the rich
flow of his discourse;" and that "the hearty, noble earnestness of his personal bearing brought back the charm
of his writing before she wearied of it."   A later visitor,

Miss Martineau, his old helper in days of struggle, was now thus esteemed : " Broken into utter wearisomeness, a mind reduced to these three elements—imbecility, dogmatism, and unlimited hope. I never in my life was more heartily bored with any creature !" In 1847 there followed the last English glimpse of Jeffrey and the last of Dr. Chalmers, who was full of enthusiasm about *Cromwell ;* then a visit to the Brights, John and Jacob, at Rochdale : with the former he had "a paltry speaking match" on topics described as "shallow, totally worthless to me," the latter he liked, recognising in him a culture and delicacy rare with so much strength of will and independence of thought. Later came a second visit from Emerson, then on a lecturing tour to England, gathering impressions revived in his *English Traits.* "His doctrines are too airy and thin," wrote Carlyle, "for the solid, practical heads of the Lancashire region. We had immense talkings with him here, but found that he did not give as much to chew the cud upon. He is a pure-minded man, but I think his talent is not quite so high as I had anticipated." They had an interesting walk to Stonehenge together, and Carlyle attended one of his friend's lectures, but with modified approval, finding this serene "spiritual son" of his own rather "gone into philanthropy and moonshine." Emerson's notes of this date, on the other hand, mark his emancipation from mere discipleship. "Carlyle had all the kleinstädtlicher traits of an islander and a Scotsman, and reprimanded with severity the rebellious instincts of the native of a vast continent. . . . In him, as in Byron, one is more struck with the rhetoric than with the matter. . . . There is more character than intellect in every sentence, therein strangely resembling Samuel Johnson." The same year Carlyle perpetrated one of his worst criticisms, that on Keats :

The kind of man he was gets ever more horrible to me. Force of hunger for pleasure of every kind, and want of all other force. . . . Such a structure of soul, it would once have been very evident, was a chosen " Vessel of Hell."

And in the next an ungenerously contemptuous reference to Macaulay's *History :*

The most popular ever written. Fourth edition already, within perhaps four months. Book to which four hundred editions could not add any value, there being no depth of sense in it at all, and a very great quantity of rhetorical wind.

Landor, on the other hand, whom he visited later at Bath, he appreciated, being " much taken with the gigantesque, explosive but essentially chivalrous and almost heroic old man." [1] He was now at ease about the sale of his books, having, *inter alia*, received £600 for a new edition of the *French Revolution* and the *Miscellanies.* His Journal is full of plans for new work on democracy, organisation of labour, and education, and his letters of the period to Thomas Erskine and others are largely devoted to politics.

In 1846 he spent the first week of September in Ireland, crossing from Ardrossan to Belfast, and then driving to Drogheda, and by rail to Dublin, where in Conciliation

[1] This is one of the few instances in which further knowledge led to a change for the better in Carlyle's judgment. In a letter to Emerson, 1840, he speaks disparagingly of Landor as "a wild man, whom no extent of culture had been able to tame! His intellectual faculty seemed to me to be weak in proportion to his violence of temper : the judgment he gives about anything is more apt to be wrong than right—as the inward whirlwind shows him this side or the other of the object : and *sides* of an object are all that he sees." *De te fabula.* Emerson answers defending Landor, and indicating points of likeness between him and Carlyle.

Hall he saw O'Connell for the first time since a casual glimpse at a radical meeting arranged by Charles Buller— a meeting to which he had gone out of curiosity in 1834. O'Connell was always an object of Carlyle's detestation, and on this occasion he does not mince his words.

> Chief quack of the then world . . . first time I had ever heard the lying scoundrel speak. . . . Demosthenes of blarney. . . . The big beggar-man who had £15,000 a year, and, *proh pudor!* the favour of English ministers instead of the pillory.

At Dundrum he met by invitation Carleton the novelist, with Mitchell and Gavan Duffy,[1] the young Ireland leaders whom he seems personally to have liked, but he told Mitchell that he would probably be hanged, and said during a drive about some flourishing and fertile fields of the Pale, "Ah! Duffy, there you see the hoof of the bloody Saxon." He returned from Kingston to Liverpool on the 10th, and so closed his short and unsatisfactory trip. Three years later, July to August 6th, 1849, he paid a longer and final visit to the "ragged commonweal" or "common woe," as Raleigh called it, landing at Dublin, and after some days there passing on to Kildare, Kilkenny, Lismore, Waterford, beautiful Killarney and its

---

[1] Sir C. Gavan Duffy, in the "Conversations and Correspondence," now being published in the *Contemporary Review*, naturally emphasises Carlyle's politer, more genial side, and prints several expressions of sympathy with the "Tenant Agitations;" but his demur to the *Reminiscences of My Irish Journey* being accepted as an accurate account of the writer's real sentiments is of little avail in face of the letters to Emerson, more strongly accentuating the same view, *e.g.*, "Bothered almost to madness with Irish balderdash. . . . '*Blacklead* these two million idle beggars,' I sometimes advised, 'and sell them in Brazil as niggers!'—perhaps Parliament on sweet constraint will allow you to advance them to be niggers!"

beggar hordes, and then to Limerick, Clare, Castlebar,
where he met W. E. Foster, whose acquaintance he had
made two years earlier at Matlock.   At Gweedore in
Donegal he stayed with Lord George Hill, whom he respected, though persuaded that he was on the wrong road
to Reform by Philanthropy in a country where it had
never worked; and then on to half Scotch Derry.   There,
August 6th, he made an emphatic after-breakfast speech
to a half sympathetic audience ; the gist of it being that
the remedy for Ireland was not "emancipation" or
"liberty," but to "cease following the devil, as it had
been doing for two centuries."   The same afternoon he
escaped on board a Glasgow steamer, and landed safe at
2 A.M. on the morning of the 7th.   The notes of the tour,
set down on his return to Chelsea and republished in
1882, having only the literary merit of the vigorous descriptive touches inseparable from the author's lightest
writing; otherwise they are mere rough and tumble jottings, with no consecutive meaning, of a rapid hawk's-eye
view of the four provinces.

   But Carlyle never departed from the views they set
forth, that Ireland is in the main a country of idle semi-
savages, whose staple trade is begging, whose practice is
to lie, unfit not only for self-government but for what is
commonly called constitutional government, whose ragged
people must be coerced, by the methods of Raleigh, of
Spenser, and of Cromwell, into reasonable industry and
respect for law.   At Westport, where "human swinery has
reached its acme," he finds "30,000 paupers in a population of 60,000, and 34,000 kindred hulks on out-door relief,
lifting each an ounce of mould with a shovel, while 5000
lads are pretending to break stones," and exclaims, "Can
it be a charity to keep men alive on these terms?   In face

of all the twaddle of the earth, shoot a man rather than train him (with heavy expense to his neighbours) to be a deceptive human swine." Superficial travellers generally praise the Irish. Carlyle had not been long in their country when he formulated his idea of the Home Rule that seemed to him most for their good.

Kildare Railway: big blockhead sitting with his dirty feet on seat opposite, not stirring them for one who wanted to sit there. "One thing we're all agreed on," said he; "we're very ill-governed: Whig, Tory, Radical, Repealer, all, all admit we're very ill-governed!" I thought to myself, "Yes, indeed; you govern yourself! He that would govern you well would probably surprise you much, my friend —laying a hearty horsewhip over that back of yours."

And a little later at Castlebar he declares, "Society here would have to eat itself and end by cannibalism in a week, if it were not held up by the rest of our Empire standing afoot." These passages are written in the spirit which inspired his paper on "The Nigger Question" and the aggressive series of assaults to which it belongs, on what he regarded as the most prominent quackeries, shams, and pretence philanthropies of the day. His own account of the reception of this work is characteristic:

In 1849, after an interval of deep and gloom and bottomless dubitation came *Latter-Day Pamphlets*, which unpleasantly astonished everybody, set the world upon the strangest suppositions—" Carlyle got deep into whisky," said some—ruined my reputation according to the friendliest voices, and in effect divided me altogether from the mob of "Progress-of-the-species" and other vulgar; but were a great relief to my own conscience as a faithful citizen, and have been ever since.

These pamphlets alienated Mazzini and Mill, and provoked the assault of the newspapers; which, by the author's

confession, did something to arrest and restrict the sale.
Nor was this indignation wholly unnatural. Once in his
life, on occasion of his being called to serve at a jury trial,
Carlyle, with remarkable adroitness, coaxed a recalcitrant
juryman into acquiescence with the majority; but coaxing
as a rule was not his way. When he found himself in
front of what he deemed to be a falsehood his wont was
to fly in its face and tear it to pieces. His satire was not
like that of Horace, who taught his readers *ridendo dicere
verum*, it was rather that of the elder Lucilius or the later
Juvenal; not that of Chaucer, who wrote:

> That patience is a virtue high is plain,
> Because it conquers, as the clerks explain,
> Things that rude valour never could attain,

but that of *The Lye*, attributed to Raleigh, or Swift's *Gulliver*, or the Letters of Junius. The method of direct denunciation has advantages: it cannot be mistaken, nor, if
strong enough, ignored; but it must lay its account with
consequences, and Carlyle in this instance found them so
serious that he was threatened at the height of his fame
with dethronement. Men said he had lost his head, gone
back to the everlasting " No," and mistaken swearing all
round for political philosophy. The ultimate value attached to the *Latter-Day Pamphlets* must depend to a
large extent on the view of the critic. It is now, however,
generally admitted on the one hand that they served in
some degree to counteract the rashness of Philanthropy;
on the other, that their effect was marred by more than
the writer's usual faults of exaggeration. It is needless to
refer the temper they display to the troubles then gathering about his domestic life. A better explanation is to
be found in the public events of the time.

The two years previous to their appearance were the
Revolution years, during which the European world seemed
to be turned upsidedown. The French had thrown out
their *bourgeois* king, Louis Philippe—"the old scoundrel,"
as Carlyle called him—and established their second Republic. Italy, Hungary, and half Germany were in revolt
against the old authorities; the Irish joined in the chorus,
and the Chartist monster petition was being carted to
Parliament. Upheaval was the order of the day, kings
became exiles and exiles kings, dynasties and creeds were
being subverted, and empires seemed rocking as on the
surface of an earthquake. They were years of great aspirations, with beliefs in all manner of swift regeneration:

Magnus ab integro sæclorum nascitur ordo,

all varieties of doctrinaire idealisms. Mazzini failed at
Rome, Kossuth at Pesth; the riots of Berlin resulted in
the restoration of the old dull bureaucratic regime; Smith
O'Brien's bluster exploded in a cabbage garden; the Railway Bubble burst in the fall of the bloated king Hudson,
and the Chartism of the time evaporated in smoke. The
old sham gods, with Buonaparte of the stuffed eagle in
front, came back; because, concluded Carlyle, there was no
man in the front of the new movement strong enough to
guide it; because its figure-heads were futile sentimental-
ists, insurgents who could not win. The reaction produced by their failure had somewhat the same effect on
his mind that the older French Revolution had on that of
Burke: he was driven back to a greater degree than Mr.
Froude allows on practical conservatism and on the nega-
tions of which the *Latter-Day Pamphlets* are the expression. To this series of *pronunciamentos* of political scep-

ticism he meant to add another, of which he often talks
under the name of "Exodus from Houndsditch," boldly
stating and setting forth the grounds of his now complete
divergence from all forms of what either in England or
Europe generally could be called the Orthodox faith in
Religion.   He was, we are told, withheld from this by the
feeling that the teaching even of the priests he saw and
derided in Belgium or in Galway was better than the
atheistic materialism which he associated with the domin-
ion of mere physical science.   He may have felt he had
nothing, definite enough to be understood by the people,
to substitute for what he proposed to destroy; and he
may have had a thought of the reception of such a work
at Scotsbrig.   Much of the *Life of Sterling*, however, is
somewhat less directly occupied with the same question,
and though gentler in tone it excited almost as much
clamour as the *Pamphlets*, especially in the north.   The
book, says Carlyle himself, was "utterly revolting to the
religious people in particular (to my surprise rather than
otherwise).   'Doesn't believe in us either!'   Not he for
certain; can't, if you will know."   During the same year
his almost morbid dislike of materialism found vent in
denunciations of the "Crystal Palace" Exhibition of Industry; though for its main promoter, Prince Albert, he
subsequently entertained and expressed a sincere respect.

In the summer of 1851 the Carlyles went together to
Malvern, where they met Tennyson (whose good-nature
had been proof against some slighting remarks on his
verses), Sydney Dobell, then in the fame of his "Roman,"
and other celebrities.   They tried the "Water Cure,"
under the superintendence of Dr. Gully, who received and
treated them as guests; but they derived little good from
the process.   "I found," says Carlyle, "water taken as

medicine to be the most destructive drug I had ever tried."
Proceeding northward, he spent three weeks with his
mother, then in her eighty-fourth year and at last growing
feeble; a quiet time only disturbed by indignation at
"one ass whom I heard the bray of in some Glasgow newspaper," comparing "our grand hater of shams," to Father
Gavazzi. His stay was shortened by a summons to spend
a few days with the Ashburtons at Paris on their return
from Switzerland. Though bound by a promise to respond
to the call, Carlyle did not much relish it. Travelling
abroad was always a burden to him, and it was aggravated
in this case by his very limited command of the language
for conversational purposes. Fortunately, on reaching
London he found that the poet Browning and his wife,
whose acquaintance he had made ten years before, were
about to start for the same destination, and he prevailed
upon them, though somewhat reluctant, to take charge of
him.' The companionship was, therefore, not accidental,
and it was of great service. "Carlyle," according to Mrs.
Browning's biographer, "would have been miserable without Browning, who made all the arrangements for the
party, passed luggage through the customs, saw to pass-
ports, fought the battles of all the stations, and afterwards
acted as guide through the streets of the great city." By
a curious irony, two verse-makers and admirers of George
Sand made it possible for the would-be man of action to
find his way. The poetess, recalling the trip afterwards,
wrote that she liked the prophet more than she expected,
finding his "bitterness only melancholy, and his scorn
sensibility." Browning himself continued through life to
regard Carlyle with "affectionate reverence." "He never

Mrs. Sutherland Orr's *Life of Robert Browning.*

ceased," says Mrs. Orr, "to defend him against the charge
of unkindness to his wife, or to believe that, in the matter
of their domestic unhappiness, she was the more responsi-
ble of the two. . . . He always thought her a hard, unlovable
woman, and I believe little liking was lost between them.
. . . Yet Carlyle never rendered him that service—easy as
it appears—which one man of letters most justly values
from another, that of proclaiming the admiration which
he privately professed for his work." The party started
September 24th, and reached Dieppe by Newhaven, after
a rough passage, the effects of which on some fellow-
travellers more unfortunate than himself Carlyle describes
in a series of recently - discovered jottings[1] made on his
return, October 2d, to Chelsea. On September 25th they
reached Paris. Carlyle joined the Ashburtons at Meuricé's
Hotel: there dined, went in the evening to the Theatre
Français, cursed the play, and commented unpleasantly on
General Changarnier sitting in the stalls.

During the next few days he met many of the celebrities of the time, and caricatured, after his fashion, their
personal appearance, talk, and manner. These criticisms
are for the most part of little value. The writer had in
some of his essays shown almost as much capacity of understanding the great Frenchmen of the last century as was
compatible with his Puritan vein; but as regards French
literature since the Revolution he was either ignorant or
alien. What light could be thrown on that interesting era
by a man who could only say of the authors of *La Comé-
die Humaine* and *Consuelo* that they were ministers in a
Phallus worship? Carlyle seems to have seen most of

---

[1] Partially reproduced, *Pall Mall Gazette*, April 9th, 1890, with illustrative connecting comments.

Thiers, whom he treats with good-natured condescension, but little insight: "round fat body, tapering like a nine-pin into small fat feet, placidly sharp fat face, puckered eyeward ... a frank, sociable kind of creature, who has absolutely no malignity towards any one, and is not the least troubled with self-seekings." Thiers talked with contempt of Michelet, and Carlyle, unconscious of the numerous affinities between that historian of genius and himself, half assented. Prosper Mérimée,[1] on the other hand, incensed him by some freaks of criticism, whether in badinage or earnest—probably the former. "Jean Paul," he said, getting on the theme of German literature, "was a hollow fool of the first magnitude," and Goethe was "insignificant, unintelligible, a paltry kind of Scribe manqué." "I could stand no more of it, but lighted a cigar and adjourned to the street. 'You impertinent, blasphemous blockhead!' this was sticking in my throat; better to retire without bringing it out." Of Guizot he writes, "Tartuffe, gaunt, hollow, resting on the everlasting 'No' with a haggard consciousness that it ought to be the everlasting 'Yea.'" "To me an extremely detestable kind of man." Carlyle missed General Cavaignac, "of all Frenchmen the one" he "cared to see." In the streets of Paris he found no one who could properly be called a gentleman. "The truly ingenious and strong men of France are here (i.e. among the industrial classes) making money, while the politician, literary, etc., etc. class is mere play-actorism." His summary before leaving at the close of a week, rather misspent, is: "Articulate-speaking France was altogether

---

[1] The two men were mutually antagonistic; Mérimée tried to read the *French Revolution*, but flung the book aside in weariness or disdain.

without beauty or meaning to me in my then diseased mood; but I saw traces of the inarticulate . . . much worthier."

Back in London, he sent Mrs. Carlyle to the Grange (distinguishing himself, in an interval of study at home, by washing the back area flags with his own hands), and there joined her till the close of the year. During the early part of the next he was absorbed in reading and planning work. Then came an unusually tranquil visit to Thomas Erskine, of Linlathen, during which he had only to complain that the servants were often obliged to run out of the room to hide their laughter at his humorous bursts. At the close of August, 1852, he embarked on board a Leith steamer bound for Rotterdam, on his first trip to Germany. Home once more, in October, he found chaos come, and seas of paint overwhelming everything; " went to the Grange, and back in time to witness from Bath House the funeral, November 18th, of the great Duke," remarking, "The one true man of official men in England, or that I know of in Europe, concludes his long course. . . . Tennyson's verses are naught. Silence alone is respectable on such an occasion." In March, again at the Grange, he met the Italian minister Azeglio, and when this statesman disparaged Mazzini—a thing only permitted by Carlyle to himself—he retorted with the remark, " Monsieur, vous ne le connaissez pas du tout, du tout." At Chelsea, on his return, the fowl tragic-comedy reached a crisis, " the unprotected male " declaring that he would shoot them or poison them. " A man is not a Chatham nor a Wallenstein; but a man has work, too, which the Powers would not quite wish to have suppressed by two and sixpence worth of bantams. . . . They must either withdraw or die." Ultimately his mother-wife came to the

rescue of her "babe of genius;" the cocks were bought
off, and in the long-talked-of sound-proof room the last
considerable work of his life, though painfully, proceeded.
Meanwhile "brother John" had married, and Mrs. Carlyle
went to visit the couple at Moffat. While there bad
tidings came from Scotsbrig, and she dutifully hurried off
to nurse her mother-in-law through an attack from which
the strong old woman temporarily rallied. But the final
stroke could not be long delayed. When Carlyle was pay-
ing his winter visit to the Grange in December, news came
that his mother was worse, and her recovery despaired of;
and, by consent of his hostess, he hurried off to Scotsbrig;
"mournful leave given me by the Lady A., mournful en-
couragement to be speedy, not dilatory," and arrived in
time to hear her last words. "Here is Tom come to bid
you good-night, mother," said John. "As I turned to go,
she said, 'I'm muckle obleeged to you.'" She spoke no
more, but passed from sleep after sleep of coma to that of
death, on Sunday, Christmas Day, 1853. "We can only
have one mother," exclaimed Byron on a like event—the
solemn close of many storms. But between Margaret Carlyle and the son of whom she was so proud there had
never been a shadow. "If," writes Mr. Froude, "she
gloried in his fame and greatness, he gloried more in being
her son, and while she lived she, and she only, stood between him and the loneliness of which he so often and so
passionately complained."

Of all Carlyle's letters none are more tenderly beautiful
than those which he sent to Scotsbrig. The last, written
on his fifty-eighth birthday, December 4th, which she
probably never read, is one of the finest. The close of
their wayfaring together left him solitary; his "soul all
hung with black," and, for months to come, everything

around was overshadowed by the thought of his bereavement.   In his journal of February 28th, 1854, he tells us
that he had on the Sunday before seen a vision of Mainhill
in old days, with mother, father, and the rest getting
dressed for the meeting-house.   "They are gone now,
vanished all; their poor bits of thrifty clothes, . . . their
pious struggling efforts; their little life, it is all away.   It
has all melted into the still sea, it was rounded with a
sleep."   The entry ends, as fitting, with a prayer: "O pious
mother! kind, good, brave, and truthful soul as I have ever
found, and more than I have elsewhere found in this world.
Your poor Tom, long out of his school-days now, has fallen
very lonely, very lame and broken in this pilgrimage of
his; and you cannot help him or cheer him . . . any more.
From your grave in Ecclefechan kirk-yard yonder you bid
him trust in God; and that also he will try if he can understand and do."

CHAPTER VI.

THE MINOTAUR.

[1853–1866.]

CARLYLE was now engaged on a work which required, received, and wellnigh exhausted all his strength, resulting in the greatest though the least generally read of all his books. *Cromwell* achieved, he had thrown himself for a season into contemporary politics, condescending even, contrary to his rule, to make casual contributions to the Press; but his temper was too hot for success in that arena, and his letters of the time are full of the feeling that the *Latter - Day Pamphlets* had set the world against him. None of his generous replies to young men asking his advice are more suggestive than that in which he writes from Chelsea (March 9th, 1850):

If my books teach you anything, don't mind in the least whether other people believe it or not; but lay it to heart . . . as a real message left with you, which you must set about fulfilling, whatever others do. . . . And be not surprised that "people have no sympathy with you." That is an accompaniment that will attend you all your days if you mean to live an earnest life.

But he himself, though "ever a fighter," felt that, even for him, it was not good to be alone. He decided there "was no use railing in vain like Timon;" he would go back

again from the present to the past, from the latter days of
discord to seek countenance in some great figure of history, under whose ægis he might shelter the advocacy of his
views.   Looking about for a theme, several crossed his
mind.   He thought of Ireland, but that was too burning a
subject; of William the Conqueror, of Simon de Montfort,
the Norsemen, the Cid; but these may have seemed to him
too remote.   Why, ask patriotic Scotsmen, did he not take
up his and their favourite Knox.   But Knox's life had
been fairly handled by M'Crie, and Carlyle would have
found it hard to adjust his treatment of that essentially
national "hero" to the "Exodus from Houndsditch."
"Luther" might have been an apter theme; but there
too it would have been a strain to steer clear of theological controversy, of which he had had enough.   Napoleon
was at heart too much of a gamin for his taste.   Looking
over Europe in more recent times, he concluded that the
Prussian monarchy had been the main centre of modern
stability, and that it had been made so by its virtual creator, Friedrich II., called the Great.   Once entertained, the
subject seized him as with the eye of Coleridge's mariner,
and, in spite of manifold efforts to get free, compelled him,
so that he could "not choose but" write on it.   Again and
again, as the magnitude of the task became manifest, we
find him doubting, hesitating, recalcitrating, and yet cap-
tive.   He began reading Jomini, Preuss, the king's own
Memoirs and Despatches, and groaned at the mountains
through which he had to dig.   "Prussian Friedrich and
the Pelion laid on Ossa of Prussian dry-as-dust lay crushing me with the continual question, Dare I try it?   Dare
I not?"   At length, gathering himself together for the ef-
fort, he resolved, as before in the case of Cromwell, to visit
the scenes of which he was to write.   Hence the excursion

to Germany of 1852, during which, with the kindly-offered
guidance of Mr. Neuberg, an accomplished German admirer of some fortune resident in London, he made his
first direct acquaintance with the country of whose literature he had long been himself the English interpreter.
The outlines of the trip may be shortly condensed from
the letters written during its progress to his wife and mother.   Reaching Rotterdam on September 1st, after a night
made sleepless by "noisy nocturnal travellers and the most
industrious cocks and clamorous bells" he had ever heard,
he sailed up the river to Bonn, where he consulted books,
saw "Father Arndt," and encountered some types of the
German professoriate, "miserable creatures lost in statis-
tics."   There he met Neuberg, and they went together to
Rolandseck, to the village of Hunef among the Sieben-
Gebirge, and then on to Coblenz.   After a detour to Ems,
which Carlyle, comminating the gaming-tables, compared
to Matlock, and making a pilgrimage to Nassau as the
birthplace of William the Silent, they rejoined the Rhine
and sailed admiringly up the finest reach of the river.
From Mainz the philosopher and his guide went on to
Frankfort, paid their respects to Goethe's statue and the
garret where *Werther* was written, the Judengasse, "grim-
mest section of the Middle Ages," and the Römer—election hall of the old Kaisers; then to Homburg, where
they saw an old Russian countess playing "gowpanfuls of
gold pieces every stake," and left after no long stay, Carlyle, in a letter to Scotsbrig, pronouncing the fashionable
Badeort to be the "rallying-place of such a set of empty
blackguards as are not to be found elsewhere in the world."
We find him next at Marburg, where he visited the castle
of Philip of Hesse.   Passing through Cassel, he went to
Eisenach, and visited the neighbouring Wartburg, where

he kissed the old oaken table on which the Bible was
made an open book for the German race, and noted the
hole in the plaster where the ink-stand had been thrown
at the devil and his noises: an incident to which eloquent
reference is made in the lectures on "Heroes." Hence
they drove to Gotha, and lodged in Napoleon's room after
Leipzig. Then by Erfurt, with more Luther memories,
they took rail to Weimar, explored the houses of Goethe
and of Schiller, and dined by invitation with the Augusten-
burgs; the Grand Duchess, with sons and daughters, con-
versing in a Babylonish dialect, a melange of French, English, and German. The next stage seems to have been
Leipzig, then in a bustle with the Fair. "However," says
Carlyle, "we got a book or two, drank a glass of wine in
Auerbach's keller, and at last got off safe to the comparative quiet of Dresden." He ignores the picture-galleries;
and makes a bare reference to the palaces from which they
steamed up the Elbe to the heart of Saxon Switzerland.
There he surveyed Lobositz, first battle-field of the Seven
Years' War, and rested at the romantic mountain watering-
place of Töplitz. "He seems," wrote Mrs. Carlyle, "to be
getting very successfully through his travels, thanks to the
patience and helpfulness of Neuberg. He makes in every
letter frightful *misereres* over his sleeping accommodations;
but he cannot conceal that he is really pretty well." The
writer's own *misereres* are as doleful and nearly as frequent; but she was really in much worse health. From
Töplitz the companions proceeded in weary stillwagens to
Zittau in Lusatia, and so on to

Herrnhut, the primitive city of the Moravian brethren; a place not
bigger than Annan, but beautiful, pure, and quiet beyond any town
on the earth, I dare say; and, indeed, more like a saintly dream of
ideal Calvinism made real than a town of stone and lime.

Onward by "dreary, moory Frankfurt" on the Oder, whence they reconnoitred "the field of Kunersdorf, a scraggy village where Fritz received his worst defeat," they reached the Prussian capital on the last evening of the month. From the British Hotel, Unter den Linden, we have, October 1st:

> I am dead stupid; my heart nearly choked out of me, and my head churned to pieces. . . . Berlin is loud almost as London, but in no other way great . . . about the size of Liverpool, and more like Glasgow.

They spent a week there (sight-seeing being made easier by an introduction from Lady Ashburton to the Ambassador), discovering at length an excellent portrait of Fritz, meeting Tieck, Cornelius, Rauch, Preuss, etc., and then got quickly back to London by way of Hanover, Cologne, and Ostend. Carlyle's travels are always interesting, and would be more so without the tiresome, because ever the same, complaints. Six years later (1858) he made his second expedition to Germany, in the company of two friends, a Mr. Foxton—who is made a butt—and the faithful Neuberg. Of this journey, undertaken with a more exclusively business purpose, and accomplished with greater dispatch, there are fewer notes, the substance of which may be here anticipated. He sailed (August 21st) from Leith to Hamburg, admiring the lower Elbe, and then went out of his way to accept a pressing invitation from the Baron Usedom and his wife to the Isle of Rügen, sometimes called the German Isle of Wight. He went there by Stralsund, liked his hosts and their pleasant place, where for cocks crowing he had doves cooing; but in Putbus, the Richmond of the island, he had to encounter brood sows as well as cochin-chinas. From Rügen he went quickly south by Stettin to Berlin, then to Cüstrin to survey the field of

Zorndorf, with what memorable result readers of *Friedrich* know. His next halt was at Liegnitz, headquarters for exploring the grounds of "Leuthen, the grandest of all the battles," and Molwitz—first of Fritz's fights—of which we hear so much in the *Reminiscences.* His course lay on to Breslau, "a queer old city as ever you heard of, high as Edinburgh or more so," and, by Landshut, through the picturesque villages of the Riesen-Gebirge into Bohemia. There he first put up at Pardubitz in a vile, big inn, for bed a "trough eighteen inches too short, a mattress forced into it which cocked up at both ends"—such as most travellers in remoter Germany at that period have experienced. Carlyle was unfavourably impressed by the Bohemians; and "not one in a hundred of them could understand a word of German. They are liars, thieves, slatterns, a kind of miserable, subter-Irish people—Irish with the addition of ill-nature." He and his friends visited the fields of Chotusitz and Kolin, where they found the "Golden Sun," from which "the last of the Kings" had surveyed the ground, "sunk to be the dirtiest house probably in Europe." Thence he made for Prague, whose picturesque grandeur he could not help extolling. "Here," he writes, enclosing the flower to his wife, "is an authentic wild pink plucked from the battle-field. Give it to some young lady who practises the Battle of Prague on her piano to your satisfaction." On September 15th he dates from Dresden, whence he spent a laborious day over Torgau. Thereafter they sped on, with the usual tribulations, by Hochkirk, Leipzig, Weissenfels, and Rossbach. Hurrying homeward, they were obliged to decline another invitation from the Duchess at Weimar; and, making for Guntershausen, performed the fatiguing journey from there to Aix-la-Chapelle in one day, *i.e.* travelling often in slow trains from 4 A.M.

to 7 P.M., a foolish feat even for the eupeptic. Carlyle visited the cathedral, but has left a very poor account of the
impression produced on him by the simple slab sufficiently
inscribed "Carolo Magno." "Next morning stand upon the
lid of Charlemagne, abominable monks roaring out their
idolatrous grand music within sight." By Ostend and
Dover he reached home on the 22d. A Yankee scamper
trip, one might say, but for the result testifying to the
enormous energy of the traveller. "He speaks lightly,"
says Mr. Froude, "of having seen Kolin, Torgau, etc., etc.
No one would guess from reading these short notices that
he had mastered the details of every field he visited; not
a turn of the ground, not a brook, not a wood . . . had
escaped him. . . . There are no mistakes. Military students in Germany are set to learn Frederick's battles in
Carlyle's account of them."

During the interval between those tours there are few
events of interest in Carlyle's outer, or phases of his inner,
life which have not been already noted. The year 1854
found the country ablaze with the excitement of the Crim-
ean War, with which he had as little sympathy as Cob-
den or Bright or the members of Sturge's deputation. He
had no share in the popular enthusiasm for what he regarded as a mere newspaper folly. All his political leaning was on the side of Russia, which, from a safe distance,
having no direct acquaintance with the country, he always
admired as a seat of strong government, the representative
of wise control over barbarous races. Among the worst of
these he reckoned the Turk, "a lazy, ugly, sensual, dark
fanatic, whom we have now had for 400 years. I would
not buy the continuance of him in Europe at the rate of
sixpence a century." Carlyle had no more faith in the
"Balance of power" than had Byron, who scoffed at it

from another, the Republican, side as "balancing straws on kings' noses instead of wringing them off," *e.g.* :

As to Russian increase of strength, he writes, I would wait till Russia meddled with me before I drew sword to stop his increase of strength.   It is the idle population of editors, etc., that has done all this in England.   One perceives clearly that ministers go forward in it against their will.

Even our heroisms at Alma—"a terrible, almost horrible operation"—Balaclava, and Inkermann, failed to raise a glow in his mind, though he admitted the force of Tennyson's ringing lines.   The alliance with the "scandalous copper captain," elected by the French, as the Jews chose Barabbas—an alliance at which many patriots winced—was to him only an added disgrace.   Carlyle's comment on the subsequent visit to Osborne of Victor Hugo's "brigand," and his reception within the pale of legitimate sovereignty was, "Louis Bonaparte has not been shot hitherto.   That is the best that can be said."   Sedan brought most men round to his mind about Napoleon III.: but his approval of the policy of the Czars remains open to the criticism of M. Lanin.   In reference to the next great struggle of the age, Carlyle was in full sympathy with the mass of his countrymen.   He was as much enraged by the Sepoy rebellion as were those who blew the ringleaders from the muzzles of guns.   "Tongue cannot speak," he exclaims, in the spirit that inspired Millais's picture, before it was amended or spoilt, "the horrors that were done on the English by these mutinous hyænas.   Allow hyænas to mutiny and strange things will follow."   He never seems to have revolved the question as to the share of his admired Muscovy in instigating the revolt.   For the barbarism of the north he had ready apologies, for the savagery of the

south mere execration; and he writes of the Hindoos as
he did, both before and afterwards, of the negroes in Jamaica.

Three sympathetic obituary notices of the period expressed his softer side. In April, 1854, John Wilson and
Lord Cockburn died at Edinburgh. His estimate of the
former is notable as that generally entertained, now that
the race of those who came under the personal spell of
Christopher North has passed:

We lived apart as in different centuries; though to say the truth
I always loved Wilson, he had much nobleness of heart, and many
traits of noble genius, but the central tie-beam seemed always wanting; very long ago I perceived in him the most irreconcilable contradictions—Toryism with Sansculottism, Methodism of a sort with total
incredulity, etc. . . . Wilson seemed to me always by far the most
gifted of our literary men, either then or still: and yet intrinsically
he has written nothing that can endure.

Cockburn is referred to in contrast as "perhaps the last
genuinely national type of rustic Scotch sense, sincerity,
and humour—a wholesome product of Scotch dialect, with
plenty of good logic in it." Later Douglas Jerrold is
described as "last of the London wits, I hope the last."
Carlyle's letters during this period are of minor interest:
many refer to visits paid to distinguished friends and humble relatives, with the usual complaints about health, servants, and noises. At Farlingay, where he spent some time
with Edward Fitzgerald, translator of *Omar Khayam*, the
lowing of cows took the place of cocks crowing. Here
and there occurs a criticism or a speculation. That on his
dreams is, in the days of "insomnia," perhaps worth noting (F. iv. 154, 155), *inter alia* he says: "I have an impression that one always dreams, but that only in cases

where the nerves are disturbed by bad health, which pro-
duces light, imperfect sleep, do they start into such relief as
to force themselves on our waking consciousness." Among
posthumously printed documents of Cheyne Row, to this
date belongs the humorous appeal of Mrs. Carlyle for a
larger allowance of house money, entitled "Budget of a
Femme Incomprise." The arguments and statement of accounts, worthy of a bank auditor, were so irresistible that
Carlyle had no resource but to grant the request, *i.e.* practically to raise the amount to £230, instead £200 per annum. It has been calculated that his reliable income even
at this time did not exceed £400, but the rent of the
house was kept very low, £30 : he and his wife lived
frugally, so that despite the expenses of the noise - proof
room and his German tour he could afford in 1857 to
put a stop to her travelling in second - class railway car-
riages; in 1860, when the success of the first instalment
of his great work made an end of financial fears, to keep
two servants; and in 1863 to give Mrs. Carlyle a brougham. Few men have left on the whole so unimpeachable a
record in money matters.

In November, 1854, there occurred an incident hitherto
unrecorded in any biography. The Lord Rectorship of
the University of Glasgow having fallen vacant, the "Conservative Club" of the year had put forward Mr. Disraeli
as successor to the honorary office. A small body of Mr.
Carlyle's admirers among the senior students, on the other
side, nominated him, partly as a tribute of respect and
gratitude, partly in opposition to a statesman whom they
then distrusted. The nomination was, after much debate,
adopted by the so - called "Liberal Association" of that
day; and, with a curious irony, the author of the *Latter-
Day Pamphlets* and *Friedrich II.* was pitted, as a Radi-

cal, against the future promoter of the Franchise of 1867
as a Tory. It soon appeared that his supporters had un-
derestimated the extent to which Mr. Carlyle had offend-
ed Scotch theological prejudice and outraged the current
Philanthropy. His name received some sixty adherents,
and had ultimately to be withdrawn. The nomination
was received by the Press, and other exponents of popular
opinion, with denunciations that came loudest and longest
from the leaders of orthodox dissent, then arrogating to
themselves the profession of Liberalism and the initiation
of Reform. Among the current expressions in reference
to his social and religious creeds were the following:

Carlyle's philanthropy is not that of Howard, his cure for national distress is to bury our paupers in peat bogs, driving wooden
boards on the top of them. His entire works may be described as
reiterating the doctrine that "whatever is is wrong." He has thrown
off every form of religious belief and settled down into the conviction that the Christian profession of Englishmen is a sham. . . .
Elect him and you bid God-speed to Pantheism and spiritualism.[1]
Mr. Carlyle neither possesses the talent nor the distinction, nor does
he occupy the position which entitle a man to such an honour as the
Rectorial Chair. The *Scotch Guardian* writes: But for the folly exhibited in bringing forward Mr. Disraeli, scarcely any party within
the College or out of it would have ventured to nominate a still more
obnoxious personage. This is the first instance we have been able
to discover in which the suffrages of the youth of the University have
been sought for a candidate who denied in his writings that the revealed Word of God is "the way, the truth, the life." It is impossible to separate Mr. Carlyle from that obtrusive feature of his works

---

[1] Mr. Wylie states that "twice before his election by his own University he (Carlyle) had been invited to allow himself to be nominated for the office of Lord Rector, once by students in the University
of Glasgow and once by those of Aberdeen; but both of these invitations he had declined." This as regards Glasgow is incorrect.

in which the solemn verities of our holy religion are sneered at as worn-out "biblicalities," "unbelievabilities," and religious profession is denounced as "dead putrescent cant." The reader of the *Life of Sterling* is not left to doubt for a moment the author's malignant hostility to the religion of the Bible. In that work, saving faith is described as "stealing into heaven by the modern method of sticking ostrich-like your head into fallacies on earth," that is to say, by believing in the doctrines of the Gospels. How, after this, could the Principal and Professors of the University, the guardians of the faiths and morals of its inexperienced youth, accompany to the Common Hall, and allow to address the students a man who has degraded his powers to the life-labour of sapping and mining the foundations of the truth, and opened the fire of his fiendish raillery against the citadel of our best aspirations and dearest hopes.

In the result, two men of genius[1]—however diverse— were discarded, and a Scotch nobleman of conspicuous talent, always an active, if not intrusive, champion of orthodoxy, was returned by an "overwhelming majority." In answer to intelligence transmitted to Mr. Carlyle of these events, the president of the Association of his supporters—who had nothing on which to congratulate themselves save that only the benches of the rooms in which they held their meetings had been riotously broken, received the following previously unpublished letter:

CHELSEA, 16*th December*, 1854.

DEAR SIR,—I have received your Pamphlet; and return many thanks for all your kindness to me. I am sorry to learn, as I do for the first time from this narrative, what angry nonsense some of my countrymen see good to write of me. Not being much a reader of Newspapers, I had hardly heard of the Election till after it was finished; and I did not know that anything of this melancholy element

---

[1] For the elucidation of some points of contact between Carlyle and Lord Beaconsfield, *vide* Mr. Froude's *Life* of the latter.

of Heterodoxy, "Pantheism," etc., etc., had been introduced into the matter. It is an evil, after its sort, this of being hated and denounced by fools and ignorant persons; but it cannot be mended for the present, and so must be left standing there.

That another wiser class think differently, nay, that they alone have any real knowledge of the question, or any real right to vote upon it, is surely an abundant compensation. If that be so, then all is still right; and probably there is no harm done at all!—To you, and the other young gentlemen who have gone with you on this occasion, I can only say that I feel you have loyally meant to do me a great honour and kindness; that I am deeply sensible of your genial recognition, of your noble enthusiasm (which reminds me of my own young years); and that in fine there is no loss or gain of an Election which can in the least alter these valuable facts, or which is not wholly insignificant to me in comparison with them. "Elections" are not a thing transacted by the gods, in general; and I have known very unbeautiful creatures " elected " to be kings, chief-priests, railway kings, etc., by the " most sweet voices," and the spiritual virtue that inspires these, in our time!

Leaving all that, I will beg you all to retain your honourable good feelings towards me; and to think that if anything I have done or written can help any one of you in the noble problem of living like a wise man in these evil and foolish times, it will be more valuable to me than never so many Elections or Non-elections.

With many good wishes and regards I heartily thank you all, and remain, Yours very sincerely,

T. CARLYLE.

Carlyle's letters to strangers are always valuable, for they are terse and reticent. In writing to weavers, like Bamford; to men in trouble, as Cooper; to students, statesmen, or earnest inquirers of whatever degree, a genuine sympathy for them takes the place of the sympathy for himself, often too prominent in the copious effusions to his intimates. The letter above quoted is of special interest, as belonging to a time from which comparatively few survive; when he was fairly under weigh with a task which seemed

6*

to grow in magnitude under his gaze. The *Life of Fried-rich* could not be a succession of dramatic scenes, like the *French Revolution*, nor a biography like *Cromwell*, illus-trated by the surrounding events of thirty years. Carlyle found, to his dismay, that he had involved himself in writ-ing the History of Germany, and in a measure of Europe, during the eighteenth century, a period perhaps the most tangled and difficult to deal with of any in the world's an-nals. He was like a man who, with intent to dig up a pine, found himself tugging at the roots of an Igdrasil that twined themselves under a whole Hercynian forest. His constant cries of positive pain in the progress of the work are distressing, as his indomitable determination to wrestle with and prevail over it is inspiring. There is no imaginable image that he does not press into his service in rattling the chains of his voluntary servitude. Above all, he groans over the unwieldy mass of his authorities— "anti-solar systems of chaff."

I read old German books dull as stupidity itself — nay, super-annuated stupidity—gain with labour the dreariest glimpses of un-important extinct human beings. . . . but when I begin operating: *how* to reduce that widespread black desert of Brandenburg sand to a small human garden! . . . I have no capacity of grasping the big chaos that lies around me, and reducing it to order. Order! Reducing! It is like compelling the grave to give up its dead!

Elsewhere he compares his travail with the monster of his own creation to "Balder's ride to the death kingdoms, through frozen rain, sound of subterranean torrents, leaden-coloured air;" and in the retrospect of the *Reminiscences* touchingly refers to his thirteen years of rarely relieved isolation. "A desperate dead-lift pull all that time; my whole strength devoted to it . . . withdrawn from all the

world." He received few visitors and had few correspondents, but kept his life vigorous by riding on his horse
Fritz (the gift of the Marshalls), " during that book, some
30,000 miles, much of it, all the winter part of it, under
cloud of night, sun just setting when I mounted.   All the
rest of the day I sat, silent, aloft, insisting upon work, and
such work, *invitissimâ Minervâ*, for that matter."   Mrs. Carlyle[1] had her usual share of the sufferings involved in " the
awful *Friedrich*."   " That tremendous book," she writes,
" made prolonged and entire devastation of any satisfactory
semblance of home life or home happiness."   But when
at last, by help of Neuberg and of Mr. Larkin, who made
the maps of the whole book, the first two volumes were in
type (they appeared in autumn, 1858), his wife hailed
them in a letter sent from Edinburgh to Chelsea: " Oh,
my dear, what a magnificent book this is going to be,
the best of all your books, forcible, clear, and sparkling as
the *French Revolution ;* compact and finished as *Cromwell.*
Yes, you shall see that it will be the best of all your books,
and small thanks to it, it has taken a doing."   On which
the author naïvely purrs : " It would be worth while to
write books, if mankind would read them as you."   Later
he speaks of his wife's recognition and that of Emerson
—who wrote enthusiastically of the art of the work,
though much of it was across his grain—as " the only bit

---

[1] Carlyle himself writes : " I felt well enough how it was crushing down her existence, as it was crushing down my own ; and the
thought that she had not been at the choosing of it, and yet must
suffer so for it, was occasionally bitter to me.   But the practical conclusion always was, Get done with it, get done with it !   For the saving of us both that is the one outlook.   And sure enough, I did stand
by that dismal task with all my time and all my means ; day and night
wrestling with it, as with the ugliest dragon, which blotted out the
daylight and the rest of the world to me till I should get it slain."

of human criticism in which he could discern lineaments of the thing." But the book was a swift success, two editions of 2000 and another of 1000 copies being sold in a comparatively brief space. Carlyle's references to this—after his return from another visit to the north and the second trip to Germany—seem somewhat ungracious:

Book . . . much babbled over in newspapers . . . no better to me than the barking of dogs . . . officious people put reviews into my hands, and in an idle hour I glanced partly into these; but it would have been better not, so sordidly ignorant and impertinent were they, though generally laudatory.

But these notices recall the fact familiar to every writer, that while the assailants of a book sometimes read it, favourable reviewers hardly ever do ; these latter save their time by payment of generally superficial praise, and a few random quotations.

Carlyle scarcely enjoyed his brief respite on being discharged of the first instalment of his book : the remainder lay upon him like a menacing nightmare; he never ceased to feel that the work must be completed ere he could be free, and that to accomplish this he must be alone. Never absent from his wife without regrets, lamentations, contrite messages, and childlike entreaties for her to "come and protect him," when she came it was to find that they were better apart; for his temper was never softened by success. "Living beside him," she writes in 1858, is "the life of a weathercock in high wind." During a brief residence together in a hired house near Aberdour in Fifeshire, she compares herself to a keeper in a mad-house ; and writes later from Sunnybank to her husband, "If you could fancy me in some part of the house out of sight, my absence would make little difference to you, considering.

how little I do see of you, and how preoccupied you are when I do see you." Carlyle answers in his touching strain, "We have had a sore life pilgrimage together, much bad road. Oh, forgive me!" and sends her beautiful descriptions; but her disposition, not wholly forgiving, received them somewhat sceptically. "Byron," said Lady Byron, "can write anything, but he does not feel it;" and Mrs. Carlyle on one occasion told her "harsh spouse" that his fine passages were very well written for the sake of future biographers: a charge he almost indignantly repudiates. He was then, August, 1860, staying at Thurso Castle, the guest of Sir George Sinclair; a visit that terminated in an unfortunate careless mistake about a sudden change of plans, resulting in his wife, then with the Stanleys at Alderley, being driven back to Chelsea and deprived of her promised pleasure and requisite rest with her friends in the north.

The frequency of such incidents—each apart capable of being palliated by the same fallacy of division that has attempted in vain to justify the domestic career of Henry VIII.—points to the conclusion of Miss Gully that Carlyle, though often nervous on the subject, acted to his wife as if he were "totally inconsiderate of her health," so much so that she received medical advice not to be much at home when he was in the stress of writing. In January, 1858, he writes to his brother John an anxious letter in reference to a pain about a hand-breadth below the heart, of which she had begun to complain, the premonitory symptom of the disease which ultimately proved fatal; but he was not sufficiently impressed to give due heed to the warning; nor was it possible, with his long-engrained habits, to remove the Marah spring that lay under all the wearisome bickerings, repentances, and renewals of offence. The

"very little herring" who declined to be made a part of
Lady Ashburton's luggage now suffered more than ever
from her inanimate rival. The highly-endowed wife of
one of the most eminent philanthropists of America, whose
life was devoted to the awakening of defective intellects,
thirty-five years ago murmured, "If I were only an idiot!"
Similarly Mrs. Carlyle might have remonstrated, "Why
was I not born a book?" Her letters and journal teem to
tiresomeness with the refrain, "I feel myself extremely
neglected for unborn generations." Her once considerable
ambitions had been submerged, and her own vivid personality overshadowed by a man she was afraid to meet at breakfast, and glad to avoid at dinner. A woman of immense talent and a spark of genius linked to a man of vast genius and
imperious will, she had no choice but to adopt his judgments,
intensify his dislikes, and give a sharper edge to his sneers.

Mr. Froude, who for many years lived too near the sun
to see the sun, and inconsistently defends many of the inconsistencies he has himself inherited from his master, yet
admits that Carlyle treated the Broad Church party in the
English Church with some injustice. His recorded estimates of the leading theologians of the age, and personal
relation to them, are hopelessly bewildering. His long life
friendship for Erskine of Linlathen is intelligible, though
he did not extend the same charity to what he regarded as
the muddle-headedness of Maurice (Erskine's spiritual in-
spirer), and keenly ridiculed the reconciliation pamphlet
entitled "Subscription no Bondage." The Essayists and
Reviewers, "Septem contra Christum," "should," he said,
"be shot for deserting their posts;" even Dean Stanley
their *amicus curiæ*, whom he liked, came in for a share of
his sarcasm; "there he goes," he said to Froude, "bor-
ing holes in the bottom of the Church of England." Of

Colenso, who was doing as much as any one for the
" Exodus from Houndsditch," he spoke with open contempt, saying, " he mistakes for fame an extended pillory
that he is standing on ;" and was echoed by his wife,
" Colenso isn't worth talking about for five minutes, except
for the absurdity of a man making arithmetical onslaughts
on the Pentateuch with a bishop's little black silk apron
on." This is not the place to discuss the controversy involved ; but we are bound to note the fact that Carlyle
was, by an inverted Scotch intolerance, led to revile men
rowing in the same boat as himself, but with a different
stroke. To another Broad Churchman, Charles Kingsley,
partly from sympathy with this writer's imaginative power,
he was more considerate ; and one of the still deeply religious freethinkers of the time was among his closest
friends. The death of Arthur Clough in 1861 left another blank in Carlyle's life : we have had in this century
to lament the comparatively early loss of few men of finer
genius. Clough had not, perhaps, the practical force of
Sterling, but his work is of a higher order than any of the
fragments of the earlier favourite. Among High Church-
men Carlyle commended Dr. Pusey as "solid and judicious," and fraternised with the Bishop of Oxford ; but he
called Keble "an ape," and said of Cardinal Newman that
he had " no more brains that an ordinary-sized rabbit."

These years are otherwise marked by his most glaring
political blunder. The Civil War, then raging in America,
brought, with its close, the abolition of Slavery throughout
the States, a consummation for which he cared little, for
he had never professed to regard the negroes as fit for
freedom ; but this result, though inevitable, was incidental.
As is known to every one who has the remotest knowledge
of Transatlantic history, the war was in a great measure a

struggle for the preservation of National Unity : but it was
essentially more ; it was the vindication of Law and Order
against the lawless and disorderly violence of those who,
when defeated at the polling - booth, flew to the bowie-
knife ; an assertion of Right as Might, for which Carlyle
cared everything ; yet all he had to say of it was his
"Ilias Americana in nuce," published in *Macmillan's
Magazine*, August, 1863.

Peter of the North (to Paul of the South): "Paul, you un-
accountable scoundrel, I find you hire your servants for life, not
by the month or year as I do. You are going straight to Hell,
you—"
Paul: "Good words, Peter. The risk is my own. I am willing
to take the risk. Hire you your servants by the month or the
day, and get straight to Heaven ; leave me to my own method."
Peter : "No, I won't. I will beat your brains out first !" [And
is trying dreadfully ever since, but cannot yet manage it.]

This, except the *Prinzenraub*, a dramatic presentation
of a dramatic incident in old German history, was his only
side publication during the writing of *Friedrich*.

After the war ended and Emerson's letters of remon-
strance had proved prophetic, Carlyle is said to have confessed to Mr. Moncure Conway, as well as to Mr. Froude,
that he " had not seen to the bottom of the matter." But
his republication of this nadir of his nonsense was an offence, emphasising the fact that, however inspiring, he is
not always a safe guide, even to those content to abide by
his own criterion of success.

There remains of this period the record of a triumph
and of a tragedy. After seven years more of rarely inter-
mitted toil, broken only by a few visits, trips to the sea-
shore, etc., and the distress of the terrible accident to his
wife—her fall on a curb-stone and dislocation of a limb—

which has been often sufficiently detailed, he had finished
his last great work. The third volume of *Friedrich* was
published in May, 1862, the fourth appeared in February,
1864, the fifth and sixth in March, 1865. Carlyle had at
last slain his Minotaur, and stood before the world as a
victorious Theseus, everywhere courted and acclaimed, his
hard-earned rest only disturbed by a shower of honours.
His position as the foremost prose writer of his day was as
firmly established in Germany, where his book was at once
translated and read by all readers of history, as in England.
Scotland, now fully awake to her reflected fame, made
haste to make amends. Even the leaders of the sects,
bond and "free," who had denounced him, were now
eager to proclaim that he had been intrinsically all along,
though sometimes in disguise, a champion of their faith.
No men knew better how to patronise, or even seem to
lead, what they had failed to quell. The Universities
made haste with their burnt-offerings. In 1856 a body
of Edinburgh students had prematurely repeated the attempt of their forerunners in Glasgow to confer on him
their Lord Rectorship, and failed. In 1865 he was elected, in opposition again to Mr. Disraeli, to succeed Mr.
Gladstone, the genius of elections being in a jesting mood.
He was prevailed on to accept the honour, and, later, con-
sented to deliver in the spring of 1866 the customary Inaugural Address. Mrs. Carlyle's anxiety on this occasion
as to his success and his health is a tribute to her constant
and intense fidelity. He went north to his Installation,
under the kind care of encouraging friends, imprimis of
Professor Tyndall,[1] one of his truest; they stopped on the

---

[1] For the most interesting, loyally sympathetic, and characteristic
account of Carlyle's journey north on this occasion, and of the inci-

road at Fryston, with Lord Houghton, and there met Professor Huxley, who accompanied them to Edinburgh. Carlyle, having resolved to speak and not merely to read what he had to say, was oppressed with nervousness; and of the event itself he writes: "My speech was delivered in a mood of defiant despair, and under the pressure of nightmare. Some feeling that I was not speaking lies alone sustained me. The applause, etc., I took for empty noise, which it really was not altogether." The address, nominally on the "Reading of Books," really a rapid autobiography of his own intellectual career, with references to history, literature, religion, and the conduct of life, was, as Tyndall telegraphed to Mrs. Carlyle—save for some difficulty the speaker had in making himself audible—"a perfect triumph." His reception by one of the most enthusiastic audiences ever similarly assembled marked the climax of a steadily-increasing fame. It may be compared to the late welcome given to Wordsworth in the Oxford Theatre. After four days spent with Erskine and his own brother James in Edinburgh, he went for a week's quiet to Scotsbrig, and was kept there, lingering longer than he had intended, by a sprained ankle, "blessed in the country stillness, the purity of sky and earth, and the absence of all babble." On April 20th he wrote his last letter to his wife, a letter which she never read. On the evening of Saturday, the 21st, when staying on the way south at his sister's house at Dumfries, he received a telegram informing him that the companionship of more than forty years—companionship of struggle and victory, of sad and sweet so strangely blent—was forever at an end.

deuts which followed, we may refer to *New Fragments*, by John Tyndall, just published.

Mrs. Carlyle had been found dead in her carriage when driving round Hyde Park on the afternoon of that day, her death (from heart disease) being accelerated by an accident to a favourite little dog. Carlyle felt as "one who hath been stunned," hardly able to realise his loss. "They took me out next day . . . to wander in the green sunny Sabbath fields, and ever and anon there rose from my sick heart the ejaculation, 'My poor little woman!' but no full gust of tears came to my relief, nor has yet come." On the following Monday he set off with his brother for London. "Never for a thousand years shall I forget that arrival here of ours, my first unwelcomed by her. She lay in her coffin, lovely in death. Pale death and things not mine or ours had possession of our poor darling." On Wednesday they returned, and on Thursday the 26th she was buried in the nave of the old Abbey Kirk at Haddington, in the grave of her father. The now desolate old man, who had walked with her over many a stony road, paid the first of his many regretful tributes in the epitaph inscribed over her tomb: in which follows, after the name and date of birth:

In her bright existence she had more sorrows than are common, but also a soft invincibility, a capacity of discernment, and a noble loyalty of heart which are rare. For 40 years she was the true and loving helpmate of her husband, and by act and word unweariedly forwarded him as none else could in all of worthy that he did or attempted. She died at London, 21st April, 1866, suddenly snatched from him, and the light of his life as if gone out.

CHAPTER VII.

DECADENCE.

[1866–1881.]

AFTER this shock of bereavement Carlyle's days went by " on broken wing," never brightening, slowly saddening to the close; but lit up at intervals by flashes of the indomitable energy that, starting from no vantage, had conquered a world of thought, and established in it, if not a new dynasty, at least an intellectual throne. Expressions of sympathy came to him from all directions, from the Queen herself downwards, and he received them with the grateful acknowledgment that he had, after all, been loved by his contemporaries. When the question arose as to his future life, it seemed a natural arrangement that he and his brother John, then a childless widower who had retired from his profession with a competence, should take up house together. The experiment was made, but, to the discredit of neither, it proved a failure. They were in some respects too much alike. John would not surrender himself wholly to the will or whims even of one whom he revered, and the attempt was, by mutual consent, abandoned; but their affectionate correspondence lasted through the period of their joint lives. Carlyle, being left to himself in his " gaunt and lonesome home," after a short visit to Miss Bromley, an intimate friend of his wife, at her residence in Kent, accepted the invitation of the second

Lady Ashburton to spend the winter in her house at Mentone. There he arrived on Christmas Eve, 1866, under the kind convoy of Professor Tyndall, and remained breathing the balmy air and gazing on the violet sea till March of the following year. During the interval he occupied himself in writing his *Reminiscences*, drawing pen-and-ink pictures of the country, steeped in beauty fit to soothe any sorrow save such as his, and taking notes of some of the passers-by. Of the greatest celebrity then encountered, Mr. Gladstone, he writes in his journal, in a tone intensified as time went on: "Talk copious, ingenious . . . a man of ardent faculty, but all gone irrevocably into House of Commons shape. . . . Man once of some wisdom or possibility of it, but now possessed by the Prince, or many Princes of the Air." Back in Chelsea, he was harassed by heaps of letters, most of which, we are told, he answered, and spent a large portion of his time and means in charities.

Amid Carlyle's irreconcilable inconsistencies of theory, and sometimes of conduct, he was through life consistent in practical benevolence. The interest in the welfare of the working classes that in part inspired his *Sartor*, *Chartism*, and *Past and Present* never failed him. He was among the foremost in all national movements to relieve and solace their estate. He was, further, with an amiable disregard of his own maxims, overlenient towards the waifs and strays of humanity, in some instances careless to inquire too closely into the causes of their misfortune or the degree of their demerits. In his latter days this disposition grew upon him: the gray of his own evening skies made him fuller of compassion to all who lived in the shade. Sad himself, he mourned with those who mourned; afflicted, he held out hands to all in affliction. Conse-

quently " the poor were always with him," writing, en-
treating, and personally soliciting all sorts of alms, from
advice and help to ready money. His biographer informs
us that he rarely gave an absolute refusal to any of these
various classes of beggars. He answered a letter which is
a manifest parody of his own surface misanthropy ; he
gave a guinea to a ticket-of-leave-man, pretending to be a
decayed tradesman ; and a shilling to a street sweeper, who
at once took it over his crossing to a gin-shop. Froude
remonstrated ; " poor fellow," was the answer, " I dare say
he is cold and thirsty." The memory of Wordsworth is
less warmly cherished among the dales of Westmoreland
than that of Carlyle in the lanes of Chelsea, where " his
one expensive luxury was charity."

His attitude on political questions, in which for ten years
he still took a more or less prominent part, represents him
on his sterner side. The first of these was the controversy
about Governor Eyre, who, having suppressed the Jamaica
rebellion by the violent and, as alleged, cruel use of martial
law, and hung a quadroon preacher called Gordon—the man
whether honest or not being an undoubted incendiary—
without any law at all, was by the force of popular indignation dismissed in disgrace, and then arraigned for misgovernment and illegality. In the movement which resulted in the governor's recall and impeachment, there was
doubtless the usual amount of exaggeration—represented
by the violent language of one of Carlyle's minor biographers : " There were more innocent people slain than at
Jeffrey's Bloody Assize ;" " The massacre of Glencoe was
nothing to it ;" " Members of Christian Churches were
flogged," etc., etc.—but among its leaders there were so
many men of mark and celebrity, men like John S. Mill,
T. Hughes, John Bright, Fawcett, Cairnes, Goldwin Smith,

Herbert Spencer, and Frederick Harrison, that it could not
be set aside as a mere unreasoning clamour. It was a hard
test of Carlyle's theory of strong government; and he stood
to his colours. Years before, on John Sterling suggesting
that the negroes themselves should be consulted as to
making a permanent engagement with their masters, he
had said, " I never thought the rights of the negroes worth
much discussing in any form. Quashee will get himself
made a slave again, and with beneficent whip will be compelled to work." On this occasion he regarded the black
rebellion in the same light as the Sepoy revolt. He organised and took the chair of a "Defence Committee," joined
or backed by Ruskin, Henry Kingsley, Tyndall, Sir R.
Murchison, Sir T. Gladstone, and others. " I never," says
Mr. Froude, " knew Carlyle more anxious about anything."
He drew up a petition to Government and exerted himself
heart and soul for the "brave, gentle, chivalrous, and clear
man," who when the ship was on fire "had been called to
account for having flung a bucket or two of water into the
hold beyond what was necessary." He had damaged some
of the cargo perhaps, but he had saved the ship, and deserved to be made "dictator of Jamaica for the next
twenty-five years," to govern after the model of Dr. Francia
in Paraguay. The committee failed to get Eyre reinstalled
or his pension restored; but the impeachment was unsuccessful.

The next great event was the passing of the Reform
Bill of 1867, by the Tories, educated by Mr. Disraeli to
this method of "dishing the Whigs," by outbidding them
in the scramble for votes. This instigated the famous
tract called *Shooting Niagara*, written in the spirit of the
Latter-Day Pamphlets—Carlyle's final and unqualified denunciation of this concession to Democracy and all its

works.   But the upper classes in England seemed indifferent to the warning.   "Niagara, or what you like," the
author quotes as the saying of a certain shining countess,
" we will at least have a villa on the Mediterranean when
Church and State have gone."   A *mot* emphatically of the
decadence.

Later he fulminated against the Clerkenwell explosions
being a means of bringing the Irish question within the
range of practical politics.

I sit in speechless admiration of our English treatment of those
Fenians first and last.   It is as if the rats of a house had decided to
expel and extirpate the human inhabitants, which latter seemed to
have neither rat-catchers, traps, nor arsenic, and are trying to prevail by the method of love.

Governor Eyre, with Spenser's Essay on Ireland and
Cromwell's storm of Drogheda for his texts, or Otto von
Bismarck, would have been, in his view, in place at Dublin
Castle.

In the next great event of the century, the close of the
greatest European struggle since Waterloo, the cause which
pleased Cato pleased also the gods.   Carlyle, especially in
his later days, had a deepening confidence in the Teutonic,
a growing distrust of the Gallic race.   He regarded the contest between them as one between Ormuzd and Ahriman,
and wrote of Sedan, as he had written of Rossbach, with
exultation.   When a feeling began in this country, naming
itself sympathy for the fallen—really half that, the other
half, as in the American war, being jealousy of the victor
—and threatened to be dangerous, Carlyle wrote a decisive
letter to the *Times*, November 11th, 1870, tracing the
sources of the war back to the robberies of Louis XIV.,
and ridiculing the prevailing sentiment about the recapt-

ured provinces of Lothringen and Elsass. With a possible reference to Victor Hugo and his clients, he remarks:

They believe that they are the "Christ of Nations." . . . I wish they would inquire whether there might not be a Cartouche of nations. Cartouche had many gallant qualities—had many fine ladies begging locks of his hair while the indispensable gibbet was preparing. Better he should obey the heavy-handed Teutsch police officer, who has him by the windpipe in such frightful manner, give up part of his stolen goods, altogether cease to be a Cartouche, and try to become again a Chevalier Bayard. All Europe does *not* come to the rescue in gratitude for the heavenly illumination it is getting from France: nor could all Europe if it did prevent that awful Chancellor from having his own way. Metz and the boundary fence, I reckon, will be dreadfully hard to get out of that Chancellor's hands again. . . . Considerable misconception as to Herr von Bismarck is still prevalent in England. He, as I read him, is not a person of Napoleonic ideas, but of ideas quite superior to Napoleonic. . . . That noble, patient, deep, pious, and solid Germany should be at length welded into a nation, and become Queen of the Continent, instead of vapouring, vainglorious, gesticulating, quarrelsome, restless, and over-sensitive France, seems to me the hopefulest fact that has occurred in my time.

Carlyle seldom wrote with more force, or with more justice. Only, to be complete, his paper should have ended with a warning. He has done more than any other writer to perpetuate in England the memories of the great thinkers and actors — Fichte, Richter, Arndt, Körner, Stein, Goethe—who taught their countrymen how to endure defeat and retrieve adversity. Who will celebrate their yet undefined successors, who will train Germany gracefully to bear the burden of prosperity? Two years later Carlyle wrote, or rather dictated, for his hand was beginning to shake, his historical sketch of the *Early Kings of Norway*, showing no diminution of power either of thought or expression, his estimates of the three Hakons and of the three

7

Olafs being especially notable; and a paper on *The Portraits of John Knox*, the prevailing dull gray of which is relieved by a radiant vision of Mary Stuart.

He was incited to another public protest, when, in May, 1877, towards the close of the Russo-Turkish war, he had got, or imagined himself to have got, reliable information that Lord Beaconsfield, then Prime Minister, having sent our fleet to the Dardanelles, was planning to seize Gallipoli and throw England into the struggle. Carlyle never seems to have contemplated the possibility of a Sclavo-Gallic alliance against the forces of civilised order in Europe, and he chose to think of the Czars as the representatives of an enlightened autocracy. We are here mainly interested in the letter he wrote to the *Times*, as "his last public act in this world"—the phrase of Mr. Froude, who does not give the letter, and unaccountably says it "was brief, not more than three or four lines." It is as follows:

SIR,—A rumour everywhere prevails that our miraculous Premier, in spite of the Queen's Proclamation of Neutrality, intends, under cover of care for "British interests" to send the English fleet to the Baltic, or do some other feat which shall compel Russia to declare war against England. Latterly the rumour has shifted from the Baltic and become still more sinister, on the eastern side of the scene, where a feat is contemplated that will force, not Russia only, but all Europe, to declare war against us. This latter I have come to know as an indisputable fact; in our present affairs and outlooks surely a grave one.

As to "British interests" there is none visible or conceivable to me, except taking strict charge of our route to India by Suez and Egypt, and for the rest, resolutely steering altogether clear of any co-partnery with the Turk in regard to this or any other "British interest" whatever. It should be felt by England as a real ignominy to be connected with such a Turk at all. Nay, if we still had, as we ought to have, a wish to save him from perdition and annihilation in God's world, the one future for him that has any hope in it is even now that of being conquered by the Russians, and gradually schooled and drilled into peaceable attempt at learning to be himself governed. The newspaper outcry against Russia is no more respectable to me than the howling of Bedlam, proceeding as it does from the deepest ignorance, egoism, and paltry national jealousy.

These things I write, not on hearsay, but on accurate knowledge, and to all friends of their country will recommend immediate attention to them while there is yet time, lest in a few weeks the maddest and most criminal thing that a British government could do, should be done and all Europe kindle into flames of war.—I am, etc.,

T. CARLYLE.

5 CHEYNE ROW, CHELSEA,
  May 4*th.*

Meanwhile honours without stint were being rendered to the great author and venerable sage. In 1868 he had by request a personal interview with the Queen, and has left, in a letter, a graphic account of the interview at the Deanery of Westminster. Great artists, as Millais, Watts, and Boehme, vied with each other, in painting or sculpture, to preserve his lineaments; prominent reviews to record their impression of his work, and disciples to show their gratitude. One of these, Professor Masson of Edinburgh, in memory of Carlyle's own tribute to Goethe, started a subscription for a medal, presented on his eightieth birthday; but he valued more a communication of the same date from Prince Bismarck. Count Bernstoff from Berlin wrote him (1871) a semi-official letter of thanks for the services he had conferred on Germany, and in 1874 he was prevailed on to accept the Prussian " Ordre pour lé mérite." In the same year Mr. Disraeli proposed, in courteous oblivion of by-gone hostilities, to confer on him a pension and the " Order of the Grand Cross of the Bath," an emolument and distinction which Carlyle, with equal courtesy, declined. To the Countess of Derby, whom he believed to be the originator of the scheme, he (December 30th) expressed his sense of the generosity of the Premier's letter: "It reveals to me, after all the hard things I have said of him, a new and unexpected stratum of genial dignity and manliness of character." To his brother John he wrote: "I do, however, truly admire the magnanimity of Dizzy in regard to me. He is the only man I almost never spoke of without contempt . . . and yet see here he comes with a pan of hot coals for my guilty head." That he was by no means gagged by personal feeling or seduced in matters of policy is evident from the above-quoted letter to the *Times;* but he liked Disraeli better than his great rival; the one may have bewildered his followers, the other, according to his critic's view, deceived himself— the lie, in Platonic phrase, had got into the soul, till, to borrow an epigram, "he made his conscience not his guide but his accomplice." "Carlyle," says Mr. Froude, "did not regard Mr. Gladstone merely as an orator who, knowing nothing as it ought to be known, had flung his force into specious sentiments, but as the representative of the numerous cants of the age . . . differing from others in that the cant seemed true to him. He in fact believed him to be one of those fatal figures created by England's evil genius to work irreparable mischief." It must be admitted that Carlyle's censures are so broadcast as to lose half their sting. In uncontroversial writing, it is enough to note that his methods of reforming the world and Mr. Gladstone's were as far as the poles asunder; and the admirers of the latter may console themselves with the reflection that the censor was, at the same time, talking with equal disdain of the scientific discoverers of the age—conspicuously of Mr. Darwin, whom he describes as "evolving man's soul from frog spawn," adding, "I have no patience

with these gorilla damnifications of humanity." Other
criticisms, as those of George Eliot, whose *Adam Bede* he
pronounced "simply dull," display a curious limitation or
obtuseness of mind.

One of the pleasantest features of his declining years is
the ardour of his attachment to the few staunch friends
who helped to cheer and console them. He had a sincere
regard for Fitzjames Stephen, "an honest man with heavy
strokes;" for Sir Garnet Wolseley, to whom he said in
effect, "Your duty one day will be to take away that
bauble and close the doors of the House of Discord;" for
Tyndall always; for Lecky, despite their differences; for
Moncure Conway, athwart the question of "nigger" philanthropies; for Kingsley and Tennyson and Browning,
the last of whom was a frequent visitor till near the end.
Froude he had bound to his soul by hoops of steel; and a
more faithful disciple and apostle, in intention always, in
practice in the main (despite the most perplexing errors of
judgment), no professed prophet ever had. But Carlyle's
highest praise is reserved for Ruskin, whom he regarded
as no mere art critic, but as a moral power worthy to receive and carry onward his own "cross of fire." The relationship between the two great writers is uncheckered by
any shade of patronage on the one hand, of jealousy or
adulation on the other. The elder recognised in the
younger an intellect as keen, a spirit as fearless as his own,
who in the Eyre controversy had "plunged his rapier to
the hilt in the entrails of the Blatant Beast," *i.e.* Popular
Opinion. He admired all Ruskin's books; the *Stones of
Venice*, the most solid structure of the group, he named
"Sermons in Stones;" he resented an attack on *Sesame
and Lilies* as if it had been his own; and passages of the
Queen of the Air went into his heart "like arrows." The
37

Order of the Rose has attempted a practical embodiment of the review contemplated by Carlyle, as a counteractive to the money-making practice and expediency worships of the day.

Meanwhile he had been putting his financial affairs in order. In 1867, on return from Mentone, he had recorded his bequest of the revenues of Craigenputtock for the endowment of three John Welsh bursaries in the University of Edinburgh. In 1873 he made his will, leaving John Forster and Froude his literary executors: a legacy of trust which, on the death of the former, fell to the latter, to whose discretion, by various later bequests, less and less limited, there was confided the choice—at last almost made a duty—of editing and publishing the manuscripts and journals of himself and his wife.

Early in his seventy-third year (December, 1867) Carlyle quotes, "Youth is a garland of roses," adding, "I did not find it such. 'Age is a crown of thorns.' Neither is this altogether true for me. If sadness and sorrow tend to loosen us from life, they make the place of rest more desirable." The talk of Socrates in the *Republic*, and the fine phrases in Cicero's *De Senectute*, hardly touch on the great grief, apart from physical infirmities, of old age—its increasing solitariness. After sixty, a man may make disciples and converts, but few new friends, while the old ones die daily; the "familiar faces" vanish in the night to which there is no morning, and leave nothing in their stead.

During these years Carlyle's former intimates were falling round him like the leaves from an autumn tree, and the kind care of the few survivors, with the solicitous attention of his niece, nurse, and amanuensis, Mary Aitken, left him desolate. Clough had died, and Thomas Erskine and John Forster and Wilberforce, with whom he thought

he agreed, and Mill, his old champion and ally, with whom
he so disagreed that he almost maligned his memory—
calling one of the most interesting of autobiographies "the
life of a logic-chopping machine." In March, 1876, he
attended the funeral of Lady Augusta Stanley ; in the following month his brother Aleck died in Canada ; and in
1878 his brother John at Dumfries.   He seemed destined
to be left alone ; his physical powers were waning.   In
1879 he and his last horse " Comet " had their last ride together ; later, his right hand failed, and he had to write
by dictation.   In the gathering gloom he began to look
on death as a release from the shreds of life, and to envy
the old Roman mode of shuffling off the coil.   His thoughts
turned more and more to Hamlet's question of the possible
dreams hereafter, and his longing for his lost Jeannie made
him beat at the iron gates of the " Undiscovered Country "
with a yearning cry, but he could get no answer from reason, and would not seek it in any form of superstition,
least of all the latest, that of stealing into heaven " by way
of mesmeric and spiritualistic trances."   His question and
answer are always :

Strength quite a stranger to me. . . . Life is verily a weariness on
those terms.   Oftenest I feel willing to go, were my time come.
Sweet to rejoin, were it only in eternal sleep, those that are away.
That . . . is now and then the whisper of my worn-out heart, and a
kind of solace to me.   " But why annihilation or eternal sleep ?" I
ask, too.   They and I are alike in the will of the Highest.

"When," says Mr. Froude, " he spoke of the future and
its uncertainties, he fell back invariably on the last words
of his favourite hymn :

Wir heissen euch hoffen."

His favourite quotations in those days were Macbeth's "To-morrow and to-morrow and to-morrow;" Burns's line, "Had we never lo'ed sae kindly"—thinking of the tomb which he was wont to kiss in the gloamin' in Haddington Church — the lines from "The Tempest" ending, "our little life is rounded with a sleep," and the dirge in "Cymbeline." He lived on during the last years, save for his quiet walks with his biographer about the banks of the Thames, like a ghost among ghosts, his physical life slowly ebbing till, on February 4th, 1881, it ebbed away. His remains were, by his own desire, conveyed to Ecclefechan and laid under the snow-clad soil of the rural church-yard, beside the dust of his kin. He had objected to be buried, should the request be made (as it was by Dean Stanley), in Westminster Abbey : ἀνδρῶν γὰρ ἐπιφανῶν πᾶσα γῆ τάφος.

Of no man whose life has been so laid bare to us is it more difficult to estimate the character than that of Thomas Carlyle, and regarding no one of equal eminence, with the possible exception of Byron, has opinion been so divided. After his death there was a carnival of applause from his countrymen in all parts of the globe, from Canton to San Francisco. Their hot zeal, only equalled by that of their revelries over the memory of Burns, was unrestrained by limit, order, or degree. No nation is warmer than the Scotch in worship of its heroes when dead and buried : one perfervid enthusiast says of the former, "Atheist, Deist, and Pantheist: Carlyle is gone; his voice, pure as the naked heavens, majestic, free, will be heard no more:" the *Scotsman* newspaper writes of him as "probably the greatest of modern literary men; ... before the volcanic glare of his *French Revolution* all Epics, ancient and modern, grow pale and shadowy, ... his like is not now left in the world." More recently a stalwart Aberdonian, on helping to put a bust into a monument, exclaims in a strain of genuine ardour, "I knew Carlyle, and I aver to you that his heart was as large and generous as his brain was powerful; that he was essentially a most lovable man, and that there were depths of tenderness, kindliness, benevolence, and most delicate courtesy in him, with all his seeming ruggedness and sternness, such as I have found throughout my life rarely in any human being."

On the other side, a little later, after the publication of the *Reminiscences*, *Blackwood* denounced the "old man eloquent" as "a blatant impostor, who speaks as if he were the only person who knew good from bad. . . . Every one and everything dealt with in his *History* is treated in the tone of a virtuous Mephistopheles." The *World* remarks that Carlyle has been made to pay the penalty of a posthumous depreciation for a factitious fame; "but the game of venomous recrimination was begun by himself. . . . There is little that is extraordinary, still less that is heroic in his character. He had no magnanimity about him . . . he was full of littleness and weakness, of shallow dogmatism and of blustering conceit." The *Quarterly*, after alluding to Carlyle's style "as the eccentric expression of eccentricity," denounces his choice of "heroes" as reckless of morality. According to the same authority, he "was not a deep thinker, but he was a great word painter . . . he has the inspiration as well as the contortions of the Sibyl, the strength as well as the nodosities of the oak. . . . In the *French Revolution* he rarely condescends to plain narrative . . . it resembles a drama at the Porte St. Martin, in so many acts and tableaux. . . . The raisers of busts and statues in his honour are winging and pointing new arrows aimed at the reputation of their most distinguished contemporaries, and doing their best to perpetuate a baneful influence."

7*   L

Fraser, no longer edited by Mr. Froude, swells the chorus of dissent: "Money, for which he cared little, only came in quantity after the death of his wife, when everything became indifferent to an old and life-weary man. Who would be great at such a price? Who would buy so much misery with so much labour? Most men like their work. In his Carlyle seems to have found the curse imposed upon Adam. . . . He cultivated contempt of the kindly race of men."

Ample texts for these and similar censures are to be found in the pages of Mr. Froude, and he has been accused by Carlyle's devotees of having supplied this material of malice prepense. No accusation was ever more ridiculously unjust. To the mind of every impartial reader, Froude appears as one of the loyallest if one of the most infatuated of friends. Living towards the close in almost daily communion with his master, and in inevitable contact with his numerous frailties, he seems to have revered him with a love that passeth understanding, and attributed to him in good faith, as Dryden did in jest to the objects of his mock heroics, every mental as well as every moral power, *e.g.*, "Had Carlyle turned his mind to it he would have been a great philologer." "A great diplomatist was lost in Carlyle." "He would have done better as a man of action than a man of words." By kicking the other diplomatists into the sea, as he threatened to do with the urchins of Kirkcaldy? Froude's panegyrics are in style and tone worthy of that put into the mouth of Pericles by Thucydides, with which the modern biographer closes his only too faithful record. But his claims for his hero —amounting to the assertions that he was never seriously wrong; that he was as good as he was great; that "in the weightier matters of the law his life had been without speck or flaw;" that "such faults as he had were but as the vapours which hang about a mountain, inseparable from the nature of the man;" that he never, in their intercourse, uttered a "trivial word, nor one which he had better have left unuttered"—these claims will never be honoured, for they are refuted in every third page after that on which they appear: *e.g.* in the Biography, vol. iv., p. 258, we are told that Carlyle's "knowledge was not in points or lines but complete and solid:" facing the remarks we read, "He liked *ill* men like Humboldt, Laplace, or the author of the *Vestiges.* He refused Darwin's transmutation of species as unproved; he fought against it, though I could see he dreaded that it might turn out true." The statement that " he always spoke respectfully of Macaulay " is soon followed by criticisms that make us exclaim, " Save us from such respect." The extraordinary assertion that Carlyle was " always just in speaking of living men " is safeguarded by the quotation of large utterances of injustice and contempt for Coleridge, Byron, Shelley, Keats, Comte, Balzac, Hugo, Lamb, George Eliot, and disparaging patronage¹ of Scott, of Jeffrey, of Mazzini, and of Mill. The dog-like fidelity of Boswell and Eckermann was fitting to their attitude and capacity; but the spectacle of one great writer surrendering himself to another is a new testimony to the glamour of conversational genius.

Carlyle was a great man, but a great man spoiled—that is, largely soured. He was never a Timon; but, while at

---

¹ This patronage of men, some quite, others nearly on his own level, whom he delights in calling "small," "thin," and "poor," as if he were the only big, fat, and rich, is more offensive than spurts of merely dyspeptic abuse. As regards the libels on Lamb, Dr. Ireland has endeavoured to establish that they were written in ignorance of the noble tragedy of "Elia's" life; but this contention cannot be made good as regards the later attacks.

best a Stoic, he was at worst a Cynic, emulous though disdainful, trying all men by his own standard, and intolerant of a rival on the throne. To this result there contributed the bleak though bracing environment of his early years, amid kindred more noted for strength than for amenity, whom he loved, trusted, and revered, but from whose grim creed, formally at least, he had to tear himself with violent wrenches apart; his purgatory among the border-ruffians of Annan school; his teaching drudgeries; his hermit college days; ten years' struggle for a meagre competence; a life-long groaning under the Nemesis shirt of the irritable yet stubborn constitution to which genius is often heir; and above all his unusually late recognition. There is a good deal of natural bitterness in reference to the long refusal by the publishers of his first original work—an idyll like Goldsmith's *Vicar of Wakefield*, and our finest prose poem in philosophy. "Popularity," says Emerson, "is for dolls;" but it remains to find the preacher, prophet, or poet wholly impervious to unjust criticism. Neglect which crushes dwarfs only exasperates giants, but to the latter also there is great harm done. Opposition affected Carlyle as it affected Milton; it made him defiant, at times even fierce, to those beyond his own inner circle. When he triumphed, he accepted his success without a boast, but not without reproaches for the past. He was crowned; but his coronation came too late, and the death of his wife paralysed his later years.

Let those who from the Clyde to the Isis, from the Forth to the Cam, make it their pastime to sneer at living worth, compare Ben Jonson's lines,

> Your praise and dispraise are to me alike,
> One does not stroke me, nor the other strike,

with Samuel Johnson's, " It has been delayed till most of those whom I wished to please are sunk into the grave, and success and failure are empty sounds," and then take to heart the following :

> The " recent return of popularity greater than ever," which I hear of, seems due alone to that late Edinburgh affair ; especially to the Edinburgh " Address," and affords new proof of the singularly dark and feeble condition of " public judgment " at this time.   No idea, or shadow of an idea, is in that Address but what had been set forth by me tens of times before, and the poor gaping sea of pruri-ent blockheadism receives it as a kind of inspired revelation, and runs to buy my books (it is said), now when I have got quite done with their buying or refusing to buy. If they would give me £10,000 a year and bray unanimously their hosannas heaven - high for the rest of my life, who now would there be to get the smallest joy or profit from it ? To me I feel as if it would be a silent sorrow rather, and would bring me painful retrospections, nothing else.

We require no open-sesame, no clumsy confidence from attachés flaunting their intimacy, to assure us that there were "depths of tenderness" in Carlyle. His susceptibility to the softer influences of nature, of family life, of his few chosen friends, is apparent in almost every page of his biography, above all in the *Reminiscences*, those supreme records of regret, remorse, and the inspiration of bereave-ment.   There is no surge of sorrow in our literature like that which is perpetually tossed up in the second chapter of the second volume, with the never-to-be-forgotten re-frain—

> Cherish what is dearest while you have it near you, and wait not till it is far away. Blind and deaf that we are ; oh, think, if thou yet love anybody living, wait not till death sweep down the paltry little dust clouds and dissonances of the moment, and all be at last so mournfully clear and beautiful, when it is too late !

Were we asked to bring together the three most pathetic sentences in our tongue since Lear asked the question, " And have his daughters brought him to this pass?" we should select Swift's comment on the lock of Stella, " Only a woman's hair;" the cry of Tennyson's Rizpah, "The bones had moved in my side;" and Carlyle's wail, "Oh, that I had you yet but for five minutes beside me, to tell you all."   But in answer we hear only the flapping of the folds of Isis, " strepitumque Acherontis avari."

All of sunshine that remained in my life went out in that sudden moment. All of strength too often seems to have gone. . . . Were it permitted, I would pray, but to whom? I can well understand the invocation of saints.   One's prayer now has to be voiceless, done with the heart still, but also with the hands still more. . . . Her birthday.   She not here—I cannot keep it for her now, and send a gift to poor old Betty, who next to myself remembers her in life-long love and sacred sorrow. This is all I can do. . . . Time was to bring relief, said everybody; but Time has not to any extent, nor, in truth, did I much wish him.

> Eurydicen vox ipsa et frigida lingua,
> Eurydicen toto referebaut flumine ripæ.

Carlyle's pathos, far from being confined to his own calamity, was ready to awake at every touch. "I was walking with him," writes Froude, "one Sunday afternoon in Battersea Park.   In the open circle among the trees was a blind man and his daughter, she singing hymns, he accompanying her on some instrument.   We stood listening.   She sang Faber's 'Pilgrims of the Night.'   The words were trivial, but the air, though simple, had something weird and unearthly about it.   'Take me away,' he said, after a few minutes, 'I shall cry if I stay longer.'"

The melancholy, " often as of deep misery frozen tor-

pid," that runs through his writing, that makes him fore-
cast death in life, and paint the springs of nature in winter
hue, the "hoarse sea," the "bleared skies," the sunsets
"beautiful and brief and wae," compels our compassion in
a manner quite different from the pictures of Sterne and
De Quincey and other colour dramatists, because we feel
it is as genuine as the melancholy of Burns. Both had
the relief of humour, but Burns only of the two was capable of gaiety. "Look up there," said Leigh Hunt, pointing to the starry skies, "look at that glorious harmony
that sings with infinite voices an eternal song of hope in
the soul of man." "Eh, it's a sair sicht," was the reply.

We have referred to a few out of a hundred instances of
Carlyle's practical benevolence. To all deserving persons
in misfortune he was a good Samaritan, and like all benefactors the dupe of some undeserving. Charity may be,
like maternal affection, a form of self-indulgence, but it is
so only to kind-hearted men. In all that relates to money
Carlyle's career is exemplary. He had too much common-
sense to affect to despise it, and was restive when he was
underpaid; he knew that the labourer was worthy of his
hire. But, after hacking for Brewster he cannot be said to
have ever worked for wages; his concern was rather with
the quality of his work, and, regardless of results, he always
did his best. A more unworldly man never lived; from
his first savings he paid ample tributes to filial piety and
fraternal kindness, and to the end of his life retained the
simple habits in which he had been trained. He hated waste
of all kinds, save in words, and carried his home frugalities
even to excess. In writing to James Aitken, engaged to
his sister, "the Craw," he says, "remember in marriage
you have undertaken to do to others as you would wish
they should do to you." But this rede he did not reck.

"Carlyle," writes Longfellow, "was one of those men
who sacrificed their happiness to their work;" the misfortune is that the sacrifice did not stop with himself. He
seemed made to live with no one but himself. Alternately
courteous and cross-grained, all his dramatic power went
into his creations; he could not put himself into the place
of those near him. Essentially perhaps the bravest man
of his age, he would turn not an inch aside for threat or
flattery; *integer vitæ*, conscience never made him a coward.
He bore great calamities with the serenity of a Marcus
Aurelius: his reception of the loss of his first volume of the
French Revolution was worthy of Sidney or of Newton:
his letters, when the successive deaths of almost all that
were dearest left him desolate, are among the noblest, the
most resigned, the most pathetic in biography. Yet, says
Mr. Froude, in a judgment which every careful reader must
endorse: "Of all men I have ever seen Carlyle was the least
patient of the common woes of humanity." "A positive
Christian," says Mrs. Carlyle, "in bearing others' pain, he
was a roaring Thor when himself pricked by a pin," and
his biographer corroborates this: "If matters went well
with himself, it never occurred to him that they could be
going ill with any one else; and, on the other hand, if he
were uncomfortable he required all the world to be uncomfortable along with him." He did his work with more than
the tenacity of a Prescott or a Fawcett, but no man ever
made so much noise over it as this apostle of silence.
"Sins of passion he could forgive, but those of insincerity
never." Carlyle has no tinge of insincerity; his writing,
his conversation, his life, is absolutely, dangerously transparent. His utter genuineness was in the long run one of the
sources of his success. He always, if we allow for a habit
of rhetorical exaggeration, felt what he made others feel.

Sullen moods, and " words at random sent," those judging him from a distance can easily condone; the errors of a hot head are pardonable to one who, in his calmer hours, was ready to confess them. "Your temptation and mine," he writes to his brother Alexander, "is a tendency to imperiousness and indignant self-help; and, if no wise theoretical, yet practical forgetfulness and tyrannical contempt of other men." His nicknaming mania was the inheritance of a family failing, always fostered by the mockingbird at his side. Humour, doubtless, ought to discount many of his criticisms. Dean Stanley, in his funeral sermon, charitably says, that in pronouncing the population of England to be "thirty millions, mostly fools," Carlyle merely meant that " few are chosen and strait is the gate," generously adding—"There was that in him, in spite of his contemptuous descriptions of the people, which endeared him to those who knew him best. The idols of their market-place he trampled underfoot, but their joys and sorrows, their cares and hopes, were to him revered things." Another critic pleads for his discontent that it had in it a noble side, like that of Faust, and that his harsh judgments of eminent men were based on the belief that they had allowed meaner to triumph over higher impulses, or influences of society to injure their moral fibre. This plea, however, fails to cover the whole case. Carlyle's ignorance in treating men who moved in spheres apart from his own, as the leaders of science, definite theological enlightenment, or even poetry and arts was an intellectual rather than a moral flaw; but in the implied assertion, "what I can't do is not worth doing," we have to regret the influence of an enormous egotism stunting enormous powers, which, beginning with his student days, possessed him to the last. The fame of Newton, Leibnitz, Gibbon,

whose works he came to regard as the spoon-meat of his
"rude untutored youth," is beyond the range of his or of
any shafts.   When he trod on Mazzini's pure patriot career, as a "rose-water imbecility," or maligned Mill's intrepid thought as that of a mere machine, he was astray
on more delicate ground, and alienated some of his truest
friends.   Among the many curses of our nineteenth-century
literature denounced by its leading Censor, the worst, the
want of loyalty among literary men, he fails to denounce
because he largely shares in it.   "No sadder proof," he
declares, "can be given by a man of his own littleness
than disbelief in great men," and no one has done more
to retrieve from misconception the memories of heroes of
the past; but rarely do either he or Mrs. Carlyle say a
good word for any considerable English writer then living.
It is true that he criticises, more or less disparagingly, all
his own works, from *Sartor*, of which he remarks that
"only some ten pages are fused and harmonious," to his
self-entitled "rigmarole on the Norse Kings:" but he would
not let his enemy say so; nor his friend.   Mill's just
strictures on the "Nigger Pamphlet" he treats as the impertinence of a boy, and only to Emerson would he grant
the privilege to hold his own.   *Per contra*, he overesti-
mated those who were content to be his echoes.   Material
help he refused with a red Indian pride; intellectual he
used and slighted.   He renders scant justice to those who
had preceded him in his lines of historical investigation,
as if they had been poachers on his premises, *e.g.* Heath,
the royalist writer of the Commonwealth time, is "carrion
Heath:" Noble, a former biographer of Cromwell, is "my
reverend imbecile friend:" his predecessors in *Friedrich*, as
Schlosser, Preuss, Ranke, Förster, Vehse, are "dark chaotic
dullards whose books are mere blotches of printed stupor,

tumbled mountains of marine stores"—criticism valueless even when it raises the laughter due to a pantomime. Carlyle assailed three sets of people :

1. Real humbugs, or those who had behaved, or whom he believed to have behaved, badly to him.
2. Persons from whom he differed, or whom he could not understand — as Shelley, Keats, Lamb, Coleridge, and the leaders of Physics and Metaphysics.
3. Persons who had befriended, but would not give him an unrestricted homage or an implicit following, as Mill, Mazzini, Miss Martineau, etc.

The last series of assaults are hard to pardon. Had his strictures been always just, so winged with humorous epigram, they would have blasted a score of reputations: as it is they have only served to mar his own. He was a typical Scotch student of the better class, stung by the οἶστρος of their ambitious competition and restless push, wanting in repose, never like

a gentleman at ease
With moral breadth of temperament,

too apt to note his superiority with the sneer, "they call this man as good as me." Bacon, in one of his finest antitheses, draws a contrast between the love of Excellence and the love of Excelling. Carlyle is possessed by both; he had none of the exaggerated caution which in others of his race is apt to degenerate into moral cowardice: but when he thought himself trod on he became, to use his own figure, "a rattlesnake," and put out fangs like those of the griffins curiously, if not sardonically, carved on the tombs of his family in the church-yard of Ecclefechan.

Truth, in the sense of saying what he thought, was one of his ruling passions.   To one of his brothers on the birth of a daughter, he writes, " Train her to this, as the corner-stone of all morality, to stand by the truth, to abhor a lie as she does hell-fire."   The "gates of hell" is the phrase of Achilles ; but Carlyle has no real point of contact with the Greek love of abstract truth.   He objects that "Socrates is terribly at ease in Zion :" he liked no one to be at ease anywhere.   He is angry with Walter Scott because he hunted with his friends over the breezy heath instead of mooning alone over twilight moors.   Read Scott's *Memoirs* in the morning, the *Reminiscences* at night, and dispute if you like about the greater genius, but never about the healthier, better, and larger man.

Hebraism, says Matthew Arnold, is the spirit which obeys the mandate, " walk by your light."   Hellenism the spirit which remembers the other, " have a care your light be not darkness ;" the former prefers doing to thinking, the latter is bent on finding the truth it loves.   Carlyle is a Hebraist unrelieved and unretrieved by the Hellene. A man of inconsistencies, egotisms, Alpine grandeurs, and crevasses, let us take from him what the gods or proto-plasms have allowed.   His way of life,[1] duly admired for

---

[1] In the *Times* of February 7th, 1881, there appeared an interesting account of Carlyle's daily routine.   "No book hack could have sur-passed the regularity and industry with which he worked early and late in his small attic.   A walk before breakfast was part of the day's duties.   At ten o'clock in the morning, whether the spirit moved him or not, he took up his pen and laboured hard until three o'clock.   Nothing, not even the opening of the morning letters, was allowed to distract him.   Then came walking, answering letters, and seeing friends. . . . In the evening he read and prepared for the work of the morrow."

its stern temperance, its rigidity of noble aim — eighty
years spent in contempt of favour, plaudit, or reward, left
him austere to frailty other than his own, and wrapt him
in the repellent isolation which is the wrong side of uncompromising dignity.   He was too great to be, in the
common sense, conceited.   All his consciousness of power
left him with the feeling of Newton, "I am a child gathering shells on the shore:" but what sense he had of fallibility arose from his glimpse of the infinite sea, never from
any suspicion that, in any circumstances, he might be
wrong and another mortal right: Shelley's lines on Byron:

> The sense that he was greater than his kind
> Had struck, methinks, his eagle spirit blind
> By gazing on its own exceeding light—

fit him, like Ruskin's verdict, "What can you say of Carlyle but that he was born in the clouds and struck by the
lightning," which withers while it immortalises.

38

CHAPTER VIII.

CARLYLE AS MAN OF LETTERS, CRITIC, AND HISTORIAN.

CARLYLE was so essentially a Preacher that the choice of a profession made for him by his parents was in some measure justified; but he was also a keen Critic, unamenable to ecclesiastic or other rule, a leader of the revolutionary spirit of the age, even while protesting against its extremes: above all, he was a literary Artist. Various opinions will continue to be held as to the value of his sermons; the excellence of his best workmanship is universally acknowledged. He was endowed with few of the qualities which secure a quick success — fluency, finish of style, the art of giving graceful utterance to current thought; he had in full measure the stronger if slower powers—sound knowledge, infinite industry, and the sympathetic insight of penetrative imagination—that ultimately hold the fastnesses of fame. His habit of startling his hearers, which for a time restricted, at a later date widened their circle. There is much, sometimes even tiresome, repetition in Carlyle's work; the range of his ideas is limited; he plays on a few strings with wonderfully versatile variations; in reading his later we are continually confronted with the "old familiar faces" of his earlier essays. But, after the perfunctory work for Brewster, he wrote nothing wholly commonplace; occasionally paradoxical to the verge of absurdity, he is never dull.

Setting aside his TRANSLATIONS, always in prose, often in verse, masterpieces of their kind, he made his first mark in CRITICISM, which may be regarded as a higher kind of translation : the great value of his work in this direction is due to his so regarding it. Most criticism has for its aim to show off the critic; good criticism interprets the author. Fifty years ago, in allusion to methods of reviewing, not even now wholly obsolete, Carlyle wrote :

The first and most convenient is for the reviewer to perch himself resolutely, as it were, on the shoulder of his author, and therefrom to show as if he commanded him and looked down upon him by natural superiority of stature. Whatsoever the great man says or does the little man shall treat with an air of knowingness and light condescending mockery, professing with much covert sarcasm that this or that is beyond *his* comprehension, and cunningly asking his readers if *they* comprehend it.

There is here, perhaps, some "covert sarcasm" directed against contemporaries who forgot that their mission was to pronounce on the merits of the books reviewed, and not to patronise their authors; it may be set beside the objection to Jeffrey's fashion of saying, "I like this; I do not like that," without giving the reason why. But in this instance the writer did reck his own rede. The temptation of a smart critic is to seek or select legitimate or illegitimate objects of attack; and that Carlyle was well armed with the shafts of ridicule is apparent in his essays as in his histories; superabundantly so in his letters and conversation. His examination of the *German Playwrights*, of *Taylor's German Literature*, and his inimitable sketch of Herr Döring, the hapless biographer of Richter, are as amusing as Macaulay's *coup-de-grâce* to Robert Montgomery. But the graver critic would have us take to heart these sentences of his essay on Voltaire:[1]

Far be it from us to say that solemnity is an essential of greatness; that no great man can have other than a rigid vinegar aspect of countenance, never to be thawed or warmed by billows of mirth. There are things in this world to be laughed at as well as things to be admired. Nevertheless, contempt is a dangerous element to sport in; a deadly one if we habitually live in it. The faculty of love, of admiration, is to be regarded as a sign and the measure of high souls; unwisely directed, it leads to many evils; but without it, there cannot be any good. Ridicule, on the other hand, is the smallest of all faculties that other men are at pains to repay with any esteem. . . . Its nourishment and essence is denial, which hovers only on the surface, while knowledge dwells far below, . . . it cherishes nothing but our vanity, which may in general be left safely enough to shift for itself.

We may compare with this one of the writer's numerous warnings to young men taking to literature, as to drinking, in despair of anything better to do, ending with the exhortation, " Witty above all things, oh, be not witty ;" or turn to the passage in the review of Sir Walter Scott:

Is it with ease or not with ease that a man shall do his best in any shape; above all, in this shape justly named of soul's travail, working in the deep places of thought? . . . Not so now nor at any time. . . . Virgil and Tacitus, were they ready writers? The whole *Prophecies of Isaiah* are not equal in extent to this cobweb of a Review article. Shakespeare, we may fancy, wrote with rapidity, but

---

[1] As an estimate of Voltaire this brilliant essay is inadequate. Carlyle's maxim, we want to be told " not what is *not* true, but what *is* true," prevented him from appreciating the great work of the Encyclopædists.

not till he had thought with intensity, . . . no easy writer he. Neither was Milton one of the mob of gentlemen that write with ease. Goethe tells us he " had nothing sent to him in his sleep," no page of his but he knew well how it came there. Schiller—" konnte nie fer- tig werden "—never could get done. Dante sees himself " growing lean " over his *Divine Comedy ;* in stern solitary death wrestle with it, to prevail over it and do it, if his uttermost faculty may ; hence, too, it is done and prevailed over, and the fiery life of it endures for evermore among men. No ; creation, one would think, cannot be easy ; your Jove has severe pains and fire flames in the head, out of which an armed Pallas is struggling ! As for manufacture, that is a different matter. . . . Write by steam if thou canst contrive it and sell it, but hide it like virtue.

In these and frequent similar passages lies the secret of Carlyle's slow recognition, long struggle, and ultimate suc- cess ; also of his occasional critical intolerance. Com- mander-in-chief of the " red artillery," he sets too little store on the graceful yet sometimes decisive charges of the light brigades of literature. He feels nothing but con- tempt for the banter of men like Jerrold ; despises the genial pathos of Lamb ; and salutes the most brilliant wit and exquisite lyrist of our century with the Puritanical comment, " Blackguard Heine." He deified work as he deified strength ; and so often stimulated his imitators to attempt to leap beyond their shadows. Hard work will not do everything : a man can only accomplish what he was born fit for. Many, in the first flush of ambition doomed to wreck, are blind to the fact that it is not in every ploughman to be a poet, nor in every prize-student to be a philosopher. Nature does half : after all, perhaps the larger half. Genius has been absurdly defined as " an infinite capacity for taking trouble ;" no amount of pump- ing can draw more water than is in the well. Himself in " the chamber of little ease," Carlyle travestied Goethe's "worship of sorrow" till it became a pride in pain. He forgot that rude energy requires restraint. Hercules Furens and Orlando Furioso did more than cut down trees; they tore them up; but to no useful end. His power is often almost Miltonic; it is never Shakespearian; and his insistent earnestness would run the risk of fatiguing us were it not redeemed by his humour. But he errs on the better side; and his example is a salutary counteractive in an age when the dust of so many skirmishers obscures the air, and laughter is too readily accepted as the test of truth. His stern conception of literature accounts for his exaltations of the ideal, and denunciations of the actual, profession of letters in passages which, from his habit of emphasising opposite sides of truth, instead of striking a balance, appear almost side by side in contradiction. The following condenses the ideal:

If the poor and humble toil that we have food, must not the high and glorious toil for him in return, that he may have guidance, freedom, immortality. These two in all degrees I honour; all else is chaff and dust, which let the wind blow whither it listeth. Doubt, desire, sorrow, remorse, indignation, despair itself—all these like hellhounds lie beleaguering the souls of the poor day worker as of every man; but he bends himself with free valour against his task, and all these are stifled—all these shrink murmuring far off in their caves.

Against this we have to set innumerable tirades on the crime of worthless writing, e.g.:

No mortal has a right to wag his tongue, much less to wag his pen, without saying something; he knows not what mischief he does, past computation, scattering words without meaning, to afflict the whole world yet before they cease. For thistle-down flies abroad on all winds and airs of wind. . . . Ship-loads of fashionable novels, sentimental rhymes, tragedies, farces . . . tales by flood and field are swallowed monthly into the bottomless pool; still does the press toil, . . . and still in torrents rushes on the great army of publications to their final home; and still oblivion, like the grave, cries Give! give! How is it that of all these countless multitudes no one can . . . produce aught that shall endure longer than "snow-flake on the river? Because they are foam, because there is no reality in them. . . ." Not by printing-ink alone does man live. Literature, as followed at present, is but a species of brewing or cooking, where the cooks use poison, and vend it by telling innumerable lies.

These passages owe their interest to the attestation of their sincerity by the writer's own practice. "Do not," he counsels one of his unknown correspondents, "take up a subject because it is singular and will get you credit, but because you *love* it," and he himself acted on the rule. Nothing more impresses the student of Carlyle's works than his *thoroughness*. He never took a task in hand without the determination to perform it to the utmost of his ability; consequently when he satisfied himself that he was master of his subject he satisfied his readers; but this mastery was only attained, as it is only attainable, by the most rigorous research. He seems to have written down his results with considerable fluency; the molten ore flowed freely forth, but the process of smelting was arduous. The most painful part of literary work is not the actual composition, but the accumulation of details, the wearisome compilation of facts, weighing of previous criticisms, the sifting of the grains of wheat from the bushels of chaff. This part of his task Carlyle performed with an admirable conscientiousness. His numerous letters applying for out-of-the-way books to buy or borrow, for every pamphlet throwing light on his subject, bear testimony to the careful exactitude which rarely permitted him to leave any record unread or any worthy opinion untested about any event of which or any person of whom he undertook to write. From Templand (1833) he applies for seven volumes of Beaumarchais, three of Bassompierre, the Memoirs of Abbé Georgel, and every attainable account of Cagliostro and the Countess de la Motte, to fuse into *The Diamond Necklace.* To write the essay on *Werner* and the *German Playwrights* he swam through seas of trash. He digested the whole of *Diderot* for one review article. He seems to have read through *Jean Paul Richter*, a feat to accomplish which Germans require a special dictionary. When engaged on the Civil War he routed up a whole shoal of obscure seventeenth - century papers from Yarmouth, the remnant of a yet larger heap, "read hundred-weights of dreary books," and endured "a hundred Museum headaches." In grappling with *Friedrich* he waded through so many gray historians that we can forgive his sweeping condemnation of their dulness. He visited all the scenes and places of which he meant to speak, from St. Ives to Prague, and explored the battle-fields. Work done after this fashion seldom brings a swift return; but if it is utilized and made vivid by literary genius it has a claim to permanence. Bating a few instances where his sense of proportion is defective, or his eccentricity is in excess, Carlyle puts his ample material to artistic use; seldom making ostentation of detail, but skilfully concentrating, so that we read easily and readily recall what he has written. Almost everything he has done has made a mark; his best work in criticism is final, it does not require to be done again. He interests us in the fortunes of his leading characters; *first*, because he feels with them; *secondly*, because he knows how to distinguish the essence from the accidents of their lives, what to forget and what to remember, where to begin and where to stop. Hence, not only his set biographies, as of Schiller and of Sterling, but the shorter notices in his Essays, are intrinsically more complete and throw more real light on character than whole volumes of ordinary memoirs.

With the limitations above referred to, and in view of his antecedents, the range of Carlyle's critical appreciation is wonderfully wide. Often perversely unfair to the majority of his English contemporaries, the scales seem to fall from his eyes in dealing with the great figures of other nations. The charity expressed in the saying that we should judge men, not by the number of their faults, but by the amount of their deflection from the circle, great or small, that bounds their being, enables him often to do justice to those most widely differing in creed, sentiment, and lines of activity from each other and from himself. When treating congenial themes he errs by overestimate rather than by depreciation : among the qualities of his early work, which afterwards suffered some eclipse in the growth of other powers, is its flexibility. It was natural for Carlyle, his successor in genius in the Scotch lowlands, to give an account of Robert Burns which throws all previous criticism of the poet into the shade. Similarly he has strong affinities to Johnson, Luther, Knox, Cromwell, to all his so-called heroes; but he is fair to the characters, if not always to the works, of Voltaire and Diderot, slurs over or makes humorous the escapades of Mirabeau, is undeterred by the mysticism of Novalis, and in the fervour of his worship fails to see the gulf between himself and Goethe.

Carlyle's ESSAYS mark an epoch, *i.e.*, the beginning of a new era, in the history of British criticism. The able and vigorous writers who contributed to the early numbers of the *Edinburgh* and *Quarterly Reviews* successfully applied their taste and judgment to such works as fell within their sphere, and could be fairly tested by their canons; but they passed an alien act on everything that lay beyond the range of their insular view. In dealing with the efforts of a nation whose literature, the most recent in Europe save that of Russia, had only begun to command recognition, their rules were at fault and their failures ridiculous. If the old formulæ have been theoretically dismissed, and a conscientious critic now endeavours to place himself in the position of his author, the change is largely due to the influence of Carlyle's *Miscellanies.* Previous to their appearance, the literature of Germany, to which half of these papers are devoted, had been (with the exception of Sir Walter Scott's translation of *Goetz von Berlichingen*, De Quincey's travesties, and Taylor's renderings from Lessing) a sealed book to English readers, save those who were willing to breathe in an atmosphere of Coleridgean mist. Carlyle first made it generally known in England, because he was the first fully to apprehend its meaning. The *Life of Schiller*, which the author himself depreciated, remains one of the best of comparatively short biographies; it abounds in admirable passages (conspicuously the contrast between the elder and the younger of the Dioscuri at Weimar), and has the advantage to some readers of being written in classical English prose.

To the essays relating to Germany, which we may accept as the *disjecta membra* of the author's unpublished History, there is little to add. In these volumes we have the best English account of the Nibelungen Lied—the most graphic and in the main most just analyses of the genius of Heyne, Richter, Novalis, Schiller, and, above all, of Goethe, who is recorded to have said, "Carlyle is almost more at home in our literature than ourselves." With the Germans he is on his chosen ground; but the range of his sympathies is most apparent in the portrait-gallery of eighteenth-century Frenchmen that forms, as it were, a proscenium to his first great History. Among other papers in the same collection the most prominent are the *Signs of the Times* and *Characteristics*, in which he first distinctly broaches some of his peculiar views on political philosophy and life.

The scope and some of the limitations of Carlyle's critical power are exhibited in his second Series[1] of Lectures, delivered in 1838, when (*æt.* 43) he had reached the maturity of his powers. The first three of these lectures, treating of Ancient History and Literature, bring into strong relief the speaker's inadequate view of Greek thought and civilisation :

Greek transactions had never anything alive, no result for us, they were dead entirely . . . all left is a few ruined towers, masses of stone, and broken statuary. . . . The writings of Socrates are made up of a few wire-drawn notions about virtue; there is no conclusion, no word of life in him.

These and similar dogmatic utterances are comments of the Hebrew on the Hellene. To the Romans, "the men of antiquity," he is more just, dwelling on their agriculture and road-making as their "greatest work written on the planet;" but the only Latin author he thoroughly appreci-

---

[1] Though a mere reproduction of the notes of Mr. Chisholm Anstley, this posthumous publication is justified by its interest and obvious authenticity. The appearance in a prominent periodical (while these sheets are passing through the press) of *Wotton Reinfred* is more open to question. This fragment of a romance, partly based on the plan of *Wilhelm Meister*, with shadowy love episodes recalling the manner of the "Minerva press," can add nothing to Carlyle's reputation.

ates is Tacitus, "a Colossus on edge of dark night." Then follows an exaltation of the Middle Ages, as those in which "we see belief getting the victory over unbelief," in a strain suitable to Cardinal Newman's *Grammar of Assent.* In the struggle between the Popes and the Hohenstaufens, Carlyle's whole sympathy is with Gregory and Hildebrand. He refers to the surrender at Canossa with the characteristic comment, "the clay that is about man is always sufficiently ready to assert its rights; the danger is always the other way, that the spiritual part of man will become overlaid with the bodily part." In the same vein is his praise of Peter the Hermit, whose motto was not the "action, action" of Demosthenes, but "belief, belief." In the brief space of those suggestive though unequal discourses the speaker allows awkward proximity to some of the self-contradictions which, even when scattered farther apart, perplex his readers, and render it impossible to credit his philosophy with more than a few strains of consistent thought.

In one page "the judgments of the heart[1] are of more value than those of the head." In the next "morals in a man are the counterpart of the intellect that is in it." The Middle Ages were "a healthy age," and therefore there was next to no Literature. "The strong warrior disdained to write." "Actions will be preserved when all writers are forgotten." Two days later, apropos of Dante, he says, "The great thing which any nation can do is to produce great men. . . . When the Vatican shall have crumbled to dust, and St. Peter's and Strassburg Minster be no more; for thousands of years to come Catholicism will survive in this sublime relic of antiquity—the *Divina Commedia.*"

---

[1] It has been suggested that Carlyle may have been in this instance a student of Vauvenargues, who in the early years of the much-maligned eighteenth century wrote "Les grandes pensées viennent du cœur."

Passing to Spain, Carlyle salutes Cervantes and the Cid, —calling Don Quixote the " poetry of comedy," "the age of gold in self-mockery "—pays a more reserved tribute to Calderon, ventures on the assertion that Cortes was "as great as Alexander," and gives a sketch, so graphic that it might serve as a text for Motley's great work, of the way in which the decayed Iberian chivalry, rotten through with the Inquisition, broke itself on the Dutch dykes. After a brief outline of the rise of the German power, which had three avatars—the overwhelming of Rome, the Swiss resistance to Austria, and the Reformation—we have a rough estimate of some of the Reformers. Luther is exalted even over Knox; Erasmus is depreciated, while Calvin and Melanchthon are passed by.

The chapter on the Saxons, in which the writer's love of the sea appears in picturesque reference to the old rover kings, is followed by unusually commonplace remarks on earlier English literature, interspersed with some of Carlyle's refrains :

The mind is one, and consists not of bundles of faculties at all . . . the same features appear in painting, singing, fighting . . . when I hear of the distinction between the poet and the thinker, I really see no difference at all. " Bacon sees, Shakespeare sees through," " Milton is altogether sectarian — a Presbyterian one might say—he got his knowledge out of Knox." "Eve is a cold statue."

Coming to the well belaboured eighteenth century— when much was done of which the nineteenth talks, and massive books were written that we are content to criticise —we have the inevitable denunciations of scepticism, materialism, argumentation, logic ; the quotation (referred to a motto in the Swiss gardens), "Speech is silvern, silence

8*

is golden," and a loud assertion that all great things are
silent. The age is commended for Watt's steam-engine,
Arkwright's spinning-jenny, and Whitfield's preaching, but
its policies and theories are alike belittled. The summaries
of the leading writers are interesting, some curious, and a
few absurd. On the threshold of the age Dryden is noted
as "a great poet born in the worst of times :" Addison as
"an instance of one formal man doing great things :"
Swift is pronounced "by far the greatest man of that time,
not unfeeling," who "carried sarcasm to an epic pitch :"
Pope, we are told, had "one of the finest heads ever known."
Sterne is handled with a tenderness that contrasts with the
death sentence pronounced on him by Thackeray, "much
is forgiven him because he loved much, . . . a good, simple
being after all." Johnson the "much enduring," is treated
as in the *Heroes* and the Essay. Hume, with "a far dull-
er kind of sense," is commended for "noble perseverance
and Stoic endurance of failure ; but his eye was not open
to faith," etc. On which follows a stupendous criticism
of Gibbon, whom Carlyle, returning to his earlier and
juster view, ended by admiring :

> With all his swagger and bombast, no man ever gave a more
> futile account of human things than he has done of the *Decline and
> Fall of the Roman Empire.*

The sketch of the Pre-Revolution period is slight, and
marked by a somewhat shallow reference to Rousseau. The
last lecture on the recent German writers is a mere *réchauffé*
of the Essays. Carlyle closes with the famous passage
from Richter, one of those which indicate the influence in
style as in thought of the German over the Scotch humourist.
"It is now the twelfth hour of the night, birds of darkness
are on the wing, the spectres uprear, the dead walk, the

living dream. Thou, Eternal Providence, wilt cause the day to dawn." The whole volume is a testimony to the speaker's power of speech, to his often unsurpassed penetration, and to the hopeless variance of the often rapidly shifting streams of his thought.

Detailed criticism of Carlyle's HISTORIES belongs to the sphere of separate disquisitions. Here it is only possible to take note of their general characteristics. His conception of what history should be is shared with Macaulay. Both writers protest against its being made a mere record of "court and camp," of royal intrigue and state rivalry, of pageants of procession, or chivalric encounters. Both find the sources of these outwardly obtrusive events in the underground current of national sentiment, the conditions of the civilisation from which they were evolved, the prosperity or misery of the masses of the people.

> The essence of history does not lie in laws, senate-houses, or battle-fields, but in the tide of thought and action—the world of existence that in gloom and brightness blossoms and fades apart from these.

But Carlyle differs from Macaulay in his passion for the concrete. The latter presents us with pictures to illustrate his political theory; the former leaves his pictures to speak for themselves. "Give him a fact," says Emerson, "he loaded you with thanks; a theory, with ridicule or even abuse." It has been said that with Carlyle History was philosophy teaching by examples. He himself defines it as "the essence of innumerable biographies." He individualises everything he meets; his dislike of abstractions is everywhere extreme. Thus, while other writers have expanded biography into history, Carlyle condenses history into biography. Even most biographies are too vague for him. He delights in Boswell: he glides over their generalisations to pick out some previously obscure record from Clarendon or Hume. Even in the *French Revolution*, where the author has mainly to deal with masses in tumult, he gives most prominence to their leaders. They march past us, labelled with strange names, in the foreground of the scene, on which is being enacted the death wrestle of old Feudalism and young Democracy. This book is unique among modern histories for a combination of force and insight only rivalled by the most incisive passages of the seventh book of Thucydides, of Tacitus, of Gibbon, and of Michelet.[1]

The *French Revolution* is open to the charge of being a comment and a prophecy rather than a narrative: the reader's knowledge of the main events of the period is too much assumed for the purpose of a school-book. Even Dryasdust will turn when trod on, and this book has been a happy hunting-field to aggressive antiquarians, to whom the mistake of a day in date, the omission or insertion of a letter in a name, is of more moment than the difference between vitalising or petrifying an era. The lumber merchants of history are the born foes of historians who, like Carlyle and Mr. Froude, have manifested their dramatic power of making the past present and the distant near. That the excess of this power is not always compatible with perfect impartiality may be admitted; for a poetic capacity is generally attended by heats of enthusiasm, and is liable to errors of detail; but without some share of it:

> Die Zeiten der Vergangenheit
> Sind uns ein Buch mit sieben Siegeln.

---

[1] *Vide* a comparison of Carlyle and Michelet in Dr. Oswald's interesting and suggestive little volume of criticism and selection, *Thomas Carlyle, ein Lebensbild und Goldkörner aus seinen Werken.*

Mere research, the unearthing and arrangement of what Sir Philip Sidney calls "old moth-eaten records," supplies material for the work of the historian proper; and, occasionally to good purpose, corrects it, but, as a rule, with too much flourish. Applying this minute criticism to the *French Revolution*, one reviewer has found that the author has given the wrong number to a regiment: another esteemed scholar has discovered that there are seven errors in the famous account of the flight to Varennes, to wit: the delay in the departure was due to Bouillé, not to the Queen ; she did not lose her way and so delay the start; Ste. Menehould is too big to be called a village; on the arrest, it was the Queen, not the King, who asked for hot water and eggs; the coach went rather faster than is stated; and, above all, *infandum!* it was not painted yellow, but green and black. This criticism does not in any degree detract from the value of one of the most vivid and substantially accurate narratives in the range of European literature. Carlyle's object was to convey the soul of the Revolution, not to register its upholstery. The annalist, be he Dryasdust or gossip, is, in legal phrase, "the devil" of the prose artist, whose work makes almost as great a demand on the imaginative faculty as that of the poet. Historiography is related to History as the Chronicles of Hollinshed and the Voyages of Hakluyt to the Plays of Shakespeare, plays which Marlborough confessed to have been the main source of his knowledge of English history. Some men are born philologists or antiquarians; but, as the former often fail to see the books because of the words, the latter cannot read the story for the dates. The mass of readers require precisely what has been contemptuously referred to as the "Romance of History," provided it leaves with them an accurate impression, as well as an in-

39

spiring interest.   Save in his over-hasty acceptance of the
French *blague* version of " The Sinking of the Vengeur,"
Carlyle has never laid himself open to the reproach of essential inaccuracy.   As far as possible for a man of genius,
he was a devotee of facts.   He is never a careless, though
occasionally an impetuous writer; his graver errors are
those of emotional misinterpretation.   It has been observed
that, while contemning Robespierre, he has extenuated the
guilt of Danton as one of the main authors of the September massacres, and, more generally, that " his quickness
and brilliancy made him impatient of systematic thought."
But his histories remain the best illuminations of fact in
our language.   The *French Revolution* is a series of flame-
pictures; every page is on fire; we read the whole as if
listening to successive volleys of artillery; nowhere has such
a motley mass been endowed with equal life.   This book
alone vindicates Lowell's panegyric: "the figures of most
historians seem like dolls stuffed with bran, whose whole
substance runs through any hole that criticism may tear in
them; but Carlyle's are so real that if you prick them they
bleed."

When Carlyle generalises, as in the introductions to his
Essays, he is apt to thrust his own views on his subject
and on his readers; but, unlike De Quincey, who had a
like love of excursus, he comes to the point before the
close.   The one claimed the privilege, assumed by Coleridge, of starting from no premises and arriving at no conclusion; the other, in his capacity as a critic, arrives at a
conclusion, though sometimes from questionable premises.
It is characteristic of his habit of concentrating, rather than
condensing, that Carlyle abandoned his design of a history of the Civil Wars for *Oliver Cromwell's Letters and
Speeches*.   The events of the period, whose issues the writer

has firmly grasped, are brought into prominence mainly as they elucidate the career of his hero; but the "elucidations" have been accepted, with a few reservations, as final. No single work has gone so far to reverse a traditional estimate. The old current conceptions of the Protector are refuted out of his own mouth; but it was left for his editor to restore life to the half-forgotten records, and sweep away the clouds that obscured their revelations of a great though rugged character. *Cromwell* has been generally accepted in Scotland as Carlyle's masterpiece—a judgment due to the fact of its being, among the author's mature works, the least apparently opposed to the theological views prevalent in the north of our island. In reality—though containing some of his finest descriptions and battle-pieces, conspicuously that of "Dunbar"—it is the least artistic of his achievements, being overladen with detail and superabounding in extract. A good critic[1] has said that it was a labour of love, like Spedding's *Bacon;* but that the correspondence, lavishly reproduced in both works, has "some of the defects of lovers' letters to those to whom they are not addressed." Carlyle has established that Oliver was not a hypocrite, "not a man of falsehood, but a man of truth:" he has thrown doubts on his being a fanatic; but he has left it open to M. Guizot to establish that his later rule was a practical despotism.

In *Friedrich II.* he undertook a yet greater task; and his work stretching over a wide arena, is, of necessity, more of a history, less of a biography, than any of his others. In constructing and composing it he was oppressed not only by the magnitude and complexity of his theme, but, for the first time, by hesitancies as to his choice of a

---

[1] In *St. James Gazette*, February 11th, 1881.

hero. He himself confessed, "I never was admitted much to
Friedrich's confidence, and I never cared very much about
him." Yet he determined, almost of malice prepense, to
exalt the narrow though vivid Prussian as "the last of the
kings, the one genuine figure in the eighteenth century,"
and though failing to prove his case, he has, like a loyal
lawyer, made the best of his brief. The book embodies
and conveys the most brilliant and the most readable account of a great part of the century, and nothing he has
written bears such ample testimony to the writer's pictorial
genius. It is sometimes garrulous with the fluency of an
old man eloquent; parts of the third volume, with its dif-
fuse extracts from the king's survey of his realm, is hard
if not weary reading; but the rest is a masterpiece of historic restoration. The introductory portion, leading us
through one of the most tangled woods of genealogy and
political adjustment, is relieved from tedium by the procession of the half-forgotten host of German worthies—St.
Adalbert and his mission; old Barbarossa; Leopold's mystery; Conrad and St. Elizabeth; Ptolemy Alphonso; Otto
with the arrow; Margaret with the mouth; Sigismund
supra grammaticam; Augustus the physically strong; Albert Achilles and Albert Alcibiades; Anne of Cleves; Mr.
John Kepler—who move on the pages, more brightly
"pictured" than those of Livy, like marionettes inspired
with life. In the main body of the book the men and
women of the Prussian court are brought before us in fuller light and shade. Friedrich himself, at Sans Souci, with
his cocked-hat, walking-stick, and wonderful gray eyes;
Sophia Charlotte's grace, wit, and music; Wilhelmina and
her book; the old Hyperborean; the black artists Secken-
dorf and Grumkow; George I. and his blue-beard chamber; the little drummer; the Old Dessauer; the cabinet

Venus; Grävenitz Hecate; Algarotti; Goetz in his tower; the tragedy of Katte; the immeasurable comedy of Maupertuis, the flattener of the earth, and Voltaire—all these and a hundred more are summoned by a wizard's wand from the land of shadows, to march by the central figures of these volumes; to dance, flutter, love, hate, intrigue, and die before our eyes. It is the largest and most varied show-box in all history; a prelude to a series of battle-pieces — Rossbach, Leuthen, Molwitz, Zorndorf — nowhere else, save in the author's own pages, approached in prose, and rarely rivalled out of Homer's verse.

Carlyle's style, in the chiaro-oscuro of which his Histories and three-fourths of his Essays are set, has naturally provoked much criticism and some objurgation. M. Taine says it is "exaggerated and demoniacal." Hallam[1] could not read the *French Revolution* because of its "detestable" style, and Wordsworth, whose own prose was perfectly limpid, is reported to have said, "No Scotchman can write English. C—— is a pest to the language." Carlyle's style is not that of Addison, of Berkeley, or of Helps; its peculiarities are due to the eccentricity of an always eccentric being; but it is neither affected nor deliberately imitated. It has been plausibly asserted that his earlier manner of writing, as in *Schiller*, under the influence of Jeffrey, was not in his natural voice. "They forget," he said, referring to his critics, "that the style is the skin of the writer, not a coat: and the public is an old woman." Erratic, metaphorical, elliptical to excess, and therefore a dangerous model, "the mature oaken Carlylese style," with its freaks, "nodosities, and angularities," is as

---

[1] Carlyle with equal unfairness disparaged Hallam's *Literature of Europe* (containing among other fine criticisms the splendid summary of "Lear") as a valley of dry bones.

set and engrained in his nature as the *Birthmark* in Hawthorne's romance. To recast a chapter of the *Revolution*
in the form of a chapter of Macaulay would be like re-
writing Tacitus in the form of Cicero, or Browning in the
form of Pope. Carlyle is seldom obscure, the energy of
his manner is part of his matter; its abruptness corre-
sponds to the abruptness of his thought, which proceeds
often as it were by a series of electric shocks, that threaten
to break through the formal restraints of an ordinary sentence. He writes like one who must, under the spell of
his own winged words; at all hazards, determined to convey his meaning; willing, like Montaigne, to "despise no
phrase of those that run in the streets," to speak in strange
tongues, and even to coin new words for the expression of a
new emotion. It is his fashion to care as little for rounded phrase as for logical argument: and he rather con-
vinces and persuades by calling up a succession of feelings
than by a train of reasoning. He repeats himself like a
preacher, instead of condensing like an essayist. The American Thoreau writes in the course of an incisive survey:

Carlyle's . . . mastery over the language is unrivalled; it is with
him a keen, resistless weapon; his power of words is endless. All
nature, human and external, is ransacked to serve and run his er-
rands. The bright cutlery, after all the dross of Birmingham has
been thrown aside, is his style. . . . He has broken the ice, and the tor-
rent streams forth. He drives six-in-hand over ruts and streams and
never upsets. . . . With wonderful art he grinds into paint for his picture all his moods and experiences, and crashes his way through shoals
of dilettante opinions. It is not in man to determine what his style
shall be, if it is to be his own.

But though a rugged, Carlyle was the reverse of a careless or ready writer. He weighed every sentence: if in all

his works, from *Sartor* to the *Reminiscences*, you pencil-mark the most suggestive passages you disfigure the whole book. His opinions will continue to be tossed to and fro; but as an artist he continually grows. He was, let us grant, though a powerful, a one-sided historian, a twisted though in some aspects a great moralist; but he was, in every sense, a mighty painter, now dipping his pencil "in the hues of earthquake and eclipse," now etching his scenes with the tender touch of a Millet.

Emerson, in one of his early letters to Carlyle, wrote, "Nothing seems hid from those wonderful eyes of yours; those devouring eyes; those thirsty eyes; those portrait-eating, portrait-painting eyes of thine." Men of genius, whether expressing themselves in prose or verse, on canvas or in harmony, are, save when smitten, like Beethoven, by some malignity of Nature, endowed with keener physical senses than other men. They actually, not metaphorically, see more and hear more than their fellows. Carlyle's super-sensitive ear was to him, through life, mainly a torment; but the intensity of his vision was that of a born artist, and to it we owe the finest descriptive passages, if we except those of Mr. Ruskin, in English prose. None of our poets, from Chaucer and Dunbar to Burns and Tennyson, have been more alive to the influences of external nature. His early letters abound in passages like the following, on the view from Arthur's Seat:

The blue, majestic, everlasting ocean, with the Fife hills swelling gradually into the Grampians behind; rough crags and rude preci-pices at our feet (where not a hillock rears its head unsung) with Edinburgh at their base clustering proudly over her rugged founda-tions and covering with a vapoury mantle the jagged black masses of stonework that stretch far and wide, and show like a city of Faery-land. . . . I saw it all last evening when the sun was going down, and the moon's fine crescent, like a pretty silver creature as it is, was riding quietly above me.

Compare with this the picture, in a letter to Sterling, of Middlebie burn, "leaping into its caldron, singing a song better than Pasta's;" or that of the Scaur Water, that may be compared with Tennyson's verses in the valley of Cauterets; or the sketches of the Flemish cities in the tour of 1842, with the photograph of the lace-girl, recalling Sterne at his purest; or the account of the "atmosphere like silk" over the moor, with the phrase, "it was as if Pan slept;" or the few lines written at Thurso, where "the sea is always one's friend;" or the later memories of Mentone, old and new, in the *Reminiscences* (vol. ii. pp. 335–340).

The most striking of those descriptions are, however, those in which the interests of some thrilling event or crisis of human life or history steal upon the scene, and give it a further meaning, as in the dim streak of dawn rising over St. Abbs Head on the morning of Dunbar, or in the following famous apostrophe:

O evening sun of July, how at this hour thy beams fall slant on reapers amid peaceful, woody fields; on old women spinning in cottages; on ships far out in the silent main; on balls and at the Orangerie at Versailles, where high-rouged dames of the palace are even now dancing with double-jacketed Hussar officers; and also on this roaring Hell-porch of an Hotel-du-Ville.

Carlyle is, here and there, led astray by the love of contrast; but not even Heinrich Heine has employed antithesis with more effect than in the familiar passage on the sleeping city in *Sartor*, beginning, "Ach mein Lieber . . . it is a true sublimity to dwell here," and ending, "But I, mein Werther, sit above it all. I am alone with the stars."

His thought, seldom quite original, is often a resuscitation or survival, and owes much of its celebrity to its splendid brocade. *Sartor Resartus* itself escaped the failure that was at first threatened by its eccentricity partly from its noble passion, partly because of the truth of the "clothes philosophy," applied to literature as to life.

His descriptions, too often caricatures, of men are equally vivid. They set the whole great mass of *Friedrich* in a glow; they lighten the tedium of *Cromwell's* lumbering despatches; they give a heart of fire to the *French Revolution*. Dickens's *Tale of Two Cities* attempts and fulfils on a smaller what Carlyle achieved on a greater scale. The historian makes us sympathise with the real actors, even more than the novelist does with the imaginary characters on the same stage. From the account of the dying Louis XV. to the "whiff of grape-shot" which closed the last scene of the great drama, there is not a dull page. Théroigne de Méricourt, Marat, Danton, Camille Desmoulins, Mirabeau, Robespierre, Talleyrand, Louis the Simple, above all Marie Antoinette—for whom Carlyle has an affection akin to that of Mirabeau—so kindle and colour the scene that we cannot pause to feel weary of the phrases with which they are labelled. The author's letters show the same power of baptising, which he used often to unfair excess. We can no more forget Count d'Orsay as the "Phœbus Apollo of Dandyism," Daniel Webster's "brows like cliffs and huge black eyes," or Wordsworth "munching raisins" and recognising no poet but himself, or Maurice "attacked by a paroxysm of mental cramp," than we can dismiss from our memories "The Glass Coachman" or "The Tobacco Parliament."

Carlyle quotes a saying of Richter, that Luther's words were like blows; he himself compares those of Burns to cannon-balls; much of his own writing is a fusillade. All three were vehement in abuse of things and persons they did not like; abuse that might seem reckless, if not sometimes coarse, were it not redeemed, as the rogueries of Falstaff are, by strains of humour. The most Protean quality of Carlyle's genius is his humour: now lighting up the crevices of some quaint fancy, now shining over his serious thought like sunshine over the sea, it is at its best as finely quaint as that of Cervantes, more humane than Swift's. There is in it, as in all the highest humour, a sense of apparent contrast, even of contradiction, in life, of matter for laughter in sorrow and tears in joy. He seems to check himself, and as if afraid of wearing his heart in his sleeve, throws in absurd illustrations of serious propositions, partly to show their universal range, partly in obedience to an instinct of reserve, to escape the reproach of sermonising and to cut the story short. Carlyle's grotesque is, a mode of his golden silence, a sort of Socratic irony, in the indulgence of which he laughs at his readers and at himself. It appears now in the form of transparent satire, ridicule of his own and other ages, now in droll reference or mock heroic detail, in an odd conception, a character sketch, an event in parody, in an antithesis or simile— sometimes it lurks in a word, and again in a sentence. In direct pathos—the other side of humour—he is equally effective. His denunciations of sentiment remind us of Plato attacking the poets, for he is at heart the most emotional of writers, the greatest of the prose poets of England; and his dramatic sympathy extends alike to the actors in real events and to his ideal creations. Few more pathetic passages occur in literature than his "stories of the deaths of kings." The following among the less known of his eloquent passages is an apotheosis of their burials:

In this manner did the men of the Eastern Counties take up the
slain body of their Edmund, where it lay cast forth in the village of
Hoxne; seek out the severed head and reverently reunite the same.
They embalmed him with myrrh and sweet spices, with love, pity, and
all high and awful thoughts; consecrating him with a very storm of
melodious, adoring admiration, and sun-dried showers of tears; joy-
fully, yet with awe (as all deep joy has something of the awful in it),
commemorating his noble deeds and godlike walk and conversation
while on Earth. Till, at length, the very Pope and Cardinals at
Rome were forced to hear of it; and they, summing up as correctly
as they well could, with *Advocatus Diaboli* pleadings and other forms
of process, the general verdict of mankind, declared that he had in
very fact led a hero's life in this world; and, being now gone, was
gone, as they conceived, to God above and reaping his reward there.
Such, they said, was the best judgment they could form of the case,
and truly not a bad judgment.

Carlyle's reverence for the past makes him even more
apt to be touched by its sorrows than amused by its follies.
With a sense of brotherhood he holds out hands to all that
were weary; he feels even for the pedlars climbing the
Hohenzollern valley, and pities the solitude of soul on the
frozen Schreckhorn of power, whether in a dictator of
Paraguay or in a Prussian prince. He leads us to the
death-chamber of Louis XV., of Mirabeau, of Cromwell, of
Sterling, his own lost friend; and we feel with him in
the presence of a solemnising mystery. Constantly, amid
the din of arms or words, and the sarcasms by which he
satirises and contemns old follies and idle strifes, a gentler feeling wells up in his pages like the sound of the
Angelus. Such pauses of pathos are the records of real
or fanciful situations, as of Teufelsdröckh "left alone with
the night" when Blumine and Herr Towgood ride down
the valley; of Oliver recalling the old days of St. Ives;
of the Electress Louisa bidding adieu to her Elector:

At the moment of her death, it is said, when speech had fled, he felt from her hand, which lay in his, three slight pressures—farewell thrice mutely spoken in that manner, not easily to forget in this world.

There is nothing more pathetic in the range of his works, if in that of our literature, than the account of the relations of father and son in the domestic history of the Prussian Court, from the first estrangement between them —the young Friedrich in his prison at Cüstrin, the old Friedrich gliding about seeking shelter from ghosts, mourning for Absalom—to the reconciliation, the end, and the after-thoughts:

The last breath of Friedrich Wilhelm having fled, Friedrich hurried to a private room ; sat there all in tears; looking back through the gulfs of the Past, upon such a Father now rapt away forever. Sad all and soft in the moonlight of memory—the lost Loved One all in the right as we now see, we all in the wrong! This, it appears, was the Son's fixed opinion. Seven years hence here is how Friedrich concludes the *History* of his Father, written with a loyal admiration throughout: " We have left under silence the domestic chagrins of this great Prince ; readers must have some indulgence for the faults of the children, in consideration of the virtues of such a Father." All in tears he sits at present, meditating these sad things. In a little while the Old Dessauer, about to leave for Dessau, ventures in to the Crown Prince, Crown Prince no longer ; " embraces his knees," offers weeping his condolence, his congratulation ; hopes withal that his sons and he will be continued in their old posts, and that he the Old Dessauer " will have the same authority as in the late reign." Friedrich's eyes, at this last clause, flash out tearless, strangely Olympian. " In your posts I have no thought of making change ; in your posts yes ; and as to authority I know of none there can be but what resides in the king that is sovereign," which, as it were, struck the breath out of the Old Dessauer ; and sent him home with a painful miscellany of feelings, astonishment not wanting among them. At an after-hour the same night Friedrich went to Berlin, met by acclamation enough. He slept there not without tumult of dreams, one may fancy ; and on awakening next morning the first sound he beard was that of the regiment glasenap under his windows, swearing fealty to the new King.   He sprang out of bed in a tempest of emotion; bustled distractedly to and fro, wildly weeping.   Pöllnitz, who came into the anteroom, found him in this state, "half-dressed, with dishevelled hair, in tears, and as if beside himself."   "These huzzahings only tell me what I have lost," said the new King.   "He was in great suffering," suggested Pöllnitz; "he is now at rest."   True, he suffered ; but he was here with us; and now—

Carlyle has said of Dante's *Francesca*, " that it is a thing woven as of rainbows on a ground of eternal black."   The phrase, well applied to the *Inferno*, is a perhaps half-conscious verdict on his own tenderness as exhibited in his life and in his works.

9

CHAPTER IX.

CARLYLE'S POLITICAL PHILOSOPHY.

PERHAPS the profoundest of Robert Browning's critics, in the opening sentence of his work,[1] quotes a saying of Hegel's, "A great man condemns the world to the task of explaining him;" adding, "The condemnation is a double one, and it generally falls heaviest on the great man himself who has to submit to explanation." "Cousin," the graceful Eclectic is reported to have said to the great Philosopher, "Will you oblige me by stating the results of your teaching in a few sentences?" and to have received the reply, "It is not easy, especially in French."

The retort applies, with severity, to those who attempt to systematise Carlyle; for he himself was, as we have seen, intolerant of system. His mathematical attainment and his antipathy to logical methods, beyond the lines of square and circle, his love of concise fact and his often sweeping assertions are characteristic of the same contradictions in his nature as his almost tyrannical premises and his practically tender-hearted conclusions. A hard thinker, he was never a close reasoner; in all that relates to human

---

[1] *Browning as a Philosophical and Religious Teacher*, by Professor Henry Jones, of St. Andrews.

affairs he relies on nobility of feeling rather than on con-tinuity of thought. Claiming the full latitude of the prophet to warn, exhort, even to command, he declines either to preach or to accept the rubric of the partisan or of the priest.

In praise of German literature, he remarks, "One of its chief qualities is that it has no particular theory at all on the front of it;" and of its leaders, "I can only speak of the revelations these men have made to me. As to their doctrines, there is nothing definite or precise to be said;" yet he asserts that Goethe, Richter, and the rest, took him "out of the blackness and darkness of death." This is nearly the feeling that his disciples of forty years ago en-tertained towards himself; but their discipleship has rarely lasted through life. They came to his writings, inspired by the youthful enthusiasm that carries with it a vein of credulity, intoxicated by their fervour as by new wine or mountain air, and found in them the key of the perennial riddle and the solution of the insoluble mystery. But in later years the curtain to many of them became the picture.

When Carlyle was first recognised in London as a rising author, curiosity was rife as to his "opinions;" was he a Chartist at heart or an Absolutist, a Calvinist like Knox, a Deist like Hume, a Feudalist with Scott, or a Democrat with Burns—inquisitions mostly vain. He had come from the Scotch moors and his German studies, a strange ele-ment, into the midst of an almost foreign society, not so much to promulgate a new set of opinions as to infuse a new life into those already existing. He claimed to have a "mission," but it was less to controvert any form of creed than to denounce the insufficiency of shallow modes of belief. He raised the tone of literature by referring to

higher standards than these currently accepted ; he tried
to elevate men's minds to the contemplation of something
better than themselves, and impress upon them the vacuity
of lip-services ; he insisted that the matter of most consequence was the grip with which they held their convictions
and their willingness to sacrifice the interests on which
they could lay their hands in loyalty to some nobler faith.
He taught that beliefs by hearsay are not only barren but
obstructive ; that it is only

When half-gods go, the gods arrive.

But his manner of reading these important lessons admitted the retort that he himself was content rather to
dwell on what is *not* than to discover what *is* true. "Belief," he reiterates, is the cure for all the worst of human
ills ; but belief in what or in whom ? In "the eternities
and immensities," as an answer, requires definition. It
means that we are not entitled to regard ourselves as the
centres of the universe ; that we are but atoms of space
and time, with relations infinite beyond our personalities ;
that the first step to a real recognition of our duties is the
sense of our inferiority to those above us, our realisation
of the continuity of history and life, our faith and acquiescence in some universal law. This truth, often set forth

By saint, by sage, by preacher, and by poet,

no one has enforced with such eloquence as Carlyle ; but
though he founded a dynasty of ideas, they are comparatively few ; like a group of strolling players, each with a
well-filled wardrobe, and ready for many parts.

The difficulty of defining Carlyle results not merely from

his frequent golden nebulosity, but from his love of contradicting even himself. Dr. Johnson confessed to Boswell that when arguing in his dreams he was often worsted and took credit for the resignation with which he bore these defeats, forgetting that the victor and the vanquished were one and the same. Similarly his successor took liberties with himself which he would allow to no one else, and in doing so he has taken liberties with his reader. His praise and blame of the profession of letters, as the highest priesthood and the meanest trade; his early exaltation of "the writers of newspapers, pamphlets, books," as "the real effective working church of a modern country;" and his later expressed contempt for journalism as "mean and demoralising"—"we must destroy the faith in newspapers;" his alternate faith and unfaith in Individualism; the teaching of the *Characteristics* and the *Signs of the Times* that all healthy genius is unconscious, and the censure of Sir Walter Scott for troubling himself too little with mysteries; his commendation of "the strong warrior" for writing no books, and his taking sides with the mediæval monks against the king—there is no reconciliation of such contradictories. They are the expression of diverse moods and emphatically of different stages of mental progress, the later, as a rule, more negative than the earlier.

This change is most marked in the sphere of politics. At the close of his student days Carlyle was to all intents a Radical, and believed in Democracy;[1] he saw hungry masses around him, and, justly attributing some of their suffering to misgovernment, vented his sympathetic zeal for the oppressed in denunciation of the oppressors. He

[1] Passage quoted (Chap. II.) about the Glasgow Radical rising in 1819.

began not only by sympathising with the people, but by
believing in their capacity to manage best their own affairs: a belief that steadily waned as he grew older until
he denied to them even the right to choose their rulers.
As late, however, as 1830, he argued against Irving's conservatism in terms recalled in the *Reminiscences.* " He
objected clearly to my Reform Bill notions, found Democracy a thing forbidden, leading even to outer darkness: I
a thing inevitable and obliged to lead whithersoever it
could." During the same period he clenched his theory
by taking a definite side in the controversy of the age.
"This," he writes to Macvey Napier—"this is the day
when the lords are to reject the Reform Bill. The poor
lords can only accelerate (by perhaps a century) their own
otherwise inevitable enough abolition."

The political part of *Sartor Resartus*, shadowing forth
some scheme of well-organised socialism, yet anticipates,
especially in the chapter on *Organic Filaments*, the writer's
later strain of belief in dukes, earls, and marshals of men;
but this work, religious, ethical, and idyllic, contains mere
vague suggestions in the sphere of practical life. About
this time Carlyle writes of liberty: "What art thou to
the valiant and the brave when thou art thus to the weak
and timid, dearer than life, stronger than death, higher
than purest love?" and agrees with the verdict, "The slow
poison of despotism is worse than the convulsive struggles
of anarchy." But he soon passed from the mood represented by Emily Brontë to that of the famous apostrophe
of Madame Roland. He proclaimed that liberty to do as
we like is a fatal license, that the only true liberty is that
of doing what is right, which he interprets living under
the laws enacted by the wise. In 1832 he writes to his
wife, " Tell Mrs. Jeffrey that I am that monster made up

of all the Whigs hate—a radical and an absolutist." In
the result, the Absolutist, in a spirit made after Plato's
conception of various elements, devoured the Radical.
The leading counsel against the aristocracy changed his
brief and became chief advocate on their side, declaring
" we must recognise the hereditary principle if there is to
be any fixity in things." As early as 1835, he writes to
Emerson :

I believe literature to be as good as dead . . . and nothing but
hungry Revolt and Radicalism appointed us for perhaps three generations. . . . I suffer also terribly from the solitary existence I have all
along had; it is becoming a kind of passion with me to feel myself
among my brothers. And then How? Alas, I care not a doit for
Radicalism, nay, I feel it to be a wretched necessity unfit for me ;
Conservatism being not unfit only but false for me: yet these two
are the grand categories under which all English spiritual activity,
that so much as thinks remuneration possible, must range itself.

And somewhat later :

People accuse me, not of being an incendiary Sansculotte, but of
being a Tory, thank Heaven !

Some one has written with a big brush, " He who is not
a radical in his youth is a knave, he who is not a conservative in his age is a fool." The rough, if not rude, gener-
alisation has been plausibly supported by the changes in
the mental careers of Burke, Coleridge, Southey, and
Wordsworth. But Carlyle was " a spirit of another sort,"
of more mixed yarn ; and, as there is a vein of conservatism
in his early Radicalism, so there is, as also in the cases of
Landor and even of Goethe, still a revolutionary streak in
his later Conservatism. Consequently, in his instance,
there is a plea in favour of the prepossession (especially

strong in Scotland) which leads the political or religious party that a distinguished man has left still to persist in claiming him; while that which he has joined accepts him, if at all, with distrust.   Scotch Liberals will not give up Carlyle, one of his biographers keenly asseverating that he was to the last "a democrat at heart;" while the representative organ of northern Conservatism on the same ground continues to assail him—"mit der Dummheit kämpfen Götter selbst vergebens."   On all questions directly bearing on the physical welfare of the masses of the people, his speech and action remained consistent with his declaration that he had "never heard an argument for the corn laws which might not make angels weep."   From first to last, he was an advocate of Free Trade—though under the constant protest that the greatness of a nation depended in a very minor degree on the abundance of its possessions— and of free, unsectarian, and compulsory Education; while, in theology, though remote from either, he was more tolerant of the dogmatic narrowness of the Low Church of the lower, than of the Ritualism of the upper, classes.   His unwavering interest in the poor and his belief that legislation should keep them in constant view, was in accord with the spirit of Bentham's rubric; but Carlyle, rightly or wrongly, came to regard the bulk of men as children requiring not only help and guidance but control.

On the question of "the Suffrage" he completely revolved.   It appears, from the testimony of Mr. Froude, that the result of the Reform Bill of 1832 disappointed him in merely shifting the power from the owners of land to the owners of shops, and left the handicraftsmen and his own peasant class no better off.   Before a further extension became a point of practical politics he had arrived at the conviction that the ascertainment of truth and the election of the fittest did not lie with majorities. These sentences of 1835 represent a transition stage:

Conservatism I cannot attempt to conserve, believing it to be a portentous embodied sham. . . . Whether the Tories stay out or in, it will be all for the advance of Radicalism, which means revolt, dissolution, and confusion, and a darkness which no man can see through.

No one had less faith in the pæan chaunted by Macaulay and others on the progress of the nation or of the race, a progress which, without faith in great men, was to him inevitably downward; no one protested with equal emphasis against the levelling doctrines of the French Revolution. It has been observed that Carlyle's *Chartism* was " his first practical step in politics;" it is more true to say that it first embodied, with more than his usual precision, the convictions he had for some time held of the dangers of our social system; with an indication of some of the means to ward them off, based on the realisation of the interdependence of all classes in the State. This book is remarkable as containing his last, very partial, concessions to the democratic creed, the last in which he is willing to regard a wide suffrage as a possible, though by no means the best, expedient. Subsequently, in *Past and Present* and the *Latter-Day Pamphlets*, he came to hold " that with every extension of the Franchise those whom the voters would elect would be steadily inferior and more unfit." Every stage in his political progress is marked by a growing distrust in the judgment of the multitude, a distrust set forth, with every variety of metaphor, in such sentences as the following:

There is a divine message or eternal regulation of the Universe.

9*   O

How find it? All the world answers me, "Count heads, ask Universal Suffrage by the ballot-box and that will tell!" From Adam's time till now the Universe was wont to be of a somewhat abstruse nature, partially disclosing itself to the wise and noble-minded alone, whose number was not the majority. Of what use towards the general result of finding out what it is wise to do, can the fools be? . . . If of ten men nine are recognisable as fools, which is a common calculation, how in the name of wonder will you ever get a ballot-box to grind you out a wisdom from the votes of these ten men? . . . Only by reducing to zero nine of these votes can wisdom ever issue from your ten. The mass of men consulted at the hustings upon any high matter whatsoever, is as ugly an exhibition of human stupidity as this world sees. . . . If the question be asked and the answer given, I will generally consider in any case of importance that the said answer is likely to be wrong, and that I have to go and do the reverse of the same . . . for how should I follow a multitude to do evil. Cease to brag to me of America and its model institutions. . . . On this side of the Atlantic or on that, Democracy is forever impossible! The Universe is a monarchy and a hierarchy, the noble in the high places, the ignoble in the low; this is in all times and in all places the Almighty Maker's law. Democracy, take it where you will, is found a regulated method of rebellion, it abrogates the old arrangement of things, and leaves zero and vacuity. It is the consummation of no-government and *laissez faire.*

Alongside of this train of thought there runs a constant protest against the spirit of revolt. In *Sartor* we find: "Whoso cannot obey cannot be free, still less bear rule; he that is the inferior of nothing can be the superior of nothing;" and in *Chartism:*

Men who rebel and urge the lower classes to rebel ought to have other than formulas to go upon . . . those to whom millions of suffering fellow-creatures are "masses," mere explosive masses for blowing down Bastiles with, for voting at hustings for us — such men are of the questionable species. . . . Obedience . . . is the primary duty of man. . . . Of all "rights of men" this right of the ignorant

to be guided by the wiser, gently or forcibly—is the indisputablest. . . .
Cannot one discern, across all democratic turbulence, clattering of
ballot-boxes, and infinite sorrowful jangle, that this is at bottom the
wish and prayer of all human hearts everywhere, "Give me a leader."

The last sentence indicates the transition from the merely
negative aspect of Carlyle's political philosophy to the positive, which is his HERO-WORSHIP, based on the excessive
admiration for individual greatness—an admiration common to almost all imaginative writers, whether in prose or
verse; on his notions of order and fealty, and on a reverence for the past, which is also a common property of
poets.   Antiquity, then Feudalism, according to his view,
had their chiefs, captains, kings, and flourished or not as it
followed them well or ill.   Democracy, the new and dangerous force of this age, must be represented and then de-
nominated by great men raised to independence over the
arbitrary will of a multitude, to be trusted and obeyed and
followed if need be to death.

Your noblest men at the summit of affairs, is the ideal world of
poets. . . . Other aim in this earth we have none.   That we all reverence "great men" is to me the living rock amid all rushings down
whatsoever.   All that democracy ever meant lies there, the attainment
of a truer Aristocracy or Government of the Best.   Make search for
the Able man.   How to get him is the question of questions.

It is precisely the question to which Carlyle never gives,
and hardly attempts a reply; and his failure to answer inval-
idates the larger half of his politics.   Plato has at least
detailed a scheme for eliminating his philosopher guardians,
though it somewhat pedantically suggests a series of Chinese
examinations: his political, though probably unconscious
disciple has only a few negative tests.   The warrior or

sage who is to rule is *not* to be chosen by the majority, especially in our era, when they would choose the Orators who seduce and "traduce the State;" nor are we ever told that the election is to rest with either Under or Upper House: the practical conclusion is that when we find a man of great force of character, whether representing our own opinions or the reverse, we should take him on trust. This brings us to the central maxim of Carlyle's political philosophy, to which we must, even in our space, give some consideration, as its true meaning has been the theme of so much dispute.

It is a misfortune of original thought that it is hardly ever put in practice by the original thinker. When his rank as a teacher is recognised, his words have already lost half their value by repetition. His manner is aped by those who find an easy path to notoriety in imitation; the belief he held near his heart is worn as a creed like a badge; the truth he promulgated is distorted in a room of mirrors, half of it is a truism, the other half a falsism. That which begun as a denunciation of tea-table morality, is itself the tea-table morality of the next generation: an outcry against cant may become the quintessence of cant; a revolt from tyranny the basis of a new tyranny; the condemnation of sects the foundation of a new sect; the proclamation of peace a bone of contention. There is an ambiguity in most general maxims and a seed of error, which assumes preponderance over the truth when the interpreters of the maxim are men easily led by formulæ. Nowhere is this degeneracy more strikingly manifested than in the history of some of the maxims which Carlyle either first promulgated or enforced by his adoption. When he said, or quoted, "Silence is better than speech," he meant to inculcate patience and reserve. Always think before you speak: rather lose fluency than waste words: never speak for the sake of speaking. It is the best advice, but they who need it most are the last to take it; those who speak and write not because they have something to say, but because they wish to say or must say something, will continue to write and speak as long as they can spell or articulate. Thoughtful men are apt to misapply the advice, and betray their trust when they sit still and leave the "war of words to those who like it." When Carlyle condemned self-consciousness, a constant introspection and comparison of self with others, he theoretically struck at the root of the morbid moods of himself and other mental analysts; he had no intention to over-exalt mere muscularity or to deify athletic sports. It were easy to multiply instances of truths clearly conceived at first and parodied in their promulgation; but when we have the distinct authority of the discoverer himself for their correct interpretation, we can at once appeal to it. A yet graver, not uncommon, source of error arises when a great writer misapplies the maxims of his own philosophy, or states them in such a manner that they are sure to be misapplied.

Mr. Carlyle has laid down the doctrine that MIGHT IS RIGHT at various times and in such various forms, with and without modification or caveat, that the real meaning can only be ascertained from his own application of it. He has made clear, what goes without saying, that by "might" he does not intend mere physical strength.

Of conquest we may say that it never yet went by brute force; conquest of that kind does not endure. The strong man, what is he? The wise man. His muscles and bones are not stronger than ours; but his soul is stronger, clearer, nobler. . . . Late in man's history, yet clearly at length, it becomes manifest to the dullest that mind is stronger than matter, that not brute Force, but only Persuasion and Faith, is the king of this world. . . . Intellect has to govern this world and will do it.

There are sentences which indicate that he means something more than even mental force; as in a letter to Mr. Lecky, quoted by Mr. Froude (vol. iv. p. 288), "Right is the eternal symbol of Might;" and again in *Chartism*, "Might and right do differ frightfully from hour to hour; but give them centuries to try it, and they are found to be identical. The strong thing is the just thing. In kings we have either a divine right or a diabolic wrong." But, on the other hand, we read in *Past and Present :*

Savage fighting Heptarchies: their fighting is an ascertainment who has the right to rule over them.

And again :

Clear undeniable right, clear undeniable might: *either* of these, once ascertained, puts an end to battle.

And elsewhere :

Rights men have none save to be governed justly. . . . Rights I will permit thee to call everywhere correctly articulated mights. . . . All goes by wager of battle in this world, and it is, well understood, the measure of all worth. . . . By right divine the strong and capable govern the weak and foolish. . . . Strength we may say is Justice itself.

It is not left for us to balance those somewhat indefinite definitions. Carlyle has himself in his Histories illustrated and enforced his own interpretations of the summary views of his political treatises. There he has demonstrated that his doctrine, "Might is Right," is no mere unguarded expression of the truism that moral might is right. In his hands it implies that virtue is in all cases a property of strength, that strength is everywhere a property of virtue; that power of whatever sort having any considerable endurance, carries with it the seal and signal of its claim to respect, that whatever has established itself has, in the very act, established its right to be established. He is never careful enough to keep before his readers what he must himself have dimly perceived, that victory *by right* belongs not to the force of will alone, apart from clear and just conceptions of worthy ends. Even in its crude form, the maxim errs not so much in what it openly asserts as in what it implicitly denies. Aristotle (the first among ancients to *question* the institution of slavery, as Carlyle has been one of the last of moderns to defend it) more guardedly admits that strength is in itself *a good*—καὶ ἔστιν ἀεὶ τὸ κρατοῦν ἐν ὑπεροχῇ ἀγαθοῦ τινος—but leaves it to be maintained that there are forms of good which do not show themselves in excess of strength. Several of Carlyle's conclusions and verdicts seem to show that he only acknowledges those types of excellence that have already manifested themselves as powers; and this doctrine (which, if adopted in earlier ages, would practically have left possession with physical strength), colours all his History and much of his Biography. Energy of any sort compels his homage. Himself a Titan, he shakes hands with all Titans, Gothic gods, Knox, Columbus, the fuliginous Mirabeau, burly Danton dying with "no weakness" on his lips. The fulness of his charity is for the errors of Mohammed, Cromwell, Burns, Napoleon I. — whose mere belief in his own star he calls sincerity — the atrocious Francia, the Norman kings, the Jacobins, Brandenburg des-

pots; the fulness of his contempt for the conscientious in-
decision of Necker, the Girondists, the Moderates of our
own Commonwealth. He condones all that ordinary judgments regard as the tyranny of conquest, and has for the
conquered only a *væ victis*. In this spirit he writes:

> M. Thierry celebrates with considerable pathos the fate of the
> Saxons; the fate of the Welsh, too, moves him; of the Celts gen-
> erally, whom a fiercer race swept before them into the mountains,
> whither they were not worth following. What can we say, but that
> the cause which pleased the gods had in the end to please Cato also.

When all is said, Carlyle's inconsistent optimism throws
no more light than others have done on the apparent re-
lapses of history, as the overthrow of Greek civilisation,
the long night of the Dark Ages, the spread of the Russian
power during the last century, or of continental militaryism
in the present. In applying the tests of success or failure
we must bear in mind that success is from its very nature
conspicuous. We only know that brave men have failed
when they have had a "sacred bard." The good that is
lost is, *ipso facto*, forgotten. We can rarely tell of greatness unrecognised, for the very fact of our being able to
tell of it would imply a former recognition. The might
of evil walks in darkness: we remember the martyrs who,
by their deaths, ultimately drove the Inquisition from England; not those whose courage quailed. "It was their
fate," as a recent writer remarks, "that was the tragedy."
Reading Carlyle's maxim between the lines of his chapter
on the Reformation, and noting that the Inquisition triumphed in Spain, while in Austria, Bavaria, and Bohemia
the new truths were stifled by stratagem or by force; that
the massacre of St. Bartholomew was successful; and that
the revocation of the Edict of Nantes killed the France of

Henry IV., we see its limitations even in the long perspective of the past.[1] Let us, however, grant that in the ultimate issue the Platonic creed, "Justice is stronger than injustice," holds good. It is when Carlyle turns to politics and regards them as history accomplished instead of history in progress that his principle leads to the most serious error. No one has a more withering contempt for evil as meanness and imbecility; but he cannot see it in the strong hand. Of two views, equally correct, "evil is weakness," such evil as sloth, and "corruptio optimi pessima," such evil as tyranny—he only recognises the first. Despising the palpable anarchies of passion, he has no word of censure for the more settled form of anarchy which announced, "Order reigns at Warsaw." He refuses his sympathy to all unsuccessful efforts, and holds that if races are trodden underfoot, they are φύσει δοῦλοι . . . δυνάμενοι ἄλλου εἶναι; they who have allowed themselves to be subjugated deserve their fate. The cry of "oppressed nationalities" was to him mere cant. His Providence is on the side of the big battalions, and forgives very violent means to an orderly end. To his credit he declined to acknowledge the right of Louis Napoleon to rule France; but he accepted the Czars, and ridiculed Mazzini till forced to admit, almost with chagrin, that he had, "after all," substantially succeeded.

> Treason never prospers, what's the reason?
> That when it prospers, none dare call it treason.

Apprehending, on the whole more keenly than any of his contemporaries, the foundations of past greatness, his

---

[1] *Vide* Mill's *Liberty*, chap. ii., pp. 52–54.

invectives and teaching lay athwart much that is best as
well as much that is most hazardous in the new ideas of
the age.   Because mental strength, endurance, and industry
do not appear prominently in the Negro race, he looks forward with satisfaction to the day when a band of white
buccaneers shall undo Toussaint l'Ouverture's work of liber-
ation in Hayti, advises the English to revoke the Emancipation Act in Jamaica, and counsels the Americans to lash
their slaves—better, he admits, made serfs and not saleable
by auction—not more than is necessary to get from them
an amount of work satisfactory to the Anglo-Saxon mind.
Similarly he derides all movements based on a recognition
of the claims of weakness to consideration and aid.

> Fallen cherub, to be weak is miserable,
> Doing or suffering.

The application of the maxim, "Might is Right," to a
theory of government is obvious; the strongest government must be the best, *i.e.* that in which power, in the last
resort supreme, is concentrated in the hands of a single
ruler; the weakest, that in which they are most widely
diffused, is the worst.   Carlyle in his Address to the Edinburgh students commends Machiavelli for insight in attributing the preservation of Rome to the institution of the
Dictatorship.   In his last great work this view is developed
in the lessons he directs the reader to draw from Prussian
history.   The following conveys his last comparative estimate of an absolute and a limited monarchy :

This is the first triumph of the constitutional Principle which has
since gone to such sublime heights among us—heights which we begin at last to suspect may be depths leading down, all men now ask
whitherwards.   A much-admired invention in its time, that of letting

go the rudder or setting a wooden figure expensively to take care of it, and discovering that the ship would sail of itself so much the more easily. Of all things a nation needs first to be drilled, and a nation that has not been governed by so-called tyrants never came to much in the world.

Among the currents of thought contending in our age, two are conspicuously opposed. The one says: Liberty is an end, not a mere means in itself; apart from practical results the crown of life. Freedom of thought and its expression, and freedom of action, bounded only by the equal claim of our fellows, are desirable for their own sakes as constituting national vitality: and even when, as is sometimes the case, Liberty sets itself against improvements for a time, it ultimately accomplishes more than any reforms could accomplish without it. The fewer restraints that are imposed from without on human beings the better: the province of law is only to restrain men from violently or fraudulently invading the province of other men. This view is maintained and in great measure sustained by J. S. Mill in his *Liberty*, the *Areopagitica* of the nineteenth century, and more elaborately if not more philosophically set forth in the comprehensive treatise of Wilhelm von Humboldt on *The Sphere and Duties of Government*. These writers are followed with various reserves by Grote, Buckle, Mr. Herbert Spencer, and by Mr. Lecky. Mill writes:

The idea of rational Democracy is not that the people themselves govern; but that they have security for good government. This security they can only have by retaining in their own hands the ultimate control. The people ought to be masters employing servants more skilful than themselves.[1]

---

[1] It should be noted that Mill lays as great stress, and a more practical stress, on Individualism as Carlyle does. He has the same

To this Carlyle, with at least the general assent of Mr. Froude, Mr. Ruskin, and Sir James Stephen, substantially replies :

In freedom for itself there is nothing to raise a man above a fly ; the value of a human life is that of its work done ; the prime province of law is to get from its subjects the most of the best work. The first duty of a people is to find — which means to accept— their chief ; their second and last to obey him. We see to what men have been brought by " Liberty, Equality, and Fraternity," by the dreams of idealogues, and the purchase of votes.

This, the main drift of Carlyle's political teaching, rests on his absolute belief in strength (which always grows by concentration), on his unqualified admiration of order, and on his utter disbelief in what his adverse friend Mazzini was wont, with over-confidence, to appeal to as " collective wisdom."   Theoretically there is much to be said for this view : but, in practice, it involves another idealism as aerial as that of any " idealogue " on the side of Liberty. It points to the establishment of an Absolutism which must continue to exist, whether wisdom survives in the absolute rulers or ceases to survive.   Κρατεῖν δ' ἐστι καὶ μὴ δικαίως.   The rule of Cæsars, Napoleons, Czars may have been beneficent in times of revolution ; but their right to rule is apt to pass before their power, and when the latter

belief in the essential mediocrity of the masses of men whose " thinking is done for them . . . through the newspapers," and the same scorn for " the present low state of society."   He writes, " The initiation of all wise and noble things comes and must come from individuals : generally at first from some one individual ;" but adds, " I am not countenancing the sort of ' hero worship ' which applauds the strong man of genius for forcibly seizing on the government of the world. . . . All he can claim is freedom to point out the way."

descends by inheritance, as from M. Aurelius to Commodus, it commonly degenerates. It is well to learn, from a safe distance, the amount of good that may be associated with despotism : its worst evil is lawlessness, it not only suffocates freedom and induces inertia, but it renders wholly uncertain the life of those under its control. Most men would rather endure the "slings and arrows" of an irresponsible Press, the bustle and jargon of many elections, the delay of many reforms, the narrowness of many streets, than have lived from 1814 to 1840, with the noose around all necks, in Paraguay, or even precariously prospered under the paternal shield of the great Fritz's extraordinary father, Friedrich Wilhelm of Prussia.

Carlyle's doctrine of the ultimate identity of "might and right" never leads, with him, to its worst consequence, a fatalistic or indolent repose ; the withdrawal from the world's affairs of the soul "holding no form of creed but contemplating all." That he was neither a consistent optimist nor pessimist is apparent from his faith in the power of man in some degree to mould his fate. Not " belief, belief," but " action, action," is his working motto. On the title-page of the *Latter-Day Pamphlets* he quotes from Rushworth on a colloquy of Sir David Ramsay and Lord Reay in 1638 : "Then said his Lordship, 'Well, God mend all !'—'Nay, by God, Donald ; we must help Him to mend it,' said the other."

"I am not a Tory," he exclaimed, after the clamour on the publication of *Chartism*, "no, but one of the deepest though perhaps the quietest of Radicals." With the Toryism which merely says "stand to your guns" and, for the rest, "let well alone," he had no sympathy. There was nothing selfish in his theories. He felt for, and was willing to fight for mankind, though he could not trust them ;

41

even his "king" he defines to be a minister or servant of
the State. "The love of power," he says, "if thou understand what to the manful heart power signifies, is a very
noble and indispensable love;" that is, the power to raise
men above the "Pig Philosophy," the worship of clothes,
the acquiescence in wrong. "The world is not here for
me, but I for it." "Thou shalt is written upon life in
characters as terrible as thou shalt not;" are protests against
the mere negative virtues which religionists are wont unduly to exalt.

Carlyle's so-called Mysticism is a part of his German
poetry; in the sphere of common life and politics he made
use of plain prose, and often proved himself as shrewd as
any of his northern race. An excessively "good hater,"
his pet antipathies are generally bad things. In the abstract they are always so; but about the abstract there is
no dispute. Every one dislikes or professes to dislike
shams, hypocrisies, phantoms—by whatever tiresomely re-
iterated epithet he may be pleased to address things that
are not what they pretend to be. Diogenes's toil with
the lantern alone distinguished the cynic Greek, in admiration of an honest man. Similarly the genuine zeal of his
successor appears in painstaking search; his discrimination
in the detection, his eloquence in his handling of humbugs.
Occasional blunders in the choice of objects of contempt
and of worship—between which extremes he seldom halts
—demonstrate his fallibility, but outside the sphere of literary and purely personal criticism he seldom attacks any
one, or anything, without a show of reason. To all gospels
there are two sides, and a great teacher who, by reason of
the very fire that makes him great, disdains to halt and
hesitate and consider the *juste milieu*—seldom guards himself against misinterpretation or excess. Mazzini writes,

" He weaves and unweaves his web like Penelope, preaches
by turns life and nothingness, and wearies out the patience
of his readers by continually carrying them from heaven
to hell." Carlyle, like Ruskin, keeps himself right not by
caveats, but by contradictions of himself, and sometimes in
a way least to be expected. Much of his writing is a blast
of war, or a protest against the philanthropy that sets
charity before justice. Yet in a letter to the London
Peace Congress of 1851, dated 18th July, we find :

I altogether approve of your object. Clearly the less war and
cutting of throats we have among us, it will be the better for us all.
As men no longer wear swords in the streets, so neither by-and-by
will nations. . . . How many meetings would one expedition to Russia
cover the cost of ?

He denounced the Americans, in apparent ignorance of
their " Constitution," for having no Government; and yet
admitted that what he called their anarchy had done perhaps more than anything else could have done to subdue
the wilderness. He spoke with scorn of the "rights of
women," their demand for the suffrage, and the *cohue* of
female authors, expressing himself in terms of ridiculous
ridicule of such writers as Mrs. Austin, George Sand, and
George Eliot; but he strenuously advocated the claim of
women to a recognised medical education. He reviled
" Model Prisons" as pampering institutes of " a universal
sluggard and scoundrel amalgamation society," and yet seldom passed on the streets one of the " Devil's elect" without giving him a penny. He set himself against every law
or custom that tended to make harder the hard life of the
poor: there was no more consistent advocate of the abolition of the " Game Laws." Emerson says of the mediæval
architects, " they builded better than they knew." Carlyle

felt more softly than he said, and could not have been
trusted to execute one of his own Rhadamanthine decrees.[1]
Scratch the skin of the Tartar and you find beneath the
despised humanitarian.   Everything that he has written
on " The Condition of England Question " has a practical
bearing, and many of his suggestions have found a place
on our code, vindicating the assertion of the *Times* of the
day after his death, that " the novelties and paradoxes of
1846 are to a large extent nothing but the good-sense of
1881."   Such are :—his insistence on affording every facil-
ity for merit to rise from the ranks, partially embodied in
the Abolition of Purchase Act; his advocacy of State-
aided Emigration, of administrative and civil service Reform—the abolition of " the circumlocution office " in
Downing Street—of the institution of a Minister of Education ; his dwelling on the duties as well as the rights of
landowners—the theme of so many Land Acts; his en-
larging on the superintendence of labour—made practical
in Factory and Limited Hours' Bills—on care of the really
destitute, on the better housing of the poor, on the regulation of weights and measures; his general contention
for fixing more exactly the province of the legislative and
the executive bodies.   Carlyle's view that we should find
a way to public life for men of eminence who will not
cringe to mobs, has made a step towards realisation in the
enfranchisement of our universities.   Other of his proposals, as the employment of our army and navy in time
of peace, and the forcing of able-bodied paupers into " industrial regiments," have become matter of debate which
may pave the way to legislation.   One of his desiderata, a

---

[1] *Vide* a remarkable instance of this in the best short *Life of
Carlyle,* that by Dr. Richard Garnett, p. 147.

statute of limitations on "puffing," it has not yet been feasible, by the passing of an almost prohibitive duty on advertisements, to realise.

Besides these specific recommendations, three ideas are dominant in Carlyle's political treatises. *First*—A vehement protest against the doctrine of *Laissez faire;* which he says, "on the part of the governing classes will, we repeat again and again, have to cease; pacific mutual divisions of the spoil and a would-let-well-alone, will no longer suffice;" a doctrine to which he is disposed to trace the Trades-union wars, of which he failed to see the issue. He is so strongly in favor of *Free-trade* between nations that, by an amusing paradox, he is prepared to make it *compulsory.* "All men," he writes in *Past and Present,* "trade with all men when mutually convenient, and are even bound to do it. Our friends of China, who refused to trade, had we not to argue with them, in cannon-shot at last?" But in Free-trade between class and class, man and man, within the bounds of the same kingdom, he has no trust; he will not leave "supply and demand" to adjust their relations. The result of doing so is, he holds, the scramble between Capital for larger interest and Labour for higher wage, in which the rich if unchecked will grind the poor to starvation, or drive them to revolt.

Second—As a corollary to the abolition of *Laissez faire,* he advocates the *Organisation of Labour,* "the problem of the whole future to all who will pretend to govern men." The phrase from its vagueness has naturally provoked much discussion. Carlyle's bigoted dislike of Political Economists withheld him from studying their works; and he seems ignorant of the advances that have been made by the "dismal science," or of what it has proved and disproved. Consequently, while brought in evidence by

10   P

most of our modern Social idealists, Comtists and Communists alike, all they can say is that he has given to their protest against the existing state of the commercial world a more eloquent expression than their own. He has no compact scheme—as that of St. Simon or Fourier, or Owen—few such definite proposals as those of Karl Marx, Bellamy, Hertzka or Gronlund, or even William Morris. He seems to share with Mill the view that " the restraints of communism are weak in comparison with those of capitalists," and with Morris to look far forward to some golden age; he has given emphatic support to a copartnership of employers and employed, in which the profits of labour shall be apportioned by some rule of equity, and insisted on the duty of the State to employ those who are out of work in public undertakings.

> Enlist, stand drill, and become from banditti soldiers of industry. I will lead you to the Irish bogs . . . English fox-covers . . . New Forest, Salisbury Plains, and Scotch hill-sides which, as yet feed only sheep . . . thousands of square miles . . . destined yet to grow green crops and fresh butter and milk and beef without limit—

an estimate with the usual exaggeration. Carlyle's later work is, however, an advance on his earlier, in its higher appreciation of Industrialism. He looks forward to the boon of " one big railway right across America," a prophecy since three times fulfilled; and admits that " the new omnipotence of the steam-engine is hewing aside quite other mountains than the physical," i.e. bridging the gulf between races and binding men to men. He had found, since writing Sartor, that dear cotton and slow trains do not help one nearer to God, freedom, and immortality.

Carlyle's third practical point is his advocacy of Emigra-

tion, or rather his insistence on it as a sufficient remedy for Over-population. He writes of "Malthusianism" with his constant contempt of convictions other than his own:

A full formed man is worth more than a horse.... One man in a year, as I have understood it, if you lend him earth will feed himself and nine others (?)... Too crowded indeed!... What portion of this globe have ye tilled and delved till it will grow no more? How thick stands your population in the Pampas and Savannahs—in the Curragh of Kildare? Let there be an *Emigration Service*... so that every honest, willing workman who found England too strait, and the organisation of labour incomplete, might find a bridge to carry him to western lands. ... Our little isle has grown too narrow for us, but the world is wide enough yet for another six thousand years. ... If this small western rim of Europe is over-peopled, does not everywhere else, a whole vacant earth, as it were, call to us: "Come and till me, come and reap me."

On this follows an eloquent passage about our friendly Colonies, "overarched by zodiacs and stars, clasped by many sounding seas." Carlyle would apparently force emigration, and coerce the Australians, Americans, and Chinese, to receive our ship-loads of living merchandise; but the problem of population exceeds his solution of it. He everywhere inclines to rely on coercion till it is over-mastered by resistance, and to overstretch jurisdiction till it snaps.

His countenance of Autocracy may have disastrous results in Germany, where the latest representative of the Hohenzollerns is ostentatiously laying claim to "right divine." In England, where the opposite tide runs full, it is harmless; but, by a curious irony, our author's leaning to an organised control over social and private as well as public life, his exaltation of duties above rights, may serve as an incentive to the very force he seemed most to dread. Events are every day demonstrating the fallacy of his view

of Democracy as an embodiment of *Laissez faire.* Kant
with deeper penetration, indicated its tendency to become
despotic. Good government, according to Aristotle, is
that of one, of few, or of many, for the sake of all. A
Democracy where the many rule for the many alone, may
be a deadly engine of oppression; it may trample without
appeal on the rights of minorities, and, in the name of the
common good, establish and enforce an almost unconditioned tyranny. Carlyle's blindness to this superlative
danger—a danger to which Mill, in many respects his unrecognised coadjutor, became alive [1]—emphasises the limits
of his political foresight. He has consecrated Fraternity
with an eloquence unapproached by his peers, and with
equal force put to scorn the superstition of Equality; but
he has aimed at Liberty destructive shafts, some of which
may find a mark the archer little meant.

[1] *Vide passim* the chapter in *Liberty* entitled "Limits to the Authority of Society over the Individual," where Mill denounces the
idea of "the majority of operatives in many branches of industry...
that bad workmen ought to receive the same wages as good."

CHAPTER X.

CARLYLE'S RELIGION AND ETHICS — RELATION TO PREDE-
CESSORS — INFLUENCE.

THE same advance or retrogression that appears in Carlyle's
Politics is traceable in his Religion; though it is impossible
to record the stages of the change with even an equal ap-
proach to precision. Religion, in the widest sense—faith
in some supreme Power above us yet acting for us—was
the greater factor of his inner life. But when we further
question his Creed, he is either bewilderingly inconsistent
or designedly vague. The answer he gives is that of
Schiller: " Welche der Religionen? Keine von allen.
Warum? Aus Religion." In 1870 he writes: "I begin
to think religion again possible for whoever will piously
struggle upwards and sacredly refuse to tell lies; which
indeed will mostly mean refusal to speak at all on that
topic." This and other implied protests against intrusive
inquisition are valid in the case of those who keep their
own secrets; it is impertinence to " peer and botanise "
among the sanctuaries of a poet or politician or historian
who does not himself open their doors. But Carlyle has
done this in all his books. A reticent writer may veil his
convictions on every subject save that on which he writes.
An avowed preacher or prophet cannot escape interroga-
tion as to his text.

With all the evidence before us—his collected works,

his friendly confidences, his journals, his fragmentary papers, as the interesting series of jottings entitled "Spiritual Optics," and the partial accounts to Emerson and others of the design of the "Exodus from Houndsditch"—it remains impossible to formulate Carlyle's Theology. We know that he abandoned the ministry, for which he was destined, because, at an early date, he found himself at irreconcilable variance, not on matters of detail but on essentials, with the standards of Scotch Presbyterianism. We know that he never repented or regretted his resolve; that he went, as continuously as possible for a mind so liable to fits and starts, further and further from the faith of his fathers; but that he remained to the last so much affected by it, and by the ineffaceable impress of early associations, that he has been plausibly called "a Calvinist without dogma," "a Calvinist without Christianity," "a Puritan who had lost his creed." We know that he revered the character of Christ, and theoretically accepted the ideal of self-sacrifice; the injunction to return good for evil he never professed to accept; and vicarious sacrifice was contrary to his whole philosophy, which taught that every man must "dree his weird." We know that he not only believed in God as revealed in the larger Bible, the whole history of the human race, but that he threatened, almost with hell-fire, all who dared on this point to give refuge to a doubt. Finally, he believed both in fate and in free-will, in good and evil as powers at internecine war, and in the greater strength and triumph of good at some very far distant date. If we desire to know more of Carlyle's creed we must proceed by "the method of exclusions," and note, in the first place, what he did *not* believe. This process is simplified by the fact that he assailed all convictions other than his own.

Half his teaching is a protest, in variously eloquent phrase, against all forms of *Materialism* and *Hedonism*, which he brands as "worships of Moloch and Astarte," forgetting that progress in physical welfare may lead not only to material, but to mental, if not spiritual, gain. Similarly he denounces *Atheism*, never more vehemently than in his Journals of 1868–1869:

Had no God made this world it were an insupportable place. Laws without a lawgiver, matter without spirit is a gospel of dirt. All that is good, generous, wise, right . . . who or what could by any possibility have given it to me, but One who first had it to give! This is not logic, it is axiom. . . . Poor "Comtism, ghastliest of algebraic spectralities." . . . Canst *thou* by searching find out God ? I am not surprised thou canst not, vain fool! If they do abolish God from their poor bewildered hearts, there will be seen such a world as few are dreaming of.

Carlyle calls evidence from all quarters, appealing to Napoleon's question, "Who made all that?" and to Friedrich's belief that intellect "could not have been put into him by an entity that had none of its own," in support of what he calls the Eternal Fact of Facts, to which he clings as to the Rock of Ages, the sole foundation of hope and of morality to one having at root little confidence in his fellow-men.

If people are only driven upon virtuous conduct . . . by association of ideas, and there is no "Infinite Nature of Duty," the world, I should say, had better count its spoons to begin with, and look out for hurricanes and earthquakes to end with.

Carlyle hazardously confessed that as regards the foundations of his faith and morals, with Napoleon and Friedrich II. on his side, he had against him the advancing tide of modern *Science*. He did not attempt to disprove its

facts, or, as Emerson, to sublimate them into a new idealism ; he scoffed at and made light of them, *e.g.* :

Geology has got rid of Moses, which surely was no very sublime
achievement either. I often think . . . it is pretty much all that
science in this age has done. . . . Protoplasm (unpleasant doctrine
that we are all, soul and body, made of a kind of blubber, found in
nettles among other organisms) appears to be delightful to many.
. . . Yesterday there came a pamphlet published at Lewes, a hallelu-
jah on the advent of Atheism. . . . The real joy of Julian (the author)
was what surprised me, like the shout of a hyæna on finding that the
whole universe was actually carrion. In about seven minutes my
great Julian was torn in two and lying in the place fit for him. . . .
Descended from Gorillas ! Then where is the place for a Creator ?
Man is only a little higher than the tadpoles, says our new Evange-
list. . . . Nobody need argue with these people. Logic never will
decide the matter, or will seem to decide it their way. He who
traces nothing of God in his own soul, will never find God in the
world of matter—mere circlings of force there, of iron regulation,
of universal death and merciless indifference. . . . Matter itself is
either Nothing or else a product due to man's *mind*. . . . The fast-
increasing flood of Atheism on me takes no hold—does not even wet
the soles of my feet.[1]

"Carlyle," says one of his intimates, "speaks as if Darwin wished to rob or insult him." *Scepticism* proper fares
as hardly in his hands as definite denial. It is, he declares,
"a fatal condition," and, almost in the spirit of the inquisitors, he attributes it to moral vice as well as intellectual
weakness, calling it an "atrophy, a disease of the whole
soul," "a state of mental paralysis," etc. His fallacious
habit of appeal to consequences, which in others he would

---

[1] Cf. Othello, "Not a jot, not a jot." Carlyle writes on this
question with the agitation of one himself not quite at ease, with
none of the calmness of a faith perfectly secure.

have scouted as a commonplace of the pulpit, is conspicuous in his remark on Hume's view of life as "a most melancholy theory," according to which, in the words of Jean
Paul, "heaven becomes a gas, God a force, and the second
world a grave." He fails to see that all such appeals
are beside the question; and deserts the ground of his answer to John Sterling's expostulation, "that is downright
Pantheism." "What if it were Pot-theism if it is *true*."
It is the same inconsistency which, in practice, led his sympathy for suffering to override his Stoic theories; but it
vitiated his reasoning, and made it impossible for him to
appreciate the calm, yet legitimately emotional, religiosity
of Mill. Carlyle has vetoed all forms of so-called *Orthodoxy*—whether Catholic or Protestant, of Churches High
or Low; he abhorred Puseyism, Jesuitry, spoke of the
"Free Kirk and other rubbish," and recorded his definite
disbelief, in any ordinary sense, in Revelation and in Miracles. "It is as certain as Mathematics that no such thing
has ever been on earth." History is a perpetual revelation
of God's will and justice, and the stars in their courses
are a perpetual miracle, is his refrain. *This is not what
orthodoxy means*, and no one was more intolerant than he
of rhetorical devices, on such matters, to slur the difference
between "Yes" and "No." But having decided that his
own "Exodus from Houndsditch" might only open the
way to the wilderness, he would allow no one else to
take in hand his uncompleted task; and disliked Strauss
and Renan even more than he disliked Colenso. "He
spoke to me once," says Mr. Froude, "with loathing
of the *Vie de Jésus*." I asked if a true life could be
written. He said, "Yes, certainly, if it were right to
do so; but it is not." Still more strangely he writes to
Emerson:

You are the only man of the Unitarian persuasion whom I could unobstructedly like. The others that I have seen were all a kind of half-way-house characters, who I thought should, if they had not wanted courage, have ended in unbelief, in faint possible *Theism ;* which I like considerably worse than Atheism. Such, I could not but feel, deserve the fate they find here ; the bat fate ; to be killed among the bats as a bird, among the birds as a bat.

What, then, is left for Carlyle's Creed? Logically little, emotionally much. If it must be defined, it was that of a Theist with a difference. A spirit of flame from the empyrean, he found no food in the cold *Deism* of the eighteenth century, and brought down the marble image, from its pedestal, as by the music of the " Winter's Tale," to live among men and inspire them. He inherited and, *coûte que coûte,* determined to persist in the belief that there was a personal God—" a Maker, voiceless, formless, within our own soul." To Emerson he writes in 1836, " My belief in a special Providence grows yearly stronger, unsubduable, impregnable ;" and later, " Some strange belief in a special Providence was always in me at intervals." Thus, while asserting that " all manner of pulpits are as good as broken and abolished," he clings to the old Ecclefechan days.   .

" To the last," says Mr. Froude, " he believed as strongly as ever Hebrew prophet did in spiritual religion," but if we ask the nature of the God on whom all relies, he cannot answer even with the Apostles' Creed. Is He One or Three? " Wer darf ihn nennen." Carlyle's God is not a mere " tendency that makes for righteousness ;" He is a guardian and a guide, to be addressed in the words of Pope's *Universal Prayer,* which he adopted as his own. A personal God does not mean a great Figure-head of the Universe—Heine's fancy of a venerable old man, before he became "a knight" of the Holy Ghost—it means a Supreme Power, Love, or Justice, having relations to the individual man: in this sense Carlyle believed in Him, though more as Justice, exacting "the terriblest penalties," than as Love, preaching from the Mount of Olives. He never entered into controversies about the efficacy of prayer; but, far from deriding, he recommended it as "a turning of one's soul to the Highest." In 1869 he writes:

I occasionally feel able to wish, with my whole softened heart—it is my only form of prayer—"Great Father, oh, if Thou canst have pity on her and on me and on all such." In this at least there is no harm.

And about the same date to Erskine:

"Our Father;" in my sleepless tossings, these words, that brief and grand prayer, came strangely into my mind with an altogether new emphasis; as if written and shining for me in mild pure splendour on the black bosom of the night there; when I as it were read them word by word, with a sudden check to my imperfect wanderings, with a sudden softness of composure which was much unexpected. Not for perhaps thirty or forty years had I once formally repeated that prayer: nay, I never felt before how intensely the voice of man's soul it is, the inmost inspiration of all that is high and pious in poor human nature, right worthy to be recommended with an "After this manner pray ye."

Carlyle holds that if we do our duty—the best work we can—and faithfully obey His laws, living soberly and justly, God will do the best for us in this life. As regards the next we have seen that he ended with Goethe's hope. At an earlier date he spoke more confidently. On his father's death (*Reminiscences*, vol. i., p. 65) he wrote:

Man follows man. His life is as a tale that has been told: yet under time does there not lie eternity? ... Perhaps my father, all that essentially was my father, is even now near me, with me. Both he and I are with God. Perhaps, if it so please God, we shall in some higher state of being meet one another, recognise one another. ... The possibility, nay (in some way) the certainty, of perennial existence daily grows plainer to me.

On the death of Mrs. Welsh he wrote to his wife: "We shall yet go to her. God is great. God is good:" and earlier, in 1835-1836, to Emerson on the loss of his brother:

What a thin film it is that divides the living and the dead. Your brother is in very deed and truth with God, where both you and I are. ... Perhaps we shall all meet YONDER, and the tears be wiped from all eyes. One thing is no perhaps: surely we shall all meet, if it be the will of the Maker of us. If it be not His will, then is it not better so?

After his wife's death, naturally, the question of Immortality came uppermost in his mind; but his conclusions are, like those of Burns, never dogmatic:

The truth about the matter is absolutely hidden from us. "In my Father's house are many mansions." Yes, if you are God you may have a right to say so; if you are a man what do you know more than I, or any of us?

And later:

What if Omnipotence should actually have said, "Yes, poor mortals, such of you as have gone so far shall be permitted to go farther."

To Emerson in 1867 he writes:

I am as good as without hope and without fear; a gloomily serious, silent, and sad old man, gazing into the final chasm of things
in mute dialogue with "Death, Judgment, and Eternity" (dialogue
mute on both sides), not caring to discourse with poor articulate
speaking mortals, on their sorts of topics—disgusted with the world
and its roaring nonsense, which I have no further thought of lifting
a finger to help, and only try to keep out of the way of, and shut
my door against.

There can be no question of the sincerity of Carlyle's
conviction that he had to make war on credulity and to
assail the pretences of a *formal Belief* (which he regards
as even worse than Atheism) in order to grapple with real
Unbelief.   After all explanations of Newton or Laplace,
the Universe is, to him, a mystery, and we ourselves the
miracle of miracles; sight and knowledge leave us no " less
forlorn," and beneath all the soundings of science there is
a deeper deep.   It is this frame of mind that qualified him
to be the exponent of religious epochs in history.   " By
this alone," wrote Dr. Chalmers, " he has done so much to
vindicate and bring to light the Augustan age of Christianity in England," adding that it is the secret also of the
great writer's appreciation of the higher Teutonic literature.   His sombre rather than consolatory sense of "God
in History," his belief in the mission of righteousness to
constrain unrighteousness, and his Stoic view that good
and evil are absolute opposites, are his links with the Puritans, whom he habitually exalts in variations of the following strain :

The age of the Puritans has gone from us, its earnest purpose
awakens now no reverence in our frivolous hearts.   Not the body of
heroic Puritanism alone which was bound to die, but the soul of it
also, which was and should have been, and yet shall be immortal,
has, for the present, passed away.

42

Yet Goethe, the only man of recent times whom he regarded with a feeling akin to worship, was in all essentials
the reverse of a Puritan.

To Carlyle's, as to most substantially emotional works,
may be applied the phrase made use of in reference to the
greatest of all the series of ancient books—

> Hic liber est in quo quisquis sua dogmata quærit;
> Invenit hoc libro dogmata quisque sua.

From passages like those above quoted—his complaints
of the falling off of old Scotch faith ; his references to the
kingdom of a God who has written "in plain letters on
the human conscience a Law that all may read ;" his insistence that the great soul of the world is just ; his belief
in religion as a rule of conduct, and his sympathy with the
divine depths of sorrow—from all these many of his Scotch
disciples persist in maintaining that their master was to the
end essentially a Christian.   The question between them and
other critics who assert that "he had renounced Christianity " is to some extent, not wholly, a matter of nomencla-
ture ; it is hard exactly to decide it in the case of a man
who so constantly found again in feeling what he had
abandoned in thought.   Carlyle's Religion was to the last
an inconsistent mixture, not an amalgam, of his mother's
and of Goethe's.   The Puritan in him never dies; he attempts in vain to tear off the husk that cannot be sepa-
rated from its kernel.   He believes in no historical Resur-
rection, Ascension, or Atonement, yet hungers and thirsts
for a supramundane source of Law, and holds fast by a
faith in the Nemesis of Greek, Goth, and Jew.   He ab-
jures half-way houses; but is withheld by pathetic memories of the church-spires and village graveyards of his

youth from following his doubts to their conclusion; yet
he gives way to his negation in his reference to "old Jew
lights now burnt out," and in the half-despair of his expression to Froude about the Deity Himself, "He does nothing." Professor Masson says that "Carlyle had abandoned
the Metaphysic of Christianity while retaining much of
its Ethic." To reverse this dictum would be an overstrain
on the other side: but the *Metaphysic* of Calvinism is
precisely what he retained; the alleged *Facts* of Revelation he discarded; of the *Ethic* of the Gospels he accepted
perhaps the lesser half, and he distinctly ceased to regard
the teaching of Christ as final.[1] His doctrine of Renun-
ciation (suggested by the passage about the three Reverences in *Meister's Travels*) is Carlyle's transmutation, if
not transfiguration, of Puritanism; but it took neither in
him nor in Goethe any very consistent form, save that it
meant Temperance, keeping the body well under the control of the head, the will strong, and striving, through all
the lures of sense, to attain to some ideal life.

Both write of Christianity as "a thing of beauty," a
perennial power, a spreading tree, a fountain of youth; but
Goethe was too much of a Greek—though, as has been
said, "a very German Greek"—to be, in any proper sense
of the word, a Christian; Carlyle too much of a Goth.
His Mythology was Norse; his Ethics, despite his prejudice
against the race, largely Jewish. He proclaimed his code
with the thunders of Sinai, not in the reconciling voice of
the Beatitudes. He gives or forces on us world-old truths
splendidly set, with a leaning to strength and endurance
rather than to advancing thought. He did not, says a

---

[1] A passage in Mrs. Sutherland Orr's *Life and Letters of Robert
Browning*, p. 173, is decisive on this point, and perhaps too emphatic
for general quotation.

fine critic of morals, recognise that "morality also has passed through the straits." He did not really believe in Conteut, which has been called the Catholic, nor in Progress, more questionably styled the Protestant virtue. His often excellent practical rule to "do the duty nearest to hand" may be used to gag the intellect in its search after the goal; so that even his Everlasting Yea, as a predetermined affirmation, may ultimately result in a deeper negation.[1]

"Duty," to him as to Wordsworth, "stern daughter of the voice of God," has two aspects, on each of which he dwells with a persistent iteration. The *first* is *Surrender* to something higher and wider than ourselves. That he has nowhere laid the line between this abnegation and the self-assertion which in his heroes he commends, partly means that correct theories of our complex life are impossible; but Matthew Arnold's criticism, that his Ethics "are made paradoxical by his attack on Happiness, which he should rather have referred to as the result of Labour and of Truth," can only be rebutted by the assertion that the pursuit of pleasure as an end defeats itself. The *second* aspect of his "Duty" is *Work*. His master Goethe is to him as Apollo to Hercules, as Shakespeare to Luther; the one entire as the chrysolite, the other like the Schreckhorn rent and riven; the words of the former are oracles of the latter battles; the one contemplates and beautifies truth, the other wrestles and fights for it. Carlyle has a limited love of abstract truth; of action his love is unlimited. His lyre is not that of Orpheus, but that of Amphion which built the walls of Thebes. *Laborare est*

---

[1] *Vide* Professor Jones's *Browning as a Philosophical and Religious Teacher*, pp. 66–90.

orare.   He alone is honourable who does his day's work
by sword or plough or pen.   Strength is the crown of
toil.   Action converts the ring of necessity that girds us
into a ring of duty, frees us from dreams, and makes us
men.

> The midnight phantoms feel the spell,
> The shadows sweep away.

There are few grander passages in literature than some of
those litanies of labour.   They have the roll of music that
makes armies march, and if they have been made so familiar as to cease to seem new, it is largely owing to the power
of the writer which has compelled them to become common
property.

Carlyle's practical Ethics, though too little indulgent to
the light and play of life, in which he admitted no ἀδιαφόρα,
and only the relaxation of a rare genial laugh, are more
satisfactory than his conception of their sanction, which is
grim.   His "Duty" is a categorical imperative, imposed
from without by a taskmaster who has "written in flame
across the sky, 'Obey, unprofitable servant.'"   He saw the
infinite above and around, but not *in* the finite.   He insisted
on the community of the race, and struck with a bolt any
one who said, "Am I my brother's keeper?"

> All things, the minutest that man does, influence all men, the very
> look of his face blesses or curses. .... It is a mathematical fact that
> the casting of this pebble from my hand alters the centre of gravity
> of the universe.

But he left a great gulf fixed between man and God, and
so failed to attain to the Optimism after which he often
strove.   He held, with Browning, that "God's in His heav-
en," but not that "All's right with the world."   His view

was the Zoroastrian ἀθάνατος μάχη, "in God's world presided over by the prince of the powers of the air," a "divine infernal universe." The Calvinism of his mother, who said "The world is a lie, but God is truth," landed him in an *impasse;* he could not answer the obvious retort—Did, then, God make and love a lie, or make it hating it? There must have been some other power τὸ ἕτερον, or as Mill in his Apologia for *Theism* puts it, a limit to the assumed Omnipotence. Carlyle, accepting neither alternative, inconsequently halts between them; and his prevailing view of mankind[1] adds to his dilemma. He imposes an "infinite duty on a finite being," as Calvin imposes an infinite punishment for a finite fault. He does not see that mankind sets its hardest tasks to itself; or that, as Emerson declares, "the assertion of our weakness and deficiency is the fine innuendo by which the soul makes its enormous claim." Hence, according to Mazzini, "He stands between the individual and the infinite without hope or guide, and crushes the human being by comparing him with God. From his lips, so daring, we seem to hear every instant the cry of the Breton mariner, 'My God, protect me; my bark is so small and Thy ocean so vast.'" Similarly, the critic of Browning, above referred to, concludes of the great prose writer, whom he has called the poet's twin: "He has let loose confusion upon us. He has brought us within sight of the future: he has been our guide in the wilderness; but he died there and was denied the view from Pisgah."

Carlyle's Theism is defective because it is not sufficiently

---

[1] Some one remarked to Friedrich II. that the philanthropist Sulzer said, "Men are by nature good." "Ach, mein lieber Sulzer," ejaculated Fritz, as quoted approvingly by Carlyle, "er kennt nicht diese verdammte Rasse."

Pantheistic; but, in his view of the succession of events in the "roaring loom of time," of the diorama of majesty girt by mystery, he has found a cosmic Pantheism and given expression to it in a passage which is the culmination of the English prose eloquence as surely as Wordsworth's great Ode is the high-tide mark of the English verse of this century:

Are we not spirits shaped into a body, into an Appearance; and that fade away again into air and Invisibility? This is no metaphor, it is a simple scientific fact; we start out of Nothingness, take figure, and are Apparitions; round us as round the veriest spectre is Eternity, and to Eternity minutes are as years and æons. Come there not tones of Love and Faith as from celestial harp-strings, like the Song of beatified Souls? And again do we not squeak and gibber and glide, bodeful and feeble and fearful, and revel in our mad dance of the Dead—till the scent of the morning air summons us to our still home; and dreamy Night becomes awake and Day? Where now is Alexander of Macedon; does the steel host that yelled in fierce battle shouts at Issus and Arbela remain behind him; or have they all vanished utterly, even as perturbed goblins must? Napoleon, too, with his Moscow retreats and Austerlitz campaigns, was it all other than the veriest spectre hunt; which has now with its howling tumult that made night hideous flitted away? Ghosts! There are nigh a thousand million walking the earth openly at noontide; some half-hundred have vanished from it, some half-hundred have arisen in it, ere thy watch ticks once. O Heaven, it is mysterious, it is awful to consider that we not only carry each a future ghost within him, but are in very deed ghosts.[1] These limbs, whence had we them; this stormy Force; this life-blood with its burning passion? They are dust and shadow; a shadow system gathered round our *me*, wherein through some moments or years the Divine Essence is to be revealed in the Flesh. So has it been from the beginning, so will it be to the end. Generation after generation takes to itself the form of a body; and forth issuing

---

[1] One of the strangest freaks of literary heredity is that this phrase seems to have suggested the title of Ibsen's much debated play.

from Cimmerian Night on Heaven's mission appears. What force
and fire there is in each he expends, one grinding in the mill of
Industry; one hunter-like climbing the giddy Alpine heights of science; one madly dashed in pieces on the rocks of Strife in war with
his fellow, and then the heaven-sent is recalled; his earthly Vesture
falls away, and soon even to sense becomes a vanished shadow. Thus,
like some wild flaming, wild thundering train of Heaven's Artillery,
does this mysterious Mankind thunder and flame in long-drawn, quick
succeeding grandeur through the unknown deep. Thus, like a God-
created fire - breathing spirit host, we emerge from the Mane, haste
stormfully across the astonished earth, then plunge again into the
Mane. Earth's mountains are levelled and her seas filled up. On
the hardest adamant some footprint of us is stamped; the rear of
the host read traces of the earliest van. But whence, O Heaven,
whither? Sense knows not. Faith knows not; only that it is through
Mystery to Mystery, from God and to God.

Volumes might be written on Carlyle's relations, of sentiment, belief, opinion, method of thought, and manner of
expression, to other thinkers. His fierce independence, and
sense of his own prophetic mission to the exclusion of that
of his predecessors and compeers, made him often unconscious of his intellectual debts, and only to the Germans,
who impressed his comparatively plastic youth, is he disposed adequately to acknowledge them. Outside the Hebrew Scriptures he seems to have been wholly unaffected
by the writings and traditions of the East, which exercised
so marked an influence on his New England disciples. He
never realised the part played by the philosophers of Greece
in moulding the speculations of modern Europe. He knew
Plato mainly through the Socratic dialogues. There is,
however, a passage in a letter to Emerson (March 13th,
1853) which indicates that he had read, comparatively late
in life, some portions of *The Republic*. "I was much
struck with Plato last year, and his notions about Democ-

racy—mere *Latter-Day Pamphlets, saxa et faces* ... refined
into empyrean radiance and the lightning of the gods."
The tribute conveyed in the comparison is just; for there
is nothing but community of political view between the
bitter acorns dropped from the gnarled border oak and the
rich fruit of the finest olive in Athene's garden. But the
coincidences of opinion between the ancient and the modern writer are among the most remarkable in literary history.   We can only refer, without comments, to a few of
the points of contact in this strange conjunction of minds
far as the poles asunder.   Plato and Carlyle are both possessed with the idea that they are living in a degenerate
age, and they attribute its degeneracy to the same causes:
Laissez faire; the growth of luxury; the effeminate pref-
erence of Lydian to Dorian airs in music, education, and
life; the decay of the Spartan and growth of the Corinthian
spirit; the habit of lawlessness culminating in the excesses
of Democracy, which they describe in language as nearly
identical as the difference of the ages and circumstances
admit.   They propose the same remedies: a return to
"purer manners, nobler laws," with the best men in the
State to regulate and administer them.   Philosophers, says
Plato, are to be made guardians, and they are to govern,
not for gain or glory, but for the common-weal.   They
need not be happy in the ordinary sense, for there is a
higher than selfish happiness, the love of the good.   To
this love they must be *systematically educated* till they are
fit to be kings and priests in the ideal state; if they refuse
they *must*, when their turn comes, be *made to govern.*   Compare the following declarations of Carlyle :

Aristocracy and Priesthood, a Governing class and a Teaching class
—these two sometimes combined in one, a Pontiff King—there did

not society exist without those two vital elements, there will none exist. Whenever there are born Kings of men you had better seek them out and *breed them to the work.* . . . The few wise will have to take command of the innumerable foolish, they *must be got to do it.*

The Ancient and the Modern, the Greek and the Teuton, are further curiously at one: in their dislike of physical or mental Valetudinarianism (cf. *Rep.* Bs. ii. and iii. and *Characteristics*); in their protests against the morality of consequences, of rewards and punishments as motives for the highest life (the just man, says Plato, crucified is better than the unjust man crowned); in their contempt for the excesses of philanthropy and the pampering of criminals (cf. *Rep.* B. viii.); in their strange conjunctions of free-thinking and intolerance. Plato in the Laws enacts that he who speaks against[1] the gods shall be first fined, then imprisoned, and at last, if he persists in his impiety, put to death; yet he had as little belief in the national religion as Carlyle. They both accept Destiny—the Parcæ or the Norns spin the threads of life—and yet both admit a sphere of human choice. In the Republic the souls select their lots, with Carlyle man can modify his fate. The juxtaposition in each of Humour and Pathos (cf. Plato's account of the dogs in a Democracy, and Carlyle's "Nigger gone masterless among the pumpkins," and, for pathos, the image of the soul encrusted by the world as the marine Glaucus, or the Vision of Er and Natural Supernaturalism) is another contact. Both held that philosophers and heroes were few, and yet both leant to a sort of Socialism, under State control; they both assail Poetry and deride the Stage

---

[1] Rousseau, in the "Contrat Social," also assumes this position; allowing freedom of thought, but banishing the citizen who shows disrespect to the State Religion.

(cf. *Rep.* B. ii. and B. x. with Carlyle on "The Opera"), while each is the greatest prose poet of his race; they are united in hatred of orators, who "would circumvent the gods," and in exalting action and character over "the most sweet voices"—the one enforcing his thesis in the "language of the gods," the other preaching silence in forty volumes of eloquent English speech.

Carlyle seems to have known little of Aristotle. His Stoicism was indigenous; but he always alludes with deference to the teaching of the Porch. Marcus Aurelius, the nearest type of the Philosophic King, must have riveted his regard as an instance of the combination of thought and action; and some interesting parallels have been drawn between their views of life as an arena on which there is much to be done and little to be known, a passage from time to a vague eternity. They have the same mystical vein, alongside of similar precepts of self-forgetfulness, abnegation, and the waiving of desire, the same confidence in the power of the spirit to defy or disdain vicissitudes— ideas which brought both in touch with the ethical side of Christianity—but their tempers and manner are as far as possible apart. Carlyle speaks of no one with more admiration than of Dante, recognising in the Italian his own intensity of love and hate and his own tenacity; but beyond this there is little evidence of the "Divina Commedia" having seriously attuned his thought: nor does he seem to have been much affected by any of the elder English poets. He scarcely refers to Chaucer; he alludes to Spenser here and there with some homage, but hardly ever, excepting Shakespeare, to the Elizabethan dramatists.

Among writers of the seventeenth century, he may have found in Hobbes some support of his advocacy of a strong government; but his views on this theme came rather from a study of the history of that age.   Milton he appreciates inadequately.   To Dryden and Swift he is just; the latter, whether consciously to Carlyle or not, was in some respects his English master, and the points of resemblance in their characters suggest detailed examination.   Their styles are utterly opposed, that of the one resting almost wholly on its Saxon base, that of the other being a coat of many colours; but both are, in the front rank of masters of prose-satire, inspired by the same audacity of " noble rage." Swift's humour has a subtler touch and yet more scathing scorn; his contempt of mankind was more real; his pathos equally genuine but more withdrawn; and if a worse foe he was a better friend.   The comparisons already made between Johnson and Carlyle have exhausted the theme; they remain associated by their similar struggle and final victory, and sometimes by their tyrannous use of power; they are dissociated by the divergence of their intellectual and in some respects even their moral natures; both were forces of character rather than discoverers, both rulers of debate; but the one was of sense, the other of imagination, " all compact."   The one blew " the blast of doom" of the old patronage; the other, against heavier odds, contended against the later tyranny of uninformed and insolent popular opinion.   Carlyle did not escape wholly from the influence of the most infectious, if the most morbid, of French writers, J. J. Rousseau.   They are alike in setting Emotion over Reason : in referring to the Past as a model; in subordinating mere criticism to ethical, religious, or irreligious purpose; in being avowed propagandists; in their " deep unrest;" and in the diverse conclusions that have been drawn from their teaching.

Carlyle's enthusiasm for the leaders of the new German literature was, in some measure, inspired by the pride in a

treasure-trove, the regard of a foster-father or *chaperon*
who first substantially took it by the hand and introduced
it to English society; but it was also due to the feeling
that he had found in it the fullest expression of his own
perplexities, and at least their partial solution. His choice
of its representatives is easily explained. In Schiller he
found intellectually a younger brother, who had fought a
part of his own fight and was animated by his own aspirations; in dealing with his career and works there is a shade
of patronage. Goethe, on the other hand, he recognised
across many divergencies as his master. The attachment
of the belated Scotch Puritan to the greater German has
provoked endless comment; but the former has himself
solved the riddle. The contrasts between the teacher and
pupil remain, but they have been exaggerated by those who
only knew Goethe as one who had attained, and ignored
the struggle of his hot youth on the way to attainment.
Carlyle justly commends him, not alone for his artistic
mastery, but for his sense of the reality and earnestness of
life, which lifts him to a higher grade among the rulers
of human thought than such more perfect artists and
more passionate lyrists as Heine. He admires above all
his conquest over the world, without concession to it,
saying :

With him Anarchy has now become Peace . . . the once perturbed
spirit is serene and rich in good fruits. . . . Neither, which is most
important of all, has this Peace been attained by a surrender to Necessity, or any compact with Delusion—a seeming blessing, such as
years and dispiritment will of themselves bring to most men, and
which is indeed no blessing, since ever continued battle is better than
captivity. Many gird on the harness, few bear it warrior-like, still
fewer put it off with triumph. Euphorion still asserts " To die in
strife is the end of life."

11

Goethe only ceased to fight when he had won; his want of sympathy with the so-called Apostles of Freedom, the stump orators of his day, was genuine and shared by Carlyle. In the apologue of the *Three Reverences* in *Meister* the master indulges in humanitarian rhapsody and, unlike his pupil, verges on sentimental paradox, declaring through the lips of the Chief in that imaginary pedagogic province —which here and there closely recalls the *New Atlantis*— that we must recognise "humility and poverty, mockery and despite, disgrace and suffering, as divine—nay, even on sin and crime to look not as hindrances, but to honour them, as furtherances of what is holy." In answer to Emerson's Puritanic criticisms Carlyle replies:

Believe me, it is impossible you can be more a Puritan than I; nay, I often feel as if I were far too much so, but John Knox himself, could he have seen the peaceable impregnable *fidelity* of that man's mind, and how to him also Duty was infinite — Knox would have passed on wondering, not reproaching. But I will tell you in a word why I like Goethe. His is the only *healthy* mind, of any extent, that I have discovered in Europe for long generations; it was he who first convincingly proclaimed to me. . . . "Behold even in this scandalous Sceptico-Epicurean generation, when all is gone but hunger and cant, it is still possible that man be a man." And then as to that dark ground on which you love to see genius paint itself: consider whether misery is not ill health too, also whether good-fortune is not worse to bear than bad, and on the whole, whether the glorious serene summer is not greater than the wildest hurricane—as Light, the naturalists say, is stronger than Lightning.

Among German so-called mystics the one most nearly in accord with Carlyle was Novalis, who has left a sheaf of sayings—as "There is but one temple in the universe, and that is the body of man," "Who touches a human hand touches God"—that especially commended themselves to his commentator. Among philosophers proper, Fichte, in his assertion of the Will as a greater factor of human life and a nearer indication of personality than pure Thought, was Carlyle's nearest tutor. The *Vocation of the Scholar* and *The Way to a Blessed Life* anticipated and probably suggested much of the more speculative part of *Sartor*. But to show their relation would involve a course of Meta-physics.

We accept Carlyle's statement that he learnt most of the secret of life and its aims from his master Goethe: but the closest of his kin, the man with whom he shook hands more nearly as an equal, was Richter—*Jean Paul der ein-zige*, lord of the empire of the air, yet with feet firmly planted on German earth, a colossus of reading and indus-try, the quaintest of humourists, not excepting either Sir Thomas Browne or Laurence Sterne, a lover and painter of Nature unsurpassed in prose. He first seems to have in-fluenced his translator's style, and set to him the mode of queer titles and contortions, fantastic imaginary incidents, and endless digressions. His Ezekiel visions as the dream in the first *Flower Piece* from the life of Siebenkäs, and that on *New-year's Eve*, are like previsions of *Sartor*, and we find in the fantasies of both authors much of the same machinery. It has been asserted that whole pages of *Schmelzle's Journey to Flätz* might pass current for Car-lyle's own; and it is evident that the latter was saturated with *Quintus Fixlein*. The following can hardly be a mere coincidence. Richter writes of a dead brother, "For he chanced to leap on an ice-board that had jammed itself among several others; but these recoiled, and his shot forth with him, melted away as it floated under his feet, and so sank his heart of fire amid the ice and waves;" while in *Cui Bono* we have:

> What is life? a thawing ice-board
> On a sea with sunny shore.

Similarly, the eloquently pathetic close of *Fixlein*, especially the passage, "Then began the Æolian harp of Creation," recalls the deepest pathos of *Sartor*. The two writers,
it has been observed, had in common " reverence, humour,
vehemence, tenderness, gorgeousness, grotesqueness, and
pure conduct of life." Much of Carlyle's article in the
Foreign Quarterly of 1830 might be taken for a criticism
of himself.

Enough has been said of the limits of Carlyle's magnanimity in estimating his English contemporaries; but the
deliberate judgments of his essays were often more genial
than those of his letters and conversation; and perhaps
his overestimate of inferiors, whom in later days he drew
round him as the sun draws the mist, was more hurtful
than his severity; it is good for no man to live with sat-
ellites. His practical severance from Mazzini was mainly
a personal loss; the widening of the gulf between him and
Mill was a public calamity, for seldom have two men been
better qualified the one to correct the excesses of the other.
Carlyle was the greater genius; but the question which was
the greater mind must be decided by the conflict between
logic and emotion. They were related proximately as Plato
to Aristotle, the one saw what the other missed, and their
hold on the future has been divided. Mill had "the dry-
light," and his meaning is always clear; he is occasionally
open to the charge of being a formalist, allowing too little
for the "infusion of the affections," save when touched, as
Carlyle was, by a personal loss; yet the critical range indicated by his essay on "Coleridge" on the one side, that
on "Bentham" on the other, is as wide as that of his
friend; and while neither said anything base, Mill alone is

clear from the charge of having ever said anything absurd. His influence, though more indirect, may prove, save artistically, more lasting. The two teachers, in their assaults on *Laissez faire*, curiously combine in giving sometimes undesigned support to social movements with which the elder at least had no sympathy.

Carlyle's best, because his most independent, friend lived beyond the sea. He has been almost to weariness compared with Emerson, initial pupil later ally, but their contrasts are more instructive than their resemblances. They have both at heart a revolutionary spirit, marked originality, uncompromising aversion to illusions, disdain of traditional methods of thought and stereotyped modes of expression; but in Carlyle this is tempered by greater veneration for the past, in which he holds out models for our imitation; while Emerson sees in it only finger-posts for the future, and exhorts his readers to stay at home lest they should wander from themselves. The one loves detail, hates abstraction, delights to dwell on the minutiæ of biography, and waxes eloquent even on dates. The other, a brilliant though not always a profound generaliser, tells us that we must "leave a too close and lingering adherence to facts, and study the sentiment as it appeared in hope, not in history . . . with the ideal is the rose of joy. But grief cleaves to names and persons, and the partial interests of to-day and yesterday." The one is bent under a burden, and pores over the riddle of the earth, till, when he looks up at the firmament of the unanswering stars, he can but exclaim, "It is a sad sight." The other is blown upon by the fresh breezes of the new world; his vision ranges over her clear horizons, and he leaps up elastic under her light atmosphere, exclaiming, "Give me health and a day and I will make the pomp of emperors ridiculous." Carlyle is a

43

half-Germanised Scotchman, living near the roar of the metropolis, with thoughts of Weimar and reminiscences of the Covenanting hills. Emerson studies Swedenborg and reads the *Phædo* in his garden, far enough from the din of cities to enable him in calm weather to forget them. " Boston, London, are as fugitive as any whiff of smoke; so is society, so is the world." The one is strong where the other is weak. Carlyle keeps his abode in the murk of clouds illumined by bolts of fire; he has never seen the sun unveiled. Emerson's " Threnody " shows that he has known the shadow; but he has fought with no Apollyons, reached the Celestial City without crossing the dark river, and won the immortal garland " without the dust and heat." Self-sacrifice, inconsistently maintained, is the watchword of the one; self-reliance, more consistently, of the other. The art of the two writers is in strong contrast. The charm of Emerson's style is its precision; his sentences are like medals each hung on its own string; the fields of his thought are combed rather than ploughed: he draws outlines, as Flaxman, clear and colourless. Carlyle's paragraphs are like streams from Pactolus, that roll nuggets from their source on their turbid way. His expressions are often grotesque, but rarely offensive. Both writers are essentially ascetic—though the one swallows Mirabeau, and the other says that Jane Eyre should have accepted Rochester and "left the world in a minority." But Emerson is never coarse, which Carlyle occasionally is; and Carlyle is never flippant, as Emerson often is. In condemning the hurry and noise of mobs the American keeps his temper, and insists on justice without vindictiveness: wars and revolutions take nothing from his tranquillity, and he sets Hafiz and Shakespeare against Luther and Knox. Careless of formal consistency—" the hobgoblin of little minds "—he balances his aristocratic reserve with a belief in democracy, in progression by antagonism, and in collective wisdom as a limit to collective folly. Leaving his intellectual throne as the spokesman of a practical liberty, Emerson's wisdom was justified by the fact that he was always at first on the unpopular, and ultimately on the winning, side. Casting his vote for the diffusion of popular literature, a wide suf-frage, a mild penal code,[1] he yet endorsed the saying of an old American author, "A monarchy is a merchantman which sails well, but will sometimes strike on a rock and go to the bottom ; whilst a republic is a raft that will never sink, but then your feet are always in water." Maintaining that the State exists for its members, he holds that the enervating influences of authority are least powerful in popular governments, and that the tyranny of a public opinion not enforced by law need only be endured by vol-untary slaves. Emerson confides in great men, "to educate whom the State exists;" but he regards them as inspired mouth-pieces rather than controlling forces: their prime mission is to "fortify our hopes," their indirect services are their best. The career of a great man should rouse us to a like assertion of ourselves. We ought not to obey, but to follow, sometimes by not obeying, him. "It is the imbecility not the wisdom of men that is always inviting the impudence of power."

It is obvious that many of these views are in essential opposition to the teaching of Carlyle; and it is remarkable that two conspicuous men so differing and expressing their

---

[1] Carlyle, on the other hand, holds "that," as has been said, " we are entitled to deal with criminals as relics of barbarism in the midst of civilisation." His protest, though exaggerated, against leniency in dealing with atrocities, emphatically requisite in an age apt to ignore the rigour of justice, has been so far salutary, and may be more so.

differences with perfect candour should have lived so long
on such good terms.   Their correspondence, ranging over
thirty-eight years (begun in 1834, after Emerson's visit to
Craigenputtock, and ending in 1872, before his final trip
to England) is, on the whole, one of the most edifying in
literary history.   The fundamental accord, unshaken by
the ruffle of the visit in 1847, is a testimony to the fact
that the common preservation of high sentiments amid the
irksome discharge of ordinary duties may survive and override the most distinct antagonisms of opinion.   Matthew
Arnold has gone so far as to say that he " would not wonder if Carlyle lived in the long-run by such an invaluable
record as that correspondence between him and Emerson
and not by his works."   This is paradoxical; but the volumes containing it are in some respects more interesting
than the letters of Goethe and Schiller, as being records of
" two noble kinsmen" of nearer intellectual claims.   The
practical part of the relationship on the part of Emerson is
very beautiful; he is the more unselfish, and on the whole
appears the better man, especially in the almost unlimited
tolerance that passes with a smile even such violences as
the "Ilias in nuce;" but Carlyle shows himself to be the
stronger.   Their mutual criticisms were of real benefit.
Emerson succeeded in convincing his friend that so-called
anarchy might be more effective in subduing the wilderness
than any despotism; while the advice to descend from
" Himalaya peaks and indigo skies" to concrete life is
accepted and adopted in the later works of the American,
Society and Solitude and the *Conduct of Life*, which Carlyle praises without stint.   Keeping their poles apart they
often meet half-way; and in matters of style as well as
judgment tinge and tend to be transfused into one another,
so that in some pages we have to look to the signature to

be sure of the writer. Towards the close of the correspondence Carlyle in this instance admits his debt.

I do not know another man in all the world to whom I can speak
with clear hope of getting adequate response from him. Truly Concord seems worthy of the name: no dissonance comes to me from
that side. Ah me! I feel as if in the wide world there were still
but this one voice that responded intelligently to my own: as if the
rest were all hearsays . . . echoes: as if this alone were true and
alive. My blessings on you, good Ralph Waldo.

Emerson answers in 1872, on receipt of the completed
edition of his friend's work: "You shall wear the crown
at the Pan-Saxon games, with no competitor in sight . . .
well earned by genius and exhaustive labour, and with nations for your pupils and praisers."

The general verdict on Carlyle's literary career assigns
to him the first place among the authors of his time.
No writer of our generation, in or out of England, has
combined such abundance with such power. Regarding
his rank as a writer there is little or no dispute: it is
admitted that the irregularities and eccentricities of his
style are bound up with its richness. In estimating the
value of his thought we must distinguish between instruc-
tion and inspiration. If we ask what new truths he has
taught, what problems he has definitely solved, our answers
must be few. This is a perhaps inevitable result of the
manner of his writing, or rather of the nature of his mind.
Aside from political parties, he helped to check their exaggeration by his own; seeing deeply into the undercurrent
evils of the time, even when vague in his remedies he was
of use in his protest against leaving these evils to adjust
themselves—what has been called "the policy of drifting"—
or of dealing with them only by catchwords. No one set

11*   R

a more incisive brand on the meanness that often marks
the unrestrained competition of great cities; no one was
more effective in his insistence that the mere accumulation
of wealth may mean the ruin of true prosperity; no one
has assailed with such force the mammon-worship and the
frivolity of his age.   Everything he writes comes home to
the individual conscience: his claim to be regarded as a
moral exemplar has been diminished, his hold on us as an
ethical teacher remains unrelaxed.   It has been justly
observed that he helped to modify "the thought rather
than the opinion of two generations."   His message, as
that of Emerson, was that "life must be pitched on a
higher plane."   Goethe said to Eckermann in 1827 that
Carlyle was a moral force so great that he could not tell
what he might produce.   His influence has been, though
not continuously progressive, more marked than that of any
of his compeers, among whom he was, if not the greatest,
certainly the most imposing personality.   It had two cul-
minations; shortly after the appearance of the *French
Revolution,* and again towards the close of the seventh decade of the author's life.   To the enthusiastic reception of
his works in the Universities, Mr. Froude has borne eloquent testimony, and the more academically restrained
Arnold admits that "the voice of Carlyle, overstrained and
misused since, sounded then in Oxford fresh and comparatively sound," though, he adds, "The friends of one's
youth cannot always support a return to them."   In the
striking article in the *St. James's Gazette* of the date of the
great author's death we read: "One who had seen much
of the world, and knew a large proportion of the remarkable
men of the last thirty years, declared that Mr. Carlyle was
by far the most impressive person he had ever known, the
man who conveyed most forcibly to those who approached

him [best on resistance principles] that general impression
of genius and force of character which it is impossible
either to mistake or to define." Thackeray, as well as
Ruskin and Froude, acknowledged him as, beyond the
range of his own *métier*, his master, and the American
Lowell, penitent for past disparagement, confesses that " all
modern Literature has felt his influence in the right direction ;" while the Emersonian hermit Thoreau, a man of
more intense though more restricted genius than the poet-
politician, declares—"Carlyle alone with his wide humanity
has, since Coleridge, kept to us the promise of England.
His wisdom provokes rather than informs.   He blows
down narrow walls, and struggles, in a lurid light, like the
Jöthuns, to throw the old woman Time ; in his work there
is too much of the anvil and the forge, not enough hay-
making under the sun.   He makes us act rather than
think: he does not say, know thyself, which is impossible, but know thy work.   He has no pillars of Hercules,
no clear goal, but an endless Atlantic horizon.   He exaggerates.   Yes; but he makes the hour great, the picture
bright, the reverence and admiration strong ; while mere
precise fact is a coil of lead."   Our leading journal, on the
morning after Carlyle's death, wrote of him in a tone of
well-tempered appreciation :   "We have had no such individuality since Johnson.   Whether men agreed or not, he
was a touchstone to which truth and falsehood were
brought to be tried.   A preacher of Doric thought, always
in his pulpit and audible, he denounced wealth without
sympathy, equality without respect, mobs without leaders,
and life without aim."   To this we may add the testimony
of another high authority in English letters, politically at
the opposite pole: " Carlyle's influence in kindling enthusiasm for virtues worthy of it, and in stirring a sense of

the reality on the one hand and the unreality on the other, of all that men can do and suffer, has not been surpassed by any teacher now living. Whatever later teachers may have done in definitely shaping opinion . . . here is the friendly fire-bearer who first conveyed the Promethean spark; here the prophet who first smote the rock." Carlyle, writes one of his oldest friends, "may be likened to a fugleman; he stood up in the front of Life's Battle and showed in word and action his notion of the proper attitude and action of men. He was, in truth, a prophet, and he has left his gospels." To those who contest that these gospels are for the most part negative, we may reply that to be taught what not to do is to be far advanced on the way to do.

In nothing is the generation after him so prone to be unjust to a fresh thinker as with regard to his originality. A physical discovery, as Newton's, remains to ninety-nine out of a hundred a mental miracle; but a great moral teacher "labours to make himself forgotten." When he begins to speak he is suspected of insanity; when he has won his way he receives a Royal Commission to appoint the judges; as a veteran he is shelved for platitude. So Horace is regarded as a mere jewelry store of the Latin, Bacon, in his *Essays* of the English, wisdom, which they each in fact helped to create. Carlyle's paradoxes have been exaggerated, his partialities intensified in his followers; his critical readers, not his disciples, have learnt most from him; he has helped across the Slough of Despond only those who have also helped themselves. When all is said of his dogmatism, his petulance, his "evil behaviour," he remains the master-spirit of his time, its Censor, as Macaulay is its Panegyrist, and Tennyson its Mirror. He has saturated his nation with a wholesome tonic, and the practice of any one of his precepts for the conduct of life is ennobling. More intense than Wordsworth, more intelligible than Browning, more fervid than Mill, he has indicated the pitfalls in our civilisation. His works have done much to mould the best thinkers in two continents, in both of which he has been the Greatheart to many pilgrims. Not a few could speak in the words of the friend whose memory he has so affectionately preserved, "Towards me it is still more true than towards England that no one has been and done like you." A champion of ancient virtue, he appeared in his own phrase applied to Fichte, as "a Cato Major among degenerate men." Carlyle had more than the shortcomings of a Cato; he had all the inconsistent vehemence of an imperfectly balanced mind; but he had a far wider range and deeper sympathies. The message of the modern preacher transcended all mere applications of the text *delenda est.* He denounced, but at the same time nobly exhorted, his age. A storm-tossed spirit, "tempest buffeted," he was "citadel-crowned" in his unflinching purpose and the might of an invincible will.

APPENDIX.

CARLYLE'S RELIGION.

THE *St. James's Gazette*, February 11, 1881, writes:

"It is obvious that from an early age he entirely ceased to believe, in its only true sense, the creed he had been taught. He never affected to believe it in any other sense, for he was far too manly and simple-hearted to care to frame any of those semi-honest transmutations of the old doctrines into new-fangled mysticism which had so great a charm for many of his weaker contemporaries. On the other hand, it is equally true that he never plainly avowed his unbelief. The line he took up was that Christianity, though not true in fact, had a right to be regarded as the noblest aspiration after a theory of the Universe and of human life ever formed: and that the Calvinistic version of Christianity was on the whole the best it ever assumed; and the one which represented the largest proportion of truth and the least amount of error. He also thought that the truths which Calvinism tried to express, and succeeded in expressing in an imperfect or partially mistaken manner, were the ultimate governing principles of morals and politics, of whose systematic neglect in this age nothing but evil could come.

"Unwilling to take up the position of a rebel or revolutionist by stating his views plainly — indeed if he had done so sixty years ago he might have starved—the only resource left to him was that of approaching all the great subjects of life from the point of view of grim humour, irony, and pathos. This was the real origin of his unique style; though no doubt its special peculiarities were due to the wonderful power of his imagination, and to some extent—to a less extent we think than has been usually supposed—to his familiarity with German.

" What, then, was his creed? What were the doctrines which in
his view Calvinism shadowed forth and which were so infinitely true,
so ennobling to human life? First, he believed in God; secondly,
he believed in an absolute opposition between good and evil; thirdly,
he believed that all men do, in fact, take sides more or less decisively
in this great struggle, and ultimately turn out to be either good or
bad; fourthly, he believed that good is stronger than evil, and by infinitely slow degrees gets the better of it, but that this process is so
slow as to be continually obscured and thrown back by evil influences
of various kinds—one of which he believed to be specially powerful
in the present day.

" God in his view was not indeed a personal Being, like the Christian God—still less was He in any sense identified with Jesus Christ;
who, though always spoken of with rather conventional reverence in
his writings, does not appear to have specially influenced him. The
God in which Mr. Carlyle believed is, as far as can be ascertained, a
Being possessing in some sense or other will and consciousness, and
personifying the elementary principles of morals — Justice, Benevolence (towards good people), Fortitude, and Temperance—to such a
pitch that they may be regarded, so to speak, as forming collectively
the will of God. . . . That there is some one who—whether by the
earthquake, or the fire, or the still small voice—is continually saying
to mankind—'*Discite justitiam moniti*,' and that this Being is the
ultimate fact at which we can arrive . . . is what Mr. Carlyle seems
to have meant by believing in God. And if any one will take the
trouble to refer to the first few sentences of the Westminster Confession, and to divest them of their references to Christianity and to
the Bible, he will find that between the God of Calvin and of Carlyle
there is the closest possible similarity. . . . The great fact about each
particular man is the relation, whether of friendship or enmity, in
which he stands to God. In the one case he is on the side which
must ultimately prevail, . . . in the other . . . he will, in due time,
be crushed and destroyed. . . . Our relation to the universe can be
ascertained only by experiment. We all have to live out our lives.
. . . One man is a Cromwell, another a Frederick, a third a Goethe,
a fourth a Louis XV. God hates Louis XV. and loves Cromwell.
Why, if so, He made Louis XV., and indeed whether He made him
or not are idle questions which cannot be answered and should not
be asked. There are good men and bad men, all pass alike through

this mysterious hall of doom called life: most show themselves in their true colours under pressure. The good are blessed here and hereafter; the bad are accursed. Let us bring out as far as may be possible such good as a man has had in him since his origin. Let us strike down the bad to the hell that gapes for him. This we think, or something like this, was Mr. Carlyle's translation of election and predestination into politics and morals. . . . There is not much pity and no salvation worth speaking of in either body of doctrine; but there is a strange, and what some might regard as a terrible, parallelism between these doctrines and the inferences that may be drawn from physical science. The survival of the fittest has much in common with the doctrine of election, and philosophical necessity, as summed up in what we now call evolution, comes practically to much the same result as predestination."

THE END.

THE BRONTË NOVELS

By CHARLOTTE BRONTË (CURRER BELL)

JANE EYRE. Illustrated. 12mo, Cloth, $1 00; 8vo Paper 40 cents.

SHIRLEY. Illustrated. 12mo, Cloth, $1 00.

THE PROFESSOR. Illustrated. 12mo, Cloth, $1 00.

VILLETTE. Illustrated. 12mo, Cloth, $1 00.

Almost all that we require in a novelist, the writer has—perception of character and knowledge of delineating it, picturesqueness, passion, and knowledge of life. Reality—deep, significant reality—is the characteristic of this book.—*Fraser's Magazine.*

By ANNE BRONTË (ACTON BELL)

THE TENANT OF WILDFELL HALL. Illustrated. 12mo, Cloth, $1 00.

We give our honest recommendation of "Wildfell Hall" as being the most interesting novel we have read for a month past. —*Athenæum,* London.

By EMILY BRONTË (ELLIS BELL)

WUTHERING HEIGHTS. Illustrated. 12mo, Cloth, $1 00.

We strongly recommend it to all, for we can promise our readers that they never read anything like it before.—*From a review by* DOUGLAS JERROLD.

HARPER & BROTHERS, PUBLISHERS
NEW YORK AND LONDON

☞ *Any of the above works will be sent by mail, postage prepaid, to any part of the United States, Canada, or Mexico, on receipt of the price.*

Made in the USA
Middletown, DE
13 January 2023

22081365R00152